SELF CONCEPT SOURCEBOOK

Ideas and Activities for Building Self-Esteem

EDITED BY
DOV PERETZ ELKINS, M.H.L., D. Min.

GROWTH ASSOCIATES
Human Relations Consultants & Publishers
P. O. Box 8429
Rochester, New York 14618
(716) 244-1225

Growth Associates
Human Relations Publishers and Consultants
P.O. Box 8429
Rochester, NY 14618
(716) 244-1225

Other volumes by Dr. Elkins in the Growth Associates Self-Concept Development Series:
    TEACHING PEOPLE TO LOVE THEMSELVES: A LEADER'S HANDBOOK OF THEORY AND TECHNIQUE FOR SELF-ESTEEM & AFFIRMATION TRAINING
    TWELVE PATHWAYS TO FEELING BETTER ABOUT YOURSELF
    GLAD TO BE ME: BUILDING SELF-ESTEEM IN YOURSELF & OTHERS

For order blank see end of this book.

For Information about training workshops and consultation in the field of self concept development, human relations training, organizational development, humanistic education, family enrichment, in-service training, and other areas, led by Dr. Elkins, write or call Growth Associates

****

This book is dedicated to
Darrell & Mona Friedman
for the past seven years of fun, friendship and love

Table of Contents

*****

Introduction

The Need For Self-Esteem

Although he was not a psychologist, Goethe, the great German writer, intuited that "the greatest evil that can befall man is that he should come to think ill of himself." Other creative spirits have come to the same recognition. In his *Paradise Lost*, John Milton wrote: "Oft-times nothing profits more than self-esteem..." And in George Bernard Shaw's words, "A man's interest in the world is only the overflow of his interest in himself." Apparently the notion of the significance of loving oneself and accepting oneself reached down into the masses, because it has become a commonly-accepted idea that self-love is the beginning of all love and happiness. An old weaver in Edinburgh prayed each Sunday morning in church: "O Lord, grant me a high opinion of myself."

Within recent decades leading psychologists have substantiated the importance of self-esteem for healthy personality in their own practice of psychotherapy, as well as in their theoretical formulations of the principles of psychological well-being. A few brief statements will demonstrate this:

1) Carl Rogers
"If I were to search for the central core of difficulty in people as I have come to know them, it is that in the great majority of cases they despise themselves, regarding themselves as worthless and unlovable."

2) Erich Fromm
"Love of others and love of ourselves are not alternatives. On the contrary, an attitude of love towards themselves will be found in all those who are capable of loving others."

3) Stanley Coopersmith
"Probably the most important requirement for effective behavior, central to the whole problem, is self-esteem."

4) Virginia Satir
"My dream is to make families a place where adults with high self-esteem can develop. I think we have reached a point where if we don't get busy on dreams of this sort, our end is in sight. We need a world that is as good for human beings as it is for technology."

5) Bruno Bettelheim
"With some qualifications I suggest that nothing is more characteristic

of mental well-being than a healthy self-respect, a regard for one's body and its functions, and a reasonably optimistic outlook on life."

Dr. Stanley Coopersmith, who did some of the most seminal and widely-quoted research on the antecedents of self-esteem, defines the concept as follows:

By self-esteem we refer to the evaluation which the individual makes and customarily maintains with regard to himself: it expresses an attitude of approval or disapproval, and indicates the extent to which the individual believes himself to be capable, significant, successful, and worthy. In short, self-esteem is a personal judgment of worthiness that is expressed in the attitudes the individual holds toward himself. It is a subjective experience which the individual conveys to others by verbal reports and other overt expressive behavior.

In short, our self-esteem is the index of how we feel about ourselves. Does one look upon himself as a worthy, capable, lovable, significant person, or as a useless, inept, unlovable and insignificant creature?

Some have defined self-esteem as our **inner mirror**. This is a particularly useful metaphor, since it is concrete and helps us visualize the concept of self-esteem. The inner mirror of self-esteem is created in the early years of life. It is brought about through the way we perceive the attitude toward us of our significant others, especially parents. A home in which a child finds love, warmth, unconditional acceptance, and mature nurturing, will foster a sense of high self-esteem.

Even though the basic sense of self-esteem, high or low, is created in early life, it can most definitely be changed. It is never too late to change. In the Bible, for example, the word "teshuva" translated generally as "repentance," means "turning." Implied in this idea is that one's life is in one's own hands. One's life and being, and therefore one's inner mirror, are up to oneself to fashion as one sees fit.

One's self-esteem is in a constant state of flux. It never remains exactly the same. When we have good days and feel good about ourselves, our self-esteem rises. On days when things go badly at home, office, school or wherever, our self-esteem drops. While the range of rising and falling may not be as great as the fluctuations of the Dow-Jones Industrials Average, it does bounce up and down as our moods and fortunes. On rare occasions, when major changes in our lives take place, through opportunities of personality growth, significant changes can be made in our inner mirror.

For example, a person who thinks he is dumb, incapable and intellectually inferior, might improve his self-image through a positive experience, such as receiving an "A" in a college course. The process is a slow and gradual one, but sometimes one event or experience can catapult a person to a new level of self-esteem. Progress, of course, is usually two steps forward and one step backward, and personality gains are solidified only after long-term reinforcement. But the important thing is that the self-esteem index, our inner mirror, can rise and fall. The Law of Change is that no one stays in the same place. The Greek philosopher, Heraclitus, said it most effectively when he stated that one cannot step into the same river twice. Why? Because the river has changed and we have changed!

Some raise the objection that self-love is selfish and unworthy of good people. It smacks of boasting and pride, two leading "sins." By looking beneath the surface we generally find that a selfish or boasting person is one with low self-esteem who is trying to convince himself as well as others of his own worth.

The following are some of the factors important in helping achieve high self-esteem:

1) Develop accurate perception of how others see us
2) Be with people who communicate clearly, openly, honestly, helpfully
3) Make realistic assessment of such judgments and evaluations of ourselves by others
4) Develop accurate perception of our abilities and characteristics
5) Establish **realistic** and **appropriate** expectations and goals for ourselves
6) Develop accurate perception of where we are in relation to our goals
7) Find new ways to achieve our appropriate goals and expectations
8) Work to maintain a process of on-going personal growth, constant re-evaluation of where we stand in relation to our goals, and maintain adequate standards of achievement, and achieve our potential.

Self-esteem is the key to a successful, happy, fulfilled, and productive life. It is one of the foundation stones of mature, useful, self-actualizing living. It affects the state of our personal happiness, for we cannot be happy if we do not like ourselves. It affects the way we relate to others. A person who does not like oneself will not like others and will not be able to relate effectively. It influences the way we learn, the way we do our job, the kind of marriage we have, the success or failure of raising our children, and just about everything we do in life.

If a human being can be compared to a generator of power, then self-esteem is the switch that turns it on. Without that first step, nothing else works well, if at all.

All of us should want to find ways to **assess** and **improve** our self-esteem. With a heightened understanding of its importance in our lives, and some practice in raising it and strengthening it, we can become happier, more creative, energetic, fulfilled and productice human beings.

Dov Peretz Elkins
Summer, 1979.

I / Self Theory

If I am not for myself, who will be?
Hillel, from the Talmud

True dignity abides with him only, who, in the silent hour of inward thought, can still respect and still revere himself, in lowliness of heart.
William Wordsworth

A Theory of Personality

Carl R. Rogers

In endeavoring to order our perceptions of the individual as he appears in therapy, a theory of the development of personality, and of the dynamics of behavior, has been constructed. It may be well to repeat the warning previously given, and to note that the initial propositions of this theory are those which are furthest from the matrix of our experience and hence are most suspct. As one reads on, the propositions become steadily closer to the experience of therapy. As before, the defined terms and constructs are italicized, and are to be understood as previously defined.

A. POSTULATED CHARACTERISTICS OF THE HUMAN INFANT

It is postulated that the individual, during the period of infancy, has at least these attributes.

1. He perceives his *experience* as reality. His *experience* is his reality.
   a. As a consequence he has greater potential *awareness* of what reality is for him than does anyone else, since no one else can completely assume his *internal frame of reference.*
2. He has an inherent tendency toward *actualizing* his organism.
3. He interacts with his reality in terms of his basic *actualizing* tendency. Thus his behavior is the goal-directed attempt of the organism to satisfy the experienced needs for *actualization* in the reality as *perceived.*
4. In this interaction he behaves as an organized whole, as a gestalt.
5. He engages in an *organismic valuing process,* valuing *experience* with reference to the *actualizing tendency* as a criterion. *Experiences* which are *perceived* as negating such maintenance or enhancement are valued negatively.
6. He behaves with adience toward positively valued *experiences* and with avoidance toward those negatively valued.

Comment. In this view as formally stated, the human infant is seen as having an inherent motivational system (which he shares in common with all living things) and a regulatory system (the valuing process) which by its "feedback" keeps the organism "on the beam" of satisfying his motivational needs. He lives in an environment which for theoretical purposes may be said to exist only in him, or to be of his own creation.

Reprinted by permission from PSYCHOLOGY: A STUDY OF A SCIENCE, Volume 3, ed. S. Koch, by permission of McGraw-Hill Book Company, © 1959.

This last point seems difficult for some people to comprehend. It is the perception of the environment which constitutes the environment, regardless as to how this relates to some "real" reality which we may philosophically postulate. The infant may be picked up by a friendly, affectionate person. If his perception of the situation is that this is a strange and frightening experience, it is this perception, not the "reality" or the "stimulus" which will regulate his behavior. To be sure, the relationship with the environment is a transactional one, and if his continuing experience contradicts his initial perception, then in time his perception will change. But the effective reality which influences behavior is at all times the perceived reality. We can operate theoretically from this base without having to resolve the difficult question of what "really" constitutes reality.

Another comment which may be in order is that no attempt has been made to supply a complete catalogue of the equipment with which the infant faces the world. Whether he possesses instincts, or an innate sucking reflex, or an innate need for affection, are interesting questions to pursue, but the answers seem peripheral rather than essential to a theory of personality.

B. THE DEVELOPMENT OF THE SELF

1. In line with the tendency toward differentiation which is a part of the *actualizing tendency,* a portion of the individual's *experience* becomes differentiated and *symbolized* in an *awareness* of being, *awareness* of functioning. Such awareness may be described as *self-experience.*

2. This representation in *awareness* of being and functioning becomes elaboated through interaction with the environment, particularly the environment comosed of significant others, into a *concept of self,* a perceptual object in his *experiental field.*

Comment. These are the logical first steps in the development of the self. It is by no means the construct developed in our own thinking, as has been indicated in the section of definitions.

C. THE NEED FOR POSITIVE REGARD

1. As the awareness of self emerges, the individual develops a *need for positive regard.* This need is universal in human beings, and in the individual is pervasive and persistent. Whether it is an inherent or learned need is irrelevant to the theory. Standal, who formulated the concept, regards it as the latter.

a. The satisfaction of this need is necessarily based upon inferences regarding the experiential field of another.

(1) Consequently it is often ambiguous.

b. It is associated with a very wide range of the individual's *experiences.*

c. It is reciprocal, in that when an individual discriminates himself as satisfying another's need for *positive regard,* he necessarily experiences satisfaction of his own need for *positive regard.*

(1) Hence it is rewarding both to satisfy this need in another, and to experience the satisfaction of one's own need by another.

d. It is potent, in that the *positive regard* of any social other is communicated to the total *regard complex* which the individual associates with that social other.

(1) Consequently the expression of positive regard by a significant social other can become more compelling than the *organismic valuing process*, and the individual becomes more adient to the *positive regard* of such others than toward *experiences* which are of positive value in *actualizing* the organism.

D. THE DEVELOPMENT OF THE NEED FOR SELF-REGARD

1. **The positive regard satisfactions or frustrations associated with any particular** *self-experience* or group of *self-experiences* come to be experienced by the individual independently of *positive regard* transactions with social others. *Positive regard experienced* in this fashion is termed *self-regard*.

2. A *need for self-regard* develops as a learned need developing out of the association of *self-experiences* with the satisfaction or frustration of the *need for positive regard*.

3. The individual thus comes to *experience positive regard* or loss of *positive regard* independently of transactions with any social other. He becomes in a sense his own significant social other.

4. Like *positive regard, self-regard* which is *experienced* in relation to any particular *self-experience* or group of *self-experiences,* is communicated to the total *self-regard complex.*

E. THE DEVELOPMENT OF CONDITIONS OF WORTH

1.When *self-experiences* of the individual are discriminated by significant others as being more or less worthy of *positive regard,*then *self-regard* becomes similarly selective.

2. When a *self-experience* is avoided (or sought) solely because it is less (or more) worthy of *self-regard,* the individual is said to have acquired a *condition of worth.*

3. If an individual should *experience* only *unconditional positive regard,* then no *conditions of worth* would develop, *self-regard* would be unconditional, the needs for *positive regard* and *self-regard* would never be at variance with *organismic evaluation,* and the individual would continue to be *psychologically adjusted,* and would be fully functioning. This chain of events is hypothetically possible, and hence important theoretically, though it does not appear to occur in actuality.

Comment. This is an important sequence in personality development, stated more fully by Standal. It may help to restate the sequence in informal, illustrative, and much less exact terms.

The infant learns to need love. Love is very satisfying, but to know whether he is receiving it or not he must observe his mother's face, gestures, and other ambiguous signs. He develops a total gestalt as to the way he is regarded by his mother and each new experience of love or rejection tends to alter the whole gestalt. Consequently each behavior on his mother's part such as a specific disapproval of a specific behavior tends to be experienced as disapproval in general. So important is this to the infant that he comes to be guided in his behavior not by the degree to which an experience maintains or enhances the organism, but by the likelihood of receiving maternal love.

Soon he learns to view himself in much the same way, liking or disliking himself as a total configuration. He tends, quite independently of his mother or others, to view himself and his behavior in the same way they have. This means that some behaviors are regarded positively which are not actually experienced organismically as satisfying. Other behaviors are regarded negatively which are not actually experienced as unsatisfying. It is when he behaves in accordance with these introjected values that he may be said to have acquired conditions of worth. He cannot regard himself positively, as having worth, unless he lives in terms of these conditions. He now reacts with adience or avoidance toward certain behaviors solely because of these introjected conditions of self-regard, quite without reference to the organismic consequences of these behaviors. This is what is meant by living in terms of introjected values (the phrase formerly used) or conditions of worth.

It is not theoretically necessary that such a sequence develop. If the infant always felt prized, if his own feelings were always accepted even though some behaviors were inhibited, then no conditions of worth would develop. This could at least theoretically be achieved if the parental attitude was genuinely of this sort: "I can understand how satisfying it feels to you to hit your baby brother (or to defecate when and where you please, or to destroy things) and I love you and am quite willing for you to have those feelings. But I am quite willing for me to have my feelings, too, and I feel very distressed when your brother is hurt, (or annoyed or sad at other behaviors) and so I do not let you hit him. Both your feelings and my feelings are important, and each of us can freely have his own." If the child were thus able to retain his own organismic evaluation of each experience, then his life would become a balancing of these satisfactions. Schematically he might feel, "I enjoy hitting baby brother. It feels good. I do not enjoy mother's distress. That feels dissatisfying to me. I enjoy pleasing her." Thus his behavior would sometimes involve the satisfaction of hitting his brother, sometimes the satisfaction of pleasing mother. But he would never have to disown the feelings of satisfaction or dissatisfaction which he experienced in this differential way.

F. THE DEVELOPMENT OF INCONGRUENCE BETWEEN SELF AND EXPERIENCE

1. Because of the need for *self*-regard, the individual *perceives* his *experience* selectively, in terms of the *conditions of worth* which have come to exist in him.

   a. Experiences which are in accord with his *conditions of worth* are *perceived* and *symbolized* accurately in *awareness.*

   b. Experiences which run contrary to the *conditions of worth* are *perceived* selectively and distortedly as if in accord with the *conditions of worth,* or are in part or whole, *denied to awareness.*

2. Consequently some experiences now occur in the organism which are not recognized as *self-experiences,* are not accurately *symbolized,* and are not organized into the *self-structure* in *accurately symbolized* form.

3. Thus from the time of the first selective *perception* in terms of *conditions of worth,* the states of *incongruence between self and experience,* of *psychological maladjustment* and of *vulnerability,* exist to some degree.

Comment. It is thus because of the distorted perceptions arising from the conditions of worth that the individual departs from the integration which characterizes his infant state. From this point on his concept of self includes distorted perceptions which do not accurately represent his experience, and his experience includes elements which are not included in the picture he has of himself. Thus he can no longer live as a unified whole person, but various part functions now become characteristic. Certain experiences tend to threaten the self. To maintain the self-structure defensive reactions are necessary. Behavior is regulated at times by the self and at times by those aspects of the organism's experience which are not included in the self. The personality is henceforth divided, with the tensions and inadequate functioning which accompany such lack of unity.

This, as we see it, is the basic estrangement in man. He has not been true to himself, to his own natural organismic valuing of experience, but for the sake of preserving the positive regard of others has now come to falsify some of the values he experiences and to perceive them only in terms based upon their value to others. Yet this has not been a conscious choice, but a natural—and tragic—development in infancy. The path of development toward psychological maturity, the path of therapy, is the undoing of this estrangement in man's functioning, the dissolving of conditions of worth, the achievement of a self which is congruent with experience, and the restoration of a unified organismic valuing process as the regulator of behavior.

G. THE DEVELOPMENT OF DISCREPANCIES IN BEHAVIOR

1. As a consequence of the incongruence between self and experience described in *F,* a similar incongruence arises in the behavior of the individual.

a. Some behaviors are consistent with the *self-concept* and maintain and actualize and enhance it.

(1) Such behaviors are *accurately symbolized* in *awareness.*

b. Some behaviors maintain, enhance, and actualize those aspects of the experience of the organism which are not assimilated into the *self-structure.*

(1) These behaviors are either unrecognized as *self-experiences* or *perceived* in distorted or selective fashion in such a way as to be *congruent* with the *self.*

H. THE EXPERIENCE OF THREAT AND THE PROCESS OF DEFENSE

−. As the organism continues to *experience,* an *experience* which is incongruent with the self-structure (and its incororated *conditions of worth),* is *subscieved* as *threatening.*

2. The essential nature of the *threat* is that if the *experience* were *accurately symbolized* in *awareness,* the *self-concept* would no longer be a

consistent gestalt, the *conditions of worth* would be violated, and the *need for self-regard* would be frustrated. A state of *anxiety* would exist.

3. The process of *defense* is the reaction which prevents these events from occurring.

   a. This process consists of the selective *perception* or *distortion* of the *experience* and/or the *denial to awareness* of the *experience* or some portion thereof, thus keeping the total *perception* of the *experience* consistent with the individual's *self-structure,* and consistent with his *conditions of worth.*

4. The general consequences of the process of *defense,* aside from its preservation of the above consistencies, are a rigidity of *perception,* due to the necessity of distorting *perceptions,* an inaccurate *perception* of reality, due to distortion and omission of data, and *intensionality.*

Comment. Section *G* describes the psychological basis for what are usually thought of as neurotic behaviors, and Section *H* describes the mechanisms of these behaviors. From our point of view it appears more fundamental to think of defensive behaviors (described in these two sections) and disorganized behaviors (described below). Thus the defensive behaviors include not only the behaviors customarily regarded as neurotic—rationalization, fantasy, projection, compulsions, phobias, and the like—but also some of the behaviors customarily regarded as psychotic, notably paranoid behaviors and perhaps catatonic states. The disorganized category includes many of the "irrational" and "acute" psychotic behaviors, as will be explained below. This seems to be a more fundamental classification than those usually employed, and perhaps more fruitful in considering treatment. It also avoids any concept of neurosis and psychosis as entities in themselves, which we believe has been an unfortuante and misleading conception.

Let us consider for a moment the general range of the defensive behaviors from the simplest variety, common to all of us, to the more extreme and crippling varieties. Take first of all, rationalization. ("I didn't really make that mistake. It was this way...") Such excuses involve a perception of behavior distorted in such a way as to make it congruent with our concept of self (as a person who doesn't make mistakes). Fantasy is another example. ("I am a beautiful princess, and all the men adore me.") Because the actual experience is threatening to the concept of self (as an adequate person, in this example), this experience is denied, and a new symbolic world is created which enhances the self, but completely avoids any recognition of the actual experience. Where the incongruent experience is a stong need, the organism actualizes itself by finding a way of expressing this need, but it is perceived in a way which is consistent with the self. Thus an individual whose self-concept involves no "bad" sexual thoughts may feel or express the thought "I am pure, but you are trying to make me think filthy thoughts." This would be thought of as projection or as a paranoid idea. It involves the expression of the organism's need for sexual satisfactions, but it is expressed in such a fashion that this need may be denied to awareness and the behavior perceived as consistent with the self. Such examples could be continued, but perhaps the point is clear that the incongruence between self and experience is handled by the distorted perception of experience or behavior, or by the denial of experience in awareness (behavior is rarely denied, though this is possible), or by some combination of distortion and denial.

I. THE PROCESS OF BREAKDOWN AND DISORGANIZATION

Up to this point the theory of personality which has been formulated applies to every individual in a lesser or greater degree. In this and the following section certain processes are described which occur only when certain specified conditions are present.

1. If the individual has a large or significant degree of *incongruence between self and experience* and if a significant experience demonstrating this *incongruence* occurs suddenly, or with a high degree of obviousness, then the organism's process of *defense* is unable to operate successfully.

2. As a result *anxiety* is *experienced* as the *incongruence* is subceived. The degree of *anxiety* is dependent upon the extent of the *self-structure* which is *threatened*.

3. The process of *defense* being unsuccessful, the *experience* is *accurately symbolized* in *awareness,* and the gestalt of the *self-structure* is broken by this *experience* of the *incongruence* in *awareness.* A state of disorganization results.

4. In such a state of disorganization the organism behaves at times in ways which are openly consistent with experiences which have hitherto been distorted or denied to awareness.At other times the self may temporarily regain regnancy, and the organism may behave in ways consistent with it. Thus in such a state of disorganization, the tension between the concept of self (with its included distorted perceptions) and the experiences which are not accurately symbolized or included in the concept of self, is expressed in a confused regnancy, first one and then the other supplying the "feedback" by which the organism regulates behavior.

Comment. This section, as will be evident from its less exact formulation, is new, tentative, and needs much more consideration. Its meaning can be illuminated by various examples.

Statements 1 and 2 above may be illustrated by anxiety-producing experiences in therapy, or by acute psychotic breakdowns. In the freedom of therapy, as the individual expresses more and more of himself, he finds himself on the verge of voicing a feeling which is obviously and undeniably true, but which is flatly contradictory to the conception of himself which he has held. Anxiety results, and if the situation is appropriate (as described under *J*) this anxiety is moderate, and the result is constructive. But if, through overzealous and effective interpretation by the therapist, or through some other means, the individual is brought face to face with more of his denied experiences than he can handle, disorganization ensues and a psychotic break occurs, as described in statement 3. We have known this to happen when an individual has sought "therapy" from several different sources simultaneously. It has also been illustrated by some of the early experience with sodium pentathol therapy. Under the drug the individual revealed many of the experiences which hitherto he had denied to himself, and which accounted for the incomprehensible elements in his behavior. Unwisely faced with the material in his normal state he could not deny its authenticity, his defensive processes could not deny or distort the experience, and hence the self-structure was broken, and psychotic break occurred.

Acute psychotic behaviors appear often to be describable as behaviors which are consistent with the denied aspects of experience rather than consistent with the self. Thus the person who has kept sexual impulses rigidly under control, denying them as an aspect of self, may now make open sexual overtures to those with whom he is in contact. Many of the so-called irrational behaviors of psychosis are of this order.

Once the acute psychotic behaviors have been exhibited, a process of defense again sets in to protect the organism against the exceedingly painful awareness of incongruence. Here I would voice my opinion very tentatively as to this process of defense. In some instances perhaps the denied experiences are now regnant, and the organism defends itself against the awareness of the self. In other instances the self is again regnant, and behavior is consistent with it, but the self has been greatly altered. It is now a self concept which includes the important theme, "I am a crazy, inadequate, unreliable person who contains impulses and forces beyond my control." Thus it is a self in which little or no confidence is felt.

It is hoped that this portion of the theory may be further elaborated and refined and made more testable in the future.

J. THE PROCESS OF REINTEGRATION

In the situations described under sections *G* and *H*, (and probably in situations of breakdown as described under *I*, though there is less evidence on this) a process of reintegration is possible, a process which moves in the direction of increasing the *congruence* between *self* and *experience*. This may be described as follows:

1. In order for the process of *defense* to be reversed—for a customarily *threatening experience* to be *accurately symbolized* in *awareness* and assimilated into the *self-structure*, certain conditions must exist.

a. There must be a decrease in the *conditions of worth.*

b. There must be an increase in *unconditional self-regard.*

2. The communicated *unconditional positive regard* of a significant other is one way of achieving these conditions.

a. In order for the *unconditional positive regard* to be communicated, it must exist in a context of *empathic* understanding.

b. When the individual *perceives* such *unconditional positive regard,* existing *conditions of worth* are weakened or dissolved.

c. Another consequence is the increase in his own *unconditional positive self-regard.*

d. Conditions 2a and 2b above thus being met, *threat* is reduced, the process of *defense is reversed,* and *experiences* customarily *threatening* are *accurately symbolized* and integrated into the *self-concept.*

3. The consequences of 1 and 2 above are that the individual is less likely to encounter *threatening experiences;* the process of *defense* is less frequent and its consequences reduced; *self* and *experience* are more *congruent; self-regard* is increased; *positive regard* for others is increased; *positive regard* for others is increased; *psychological adjustment* is increased; the *organismic valuing process* becomes increasingly the basis of regulating behavior; the in-

dividual becomes nearly fully functioning.

Comment. This section is simply the theory of therapy which we presented earlier, now stated in a slightly more general form. It is intended to emphasize the fact that the reintegration or restoration of personality occurs always and only (at least so we are hypothesizing) in the presence of certain definable conditions. These are essentially the same whether we are speaking of formal psychotherapy continued over a considerable period, in which rather drastic personality changes may occur or whether we are speaking of the minor constructive changes which may be brought about by contact with an understanding friend or family member.

One other brief comment may be made about item *2a* above. Empathic understanding is always necessary if unconditional positive regard is to be fully communicated. If I know little or nothing of you, and experience an unconditional positive regard for you, this means little because further knowledge of you may reveal aspects which I cannot so regard. But if I know you thoroughly, knowing and empathically understanding a wide variety of your feelings and behaviors, and still experience an unconditional positive regard, this is very meaningful. It comes close to being fully known and fully accepted.

The Self in Recent RogerianTheory

C. H. Patterson

The objective of this paper is to sketch the place of the self in the current client-centered approach to personality. While the self is today becoming of central importance in all theories of personality, it constitutes the core of the Rogerian approach which has, in fact, been designated by some writers (e.g., 9, 15) as "self-theory." Perhaps this is because client-centered theory is based upon the observations of individual clients in therapy.

ROGER'S FORMULATIONS

1947

Roger's earliest formulation was presented in 1947 (17): "The self is a basic factor in the formation of personality and in the determination of behavior." As the perception of self changes, behavior changes. The person's feeling of adequacy is basic to psychological adjustment. The absence of threat is important for the development of an adequate self-concept and is a condition for changes in the self-concept. The self-concept is, by definition, a phenomenological concept: it is the self as seen by the experiencing person.

1951

In 1951 Rogers (18) amplified and extended his discussion of the self in nineteen propositions. The point of view remained perceptual and phenomenological; there is no reality for the individual other than that given by his perceptions. The self is the central concept of personality and behavior. While the basic drive of the organism is the maintenance and enhancement of the organism, the psychological self may take precedence over the physiological organism.

Once the self has developed, experiences are perceived and evaluated in terms of their relevance and significance to the self. Behavior is normally consistent with the self-concept, even at the expense of the organism. However, organic experiences or needs which are unsymbolized (because they are unacceptable) may at times lead to behavior inconsistent with the self-concept ("I was not myself"), or to psychological tension and malad-

Reprinted from the JOURNAL OF INDIVIDUAL PSYCHOLOGY, 1961, 17, pp. 5-11, by permission.

justment. Experiences which are inconsistent with the self-concept may be perceived as threatening, and may be rejected, denied, or distorted; the self-concept is defended.

Psychological adjustment or integration, on the other hand, exists when the self-concept is congruent with all the experiences of the organism. Under conditions of absence of threat to the self, all experiences—including the organismic—may be examined and assimilated into the self-concept, leading to changes in the self-concept. This occurs in therapy.

1959

The most recent and most detailed of Rogers' theoretical discussions, a more systematic and extended formulation of earlier expressions, appeared in mimeographed form in 1955 and in print in 1959 (19). Self-actualization becomes an important aspect of a general actualizing tendency.

The self-concept is defined as "the organized, consistent conceptual Gestalt composed of characteristics of the 'I' or 'me' and the perceptions of the relationships of the 'I' or 'me' to others and to various aspects of life, together with the value attached to these perceptions" (19, p. 200). The ideal self is introduced into the theory and is defined as "the self-concept which the individual would most like to possess, upon which he places the highest value for himself" (19, p. 200).

Several concepts having to do with regard are included. Rogers postulates a basic, though secondary or learned, need for positive regard from others—that is for warmth, liking, respect, sympathy, and acceptance—and a need for positive self-regard, which is related to or dependent upon positive regard from others.

Unconditional self-regard is a state of general positive self-regard, irrespective of conditions. Positive self-regard may be conditional, however, when the individual "values an experience positively or negatively solely because of ...conditions of worth which he has taken over from others, not because the experience enhances or fails to enhance his organism" (19, p. 209) In this case the individual is vulnerable to threat and anxiety.

The central ideas in Rogers' theory of the self may be stated as follows:

1. The theory of the self, as part of the general personality theory, is phenomenological. The essence of phenomenology is that "man lives essentially in his own personal and subjective world" (19, p. 191).
2. The self becomes differentiated as part of the actualizing tendency, from the environment, through transactions with the environment—particularly the social environment. The process by which this occurs is not detailed by Rogers, but is presumably along the lines described by the sociologists Cooley (8) and Mead (13).₁
3. The self-concept is the organization of the perceptions of the self. It is the self-concept, rather than any "real" self, which is of significance in personality and behavior. As Combs and Snygg note, the existence of a "real" self is a philosophical question, since it cannot be observed directly (6, p. 123).
4. The self-concept becomes the most significant determinant of response to the environment. It governs the perceptions or meanings attributed to the environment.
5. Whether learned or inherent, a need for positive regard from others

develops or emerges with the self-concept. While Rogers leans toward attributing this need to learning, I would include it as an element of the self-actualizing tendency.

6. A need for positive self-regard, or self-esteem, according to Rogers, likewise is learned through internalization or introjection of experiences of positive regard by others. But, alternatively, it may be an aspect of the self-actualizing tendency.

7. When positive self-regard depends on evaluations by others, descrepancies may develop between the needs of the organism and the needs of the self-concept for positive self-regard. There is thus incongruence between the self and experience, or psychological maladjustment. Maladjustment is the result of attempting to preserve the existing self-concept from the threat of experiences which are inconsistent with it, leading to selective perception and distortion or denial of experience.

This highly condensed summary does not include the vicissitudes of the self through the process of disorganization, or the processes of reorganization which take place in therapy.

While a number of persons have contributed to the theory, including Raimy (16), Snygg and Combs (21), and many others who have been associated with Rogers, there has been no other comparable exposition of the theory nor are there any adequately stated alternatives or variations of it. Rogers' terminology differs in some respects from that used by other client-centered writers, but the basic concepts are similar, if not identical. For example, some theorists, including myself (14), have used the term self-esteem to refer to what Rogers designates as positive self-regard.

COMPARISON WITH OTHER FORMULATIONS

"Me" versus "I"

Several theorists (2, 4, 13, 22) have emphasized two aspects of the self, essentially distinguishing between the *self as object,* the "me," and the *self as subject,* the "I." The first is often referred to as the *self-concept,* the second as the *ego,* although, as Hall and Lindzey (9, p. 468) point out, there is no general agreement upon terms. James called the "me" the empirical self and the "I" the pure ego—the sense of personal identity or the judging thought.This personal identity, he suggested, may not exist as a fact, "but it would exist as a *feeling* all the same; the consciousness of it would be there, and the psychologist would still have to analyze that" (12, p. 333).The ego would appear to be self-consciousness. Mead's conceptions of the "I" and the "me" appear to be similar, although his discussion is difficult to follow. The "I" appears to be the awareness of the self as of the moment of action (13, pp. 173-178, 192).

These concepts, while preferable to the idea of the "I" as an executive, which lends itself to reification, are vague and difficult to pin down. At least I am not able to differentiate actually, practically, or operationally between the executive aspects of the self, and the self as an object to the self. The self of Snygg and Combs is both an object and doer. Others, including Allport (1) and Sherif and Cantril (20), also appear to adopt this view. Hilgard (10) suggests that the concept of the self as a doer is an error into which psychologists have been led by the common-sense or lay view that behavior seems to be self-determined.

In Rogers' theory the self-concept, although an important determiner of behavior, is not an executive or doer. There is no need for positing such an executive. The organism is by nature continually active, seeking its goal of actualization, and the self as part of the organism is also seeking actualization through its constant activity. The self-concept thus influences the direction of activity, rather than initiating it and directing it entirely. Thus Rogers avoids the problems of reification and the ambiguousness of the concept of the "I" or the ego as the executive. James' sense of personal identity might be considered a part of the self-concept, and the ego or "I" as the awareness of the self-concept. However, I am not sure that this solution is entirely satisfactory.

Ideal Self

In his recent formulation of the concept of the ideal self Rogers indicates that the perception of the ideal self becomes more realistic, and the self becomes more congruent with the ideal self, as an outcome of therapy. This suggests that personality disturbance is characterized by an unrealistic self-ideal, and/or incongruence between the self-concept and the self-ideal. This formulation has been the basis of some research by the client-centered school (e.g., 3). But it is not incorporated in Rogers' statement of the theory. The theory apparently does not recognize conflict between the self-concept and the self-ideal as a source of disturbance, but emphasizes the conflict between the self-concept and organismic experiences as its source. This is in contrast to some other theories in which the self-ideal is a central concept and an important factor in psychological adjustment or maladjustment, e.g. Horney (11).

The Self

The notion of the self, or the self-structure, is broader than the self-concept. It includes the self-concept and the ideal self. What else it includes is not clear. Combs and Snygg speak of the phenomenal self, defined as the "organization of all the ways an individual has of seeing himself" (6, p. 126). The self-concept includes "only those perceptions about self which seem most vital or important to the individual himself" (6, p. 127). How these are to be differentiated is not indicated. Rogers considers the self-concept to be in the person's awareness, whereas the self may include aspects not in awareness.

PROBLEMS OF OPERATIONAL DEFINITION

Rogers made an effort to keep his constructs and concepts so that they can be operationally defined. The phenomenological approach, it seems to me, fosters this effort. One is not concerned about the "real" self, the "real" environment, etc., but with the perceptions of particular individuals. The self-concept and the self-ideal are perceptions which can be studied and objectified by instruments such as the Q-sort, or by tests of the "Who am I" variety. The latter, though ideally suited for use with client-centered theory, have not, however, to my knowledge, been used in connection with this theory.

Rogers points out the problem of operationally defining the organismic experiences which, it is assumed, conflict with the self-concept. The aspects of the self other than the self-concept and the self-ideal, are also not operationally defined. Maybe we do not need these concepts. I see no need for unconscious elements of the self, for example. Aspects of the self which are not in awareness but which can be brought into awareness, can be tapped by instructions such as "Sort these statements in terms of your concept of yourself as a father." The self, insofar as it is behaviorally effective, may consist only of the various self-perceptions—thus resolving the problem posed above about the area of the self apart from the self-concept and the self-ideal. The organismic experiences, on the other hand, as an essential aspect of the theory, must be brought within the realm of measurement. The approach of Chodorkoff (5), using Q-sorts of self-referent items by clinicians as an "objective description" of the total experience of the individual, though operational, may be questioned as to its validity.

There is also the problem, pointed out by Combs and Soper (7), that although the self-concept may be operationally defined as the individual's statements about himself, these statements do not necessarily correspond to his perception of himself. His statements may be inaccurate for a number of reasons, including inability or unwillingness to give an accurate report. Yet there is no other approach to determining the self-concept, since by definition it is the perception of the self by the individual, and no one else can report upon it or describe it.

In general, what is needed is a more formal theoretical statement which would lead to testable hypotheses for research, not only with clients in therapy, but in many other situations, with many other kinds of subjects.

SUMMARY

The aspects of Rogers' theory which relate to his central formulation of the self-concept have been summarized. A comparison with the thinking of others regarding the self attempted to clarify some differences and showed other differences in need of resolution. Some problems of operational definition were briefly discussed.

1. Allport, G.W. The ego in contemporary psychology. *Psychol. Rev.*, 1943, **50**, 451-468. Also in *Personality and social encounter: selected essays.* Boston: Beacon Press, 1960, pp. 71-93.
2. Bertocci, P.A. The psychological self, the ego and personality. *Psychol. Rev.*, 1945, **52**, 91-99.
3. Butler, J.M., & Haigh, G.V. Changes in the relation between self-concepts and ideal concepts consequent upon client-centered counseling. In C.R. Rogers & R.F. Dymond (Eds.), *Psychotherapy and personality change.* Chicago: University of Chicago Press, 1954, pp. 55-76
4. Chein, I. The awareness of the self and the structure of the ego. *Psychol. Rev,* 1944, **51**, 504-514.
5. Chodorkoff, B. Self-perception, perceptual defense, and adjustment. *J. Abnorm Psychol.,* 1954, **49**, 508-512.
6. Combs, A.W., & Snygg, D. *Individual behavior,* rev. ed. New York: Harper, 1959.
7. Combs, A.W., & Soper, D.W. The self, its derivative terms, and research. *J. Indiv. Psychol.,* 1957, **13**, 134-145. Also in A.E. Kuenzli (Ed.), *The phe-*

nomenological problem. New York: Harper, 1959, pp. 31-48.

8. Cooley, C.H. *Human nature and the social order.* New York: Scribner's, 1902.
9. Hall, C.S., & Lindzey, G. *Theories of personality.* New York: Wiley, 1957.
10. Hilgard, E.R. Human motives and the concept of the self. *Amer. Psychologist,* 1949, **4,** 374-382. Also in H. Brand (Ed.), *The study of personality.* New York: Wiley, 1954, pp. 347-361.
11. Horney, K. *Neurosis and human growth.* New York: W.W. Norton, 1950.
12. James, W. *The principles of psychology.* Vol. 1. New York: Holt, 1890.
13. Mead, G.H. *Mind, self and society.* Chicago: University of Chicago Press, 1934.
14. Patterson, C.H. *Counseling and psychotherapy: theory and practice,* New York: Harper, 1959.
15. Pepinsky, H.B., & Pepinsky, P.N. *Counseling: theory and practice,* New York: Ronald Press, 1954.
16. Raimy, V.C. Self-reference in counseling interviews. *J. Consult. Psychol.,* 1948, **12,** 153-163. Also in A.E. Kuenzli (Ed.), *The phenomenological problem.* New York: Harper, 1959, pp. 76-95.
17. Rogers, C.R. Some observations on the organization of personality. *Amer. Psychologist,* 1947, **2,** 358-368. Also in A.E. Kuenzli (Ed.), *The phenomenological problem.* New York: Harper, 1959, pp. 49-75.
18. Rogers, C.R. *Client-centered therapy.* Boston: Houghton-Mifflin, 1951.
19. Rogers, C.R. A theory of therapy, personality, and interpersonal relationships, as developed in the client-centered framework. In S. Koch (Ed.), *Psychology: A study of a science.* Vol. 3. New York: McGraw-Hill, 1959, pp. 184-256.
20. Sherif, M., & Cantril, H. *The psychology of ego-involvements.* New York: Wiley, 1947.
21. Snygg, D., & Combs, A.W. *Individual behavior.* New York: Harper, 1949.
22. Symonds, P.M. *The ego and the self.* New York: Appleton-Century-Crofts, 1951.

The Idealized Image
Karen Horney

Our discussions of the neurotic's fundamental attitudes toward others has acquainted us with two of the major ways in which he attempts to solve his conflicts or, more precisely, to dispose of them. One of these consists in repressing certain aspects of the personality and bringing their opposites to the fore; the other is to put such distance between oneself and one's fellows that the conflicts are set out of operation. Both processes induce a feeling of unity that permits the individual to function, even if at considerable cost to himself.₁

A further attempt, here to be described, is the creation of an image of what the neurotic believes himself to be, or of what at the time he feels he can or ought to be. Conscious or unconscious, the image is always in large degree removed from reality, though the influence it exerts on the person's life is very real indeed. What is more, it is always flattering in character, as illustrated by a cartoon in the *New Yorker* in which a large middle-aged woman sees herself in the mirror as a slender young girl. The particular features of the image vary and are determined by the structure of the personality: beauty may be held to be outstanding, or power, intelligence, genius, saintliness, honesty, or what you will. Precisely to the extent that the image is unrealistic, it tends to make the person arrogant, in the original meaning of the word; for arrogance, though used synonymously with superciliousness, means to arrogate to oneself qualities that one does not have, or that one has potentially but not factually. And the more unrealistic the image, the more it makes the person vulnerable and avid for outside affirmation and recognition. We do not need confirmation for qualities of which we are certain, but we will be extremely touchy when false claims are questioned.

We can observe this idealized image at its most blatant in the grandiose notions of psychotics; but in principle its characteristics are the same in neurotics. It is less fantastic here, but it may be just as real to them. If we regard the degree of removal from reality as marking the difference between psychoses and neuroses, we may consider the idealized image as a bit of psychosis woven into the texture of neurosis.

In all its essentials the idealized image is an unconscious phenomenon.

Selection is reprinted from OUR INNER CONFLICTS by Karen Horney, M.D., with the permission of W.W. Norton & Company, Inc. Copyright 1945 by W.W. Norton & Company, Inc. Copyright renewed 1972 by Renate Mintz, Marianne von Eckardt, & Brigitte Horney Swarzenski.

Although his self-inflation may be most obvious even to an untrained observer, the neurotic is not aware that he is idealizing himself. Nor does he know what a bizarre conglomeration of characters is assembled here. He may have a vague sense that he is making high demands upon himself, but mistaking such perfectionist demands for genuine ideals he in no way questions their validity and is indeed rather proud of them.

How his creation affects his attitude toward himself varies with the individual and depends largely on the focus of interest. If the neurotic's interest lies in convincing himself that he *is* his idealized image, he develops the belief that he is in fact the mastermind, the exquisite human being, whose very faults are divine.[2] If the focus is on the realistic self which by comparison with the idealized image is highly despicable, self-derogatory criticism is in the foreground. Since the picture of the self that results from such disparagement is just as far removed from reality as is the idealized image, it could appropriately be called the despised image. If, finally, the focus is upon the discrepancy between the idealized image and the actual self, then all he is aware of and all we can observe are his incessant attempts to bridge the gap and whip himself into perfection. In this event he keeps reiterating the word "should" with amazing frequency. He keeps telling us what he should have felt, thought, done. He is at bottom as convinced of his inherent perfection as the naively "narcissistic" person, and betrays it by the belief that he actually could be perfect if only he were more strict with himself, more controlled, more alert, more circumspect.

In contrast to authentic ideals, the idealized image has a static qualtiy. It is not a goal toward whose attainment he strives but a fixed idea which he worships. Ideals have a dynamic quality; they arouse an incentive to approximate them; they are an indispensable and invaluable force for growth and development. The idealized image is a decided hindrance to growth because it either denies shortcomings or merely condemns them. Genuine ideals make for humility, the idealized image for arrogance.

This phenomenon — however defined — has long been recognized. It is referred to in the philosophic writings of all times. Freud introduced it into the theory of neurosis, calling it by a variety of names: ego ideal, narcissism, superego. It forms the central thesis of Adler's psychology, described there as a striving for superiority. it would lead us too far afield to point out in detail the differences and similarities between these concepts and my own[3]. Briefly, all of these are concerned only with one or another aspect of the idealized image, and fail to see the phenomenon as a whole. Hence despite pertinent comment and argument not only by Freud and Adler but by many other writers as well — among them Franz Alexander, Paul Federn, Bernard Glueck, and Ernest Jones — the full significance of the phenomenon and its functions has not been recognized. What, then, are its functions? Apparently it fulfills vital needs. No matter how the various writers account for it theoretically, they are all agreed on the one point that it constitutes a stronghold of neurosis difficult to shake or even to weaken. Freud for one regarded a deeply ingrained "narcissistic" attitude as among the most serious obstacles to therapy.

To begin with what is perhaps its most elementary function, the idealized image substitutes for realistic self-confidence and realistic pride. A person who eventually becomes neurotic has little chance to build up initial self-confidence because of the crushing experiences he has been subjected to. Such self-confidence as he may have is further weakened in the course of his neurotic development because the very conditions indispensable for self-confidence are apt to be destroyed. It is difficult to formulate these conditions briefly. The most important factors are the aliveness and availability of one's emotional energies, the development of authentic goals of one's own, and the faculty of being an active instrument in one's own life. However a neurosis develops, just these things are liable to be damaged. Neurotic trends impair self-determination because a person is then driven instead of being himself the driver. Moreover, the neurotic's capacity to determine his own paths is continually weakened by his dependence upon people, whatever form this may have assumed — blind rebellion, blind craving to excel, and a blind need to keep away from others are all forms of dependence. Further, by inhibiting great sectors of emotional energy, he puts them completely out of action. All of these factors make it nearly impossible for him to develop his own goals. Last but not least, the basic conflict makes him divided in his own house. Being thus deprived of a substantial foundation, the neurotic must inflate his feeling of significance and power. That is why a belief in his omnipotence is a never-failing component of the idealized image.

A second function is closely linked with the first. The neurotic does not feel weak in a vacuum but in a world peopled with enemies ready to cheat, humiliate, enslave, and defeat him. He must therefore constantly measure and compare himself with others, not for reasons of vanity or caprice but by bitter necessity. And since at bottom he feels weak and contemptible — as we shall see later on — he must search for something that will make him feel better, more worthy than others. Whether it takes the form of feeling more saintly or more ruthless, more loving or more cynical, he must in his own mind feel superior in some way — regardless of any particular drive to excel. For the most part such a need contains elements of wanting to triumph over others, because no matter what the structure of the neurosis there is always vulnerability and a readiness to feel looked down on and humiliated. The need for vindictive triumph as an antidote to feeling humiliated may be acted upon or may exist mainly in the neurotic's own mind; it may be conscious or unconscious, but it is one of the driving forces in the neurotic need for superiority and gives it its special coloring.[4] The competitive spirit of this civilization is not only conducive to fostering neuroses in general, through the disturbances in human relationships it creates, but it also specifically feeds this need for pre-eminence.

We have seen how the idealized image substitutes for true self-confidence and pride. But there is yet another way in which it serves as surrogate. Since the neurotic's ideals are contradictory they cannot possibly have any obligating power; remaining dim and undefined, they can give him no guidance. Hence if it were not that his endeavor to be his self-created idol gave a kind of meaning to his life he would feel wholly without purpose. This becomes particularly apparent in the course of analysis, when the undermining of his idealized image gives him for a time the feeling of being quite lost. And it is only then that he recognizes his confusion in the matter of ideals and that this begins to strike him as undesirable. Before, the whole subject was beyond his understanding and interest, no matter how much lip service he gave it; now for the first time he realizes that ideals have some meaning, and wants to discover what his own ideals really are. This kind of experience is evidence, I should say, that the idealized image substitutes for genuine ideals. An understanding of this function has significance for therapy. The analyst may point out to the patient at an earlier period the contradictions in his set of values. But he cannot expect any constructive interest in the subject and hence cannot work on it until the idealized image has become dispensable.

To a greater degree than any of the others, one particular function of the image can be held accountable for its rigidity. If in our private mirror we see ourselves as paragons of virtue or intelligence, even our most blatant faults and handicaps will disappear or acquire attractive coloration — just as in a good painting a shabby, decaying wall is no longer a shabby, decaying wall but a beautiful composite of brown and gray and reddish color values.

We can arrive at a deeper understanding of this defensive function if we raise the simple question: What does a person regard as his faults and shortcomings? It is one of those questions that at first sight does not seem to lead anywhere because one starts to think of infinite possibilities. Nevertheless there is a fairly concrete answer. What a person regards as his faults and shortcomings depends on what he accepts or rejects in himself. That, however — under similar cultural conditions — is determined by which aspect of the basic conflict predominates. The compliant type, for instance, does not regard his fears or his helplessness as a taint, whereas the aggressive type would regard any such feeling as shameful, to be hidden from oneself and others. The compliant type registers his hostile aggressions as sinful; the aggressive type looks upon his softer feelings as contemptible weakness. Each type, in addition, is driven to reject all that is actually mere pretense on the part of his more acceptable self. The compliant type, for instance, has to reject the fact that he is not a genuinely loving and generous person; the detached type does not want to see that his aloofness is not a matter of his own free choice, that he must keep apart because he cannot cope with others, and so on. Both, as a rule, reject sadistic trends (to be discussed later). We would thus arrive at the conclusion that what is regarded as a shortcoming and rejected is whatever does not fit into the consistent picture created by the predominant attitude toward others. And we could say that the defensive function of the idealized image is to negate the existence of conflicts; that is why it must of necessity remain so immovable. Before I recognized this I often wondered why it is so impossible for a patient to accept himself as a little less significant, a little less superior. But looked at this way the answer is clear. He cannot budge an inch because the recognition of certain shortcomings would confront him with his conflicts, thus jeopardizing the artificial harmony he has established. We can arrive, therefore, at a positive correlation between the intensity of the conflicts and the rigidity of the idealized image: an especially elaborate and rigid image permits us to infer especially disruptive conflicts.

Over and above the four functions already pointed out, the idealized image has still a fifth, likewise related to the basic conflict. The image has a more positive use than merely to camouflage the conflict's unacceptable parts. It represents a kind of artistic creation in which opposites appear reconciled or in which, at any rate, they no longer appear as conflicts to the individual himself. A few examples will show how this happens. In order to avoid lengthy reports I shall merely name the conflicts present and show how they appeared in the idealized image.

The predominating aspect of X's conflict was compliance — a great need for affection and approval, to be taken care of, to be sympathetic, generous, considerate, loving. Second in prominence was detachment, with the usual aversion to joining groups, emphasis on independence, fear of ties, sensitivity to coercion. The detachment constantly clashed with the need for human intimacy and created repeated disturbances in his relations with women. Aggressive drives, too, were quite apparent, manifesting themselves in his having to be first in any situation, in dominating others indirectly, occasionally exploiting them, and tolerating no interference. Naturally these tendencies detracted considerably from his capacity for love and friendship, and clashed as well with his detachment. Unaware of these drives, he had fabricated an idealized image that was a composite of three figures. He was the great lover and friend — incredible that any woman could care more for another man; nobody was so kind and good as he. He was the greatest leader of his time, a political genius held much in awe. And finally he was the great philosopher, the man of wisdom, one of the few gifted with profound insight into the meaning of life and its ultimate futility.

The image was not altogether fantastic. He had ample potentialities in all these directions. but the potentialities had been raised to the level of accomplished fact, of great and unique achievement. Moreover, the compulsive nature of the drives had been obscured and was replaced by a belief in innate qualities and gifts. Instead of a neurotic need for affection and approval there was a supposed capacity to love; instead of a drive to excel, assumed superior gifts; instead of a need for aloofness, independance and wisdom. Finally and most importantly, the conflicts were exorcized in the following way. The drives which in real life interfered with one another and prevented him from fulfilling any of his potentialities were promoted to the realm of abstract perfection, appearing as several compatible aspects of a rich personality; and the three aspects of the basic conflict which they represented were isolated in the three figures that made up his idealized-image.

Another example brings into clearer relief the importance of isolating the conflicting elements.₅ In the case of Y the predominant trend was detachment, in a rather extreme form, with all the implications described in the previous chapter. His tendency to comply was also quite marked, though Y himself shut it out from awareness because it was too incompatible with his desire for independence. Strivings to be extremely good occasionally broke forcibly through the shell of repression. A longing for human intimacy was conscious, and clashed continuously with his detachment. He could be ruthlessly aggressive only in his imagination: he indulged in fantasies of mass destruction, wishing quite frankly to kill all those who interfered with his life; he professed to believe in a jungle philosophy — the gospel of might makes right, with its ruthless pursuit of self-interest, was the only intelligent and unhypocritical way of living. In his actual living, however, he was rather timid; explosions of violence occurred under certain conditions only.

His idealized image was the following odd combination. Most of the time he was a hermit living on a mountaintop, having attained to infinite wisdom and serenity. At rare intervals he could turn into a werewolf, entirely devoid of human feelings, bent on killing. And as if these two incompatible figures were not enough, he was as well the ideal friend and lover.

We see here the same denial of neurotic trends, the same self-aggrandizement, the same mistaking of potentialities for realities. In this instance, though, no attempt has been made to reconcile the conflicts; the contradictions remain. But — in contrast to real life — they appear pure and undiluted. Because they are isolated they do not interfere with one another. And that seems to be what counts. The conflicts as such have disappeared.

One last example of a more unified idealized image: In the factual behavior of Z aggressive trends strongly predominated, accompanied by sadistic tendencies. He was domineering and inclined to exploit. Driven by a devouring ambition, he pushed ruthlessly ahead. He could plan, organize, fight, and adhered consciously to an unmitigated jungle philosophy. He was also extremely detached; but since his aggressive drives always entangled him with groups of people, he could not maintain his aloofness. He kept strict guard, though, not to get involved in any personal relationship nor to let himself enjoy anything to which people were essential contributors. In this he succeeded fairly well, because positive feelings for others were greatly repressed; desires for human intimacy were mainly channeled along sexual lines. There was present, however, a distinct tendency to comply, together with a need for approval that interfered with his craving for power. And there were underlying puritanical standards, used chiefly as a whip over others — but which of course he could not help applying to himself as well — that clashed headlong with his jungle philosophy.

In his idealized image he was the knight in shining armor, the crusader with wide and unfailing vision, ever pursuing the right. As becomes a wise leader, he was not personally attached to anyone but dispensed a stern though just discipline. He was honest without being hypocritical. Women loved him and he could be a great lover but was not tied to any woman. Here the same goal is achieved as in the other instances: the elements of the basic conflict are blended.

The idealized image is thus an attempt at solving the basic conflict, an attempt of at least as great importance as the others I have described. It has the enormous subjective value of serving as a binder, of holding together a divided individual. And although it exists only in the person's mind, it exerts a decisive influence on his relations with others.

The idealized image might be called a fictitious or illusory self, but that would be only a half truth and hence misleading. The wishful thinking operating in its creation is certainly striking, particularly since it occurs in persons who otherwise stand on a ground of firm reality. But this does not make it wholly fictitious. It is an imaginative creation interwoven with and determined by very realistic factors. It usually contains traces of the person's genuine ideals. While the grandiose achievements are illusory, the potentialities underlying them are often real. More relevant, it is born of very real inner necessities, it fulfills very real functions, and it has a very real influence on its creator. The processes operating in its creation are determined by such definite laws that a knowledge of its specific features permits us to make accurate inferences as to the true character structure of the particular person.

But regardless of how much fantasy is woven into the idealized image, for the neurotic himself it has the value of reality. The more firmly it is established the more he *is* his idealized image, while his real self is proportionately dimmed out. This reversal of the actual picture is bound to come about because of the very nature of the functions the image performs. Every one of them is aimed at effacing the real personality and turning the spotlight on itself. Looking back over the history of many patients we are led to believe that its establishment has often been literally lifesaving, and that is why the resistance a patient puts up if his image is attacked is entirely justified, or at least logical. As long as his image remains real to him and is intact, he can feel significant, superior, and harmonious, in spite of the illusory nature of those feelings. He can consider himself entitled to raise all kinds of demands and claims on the basis of his assumed superiority. But if he allows it to be undermined he is immediately threatened with the prospect of facing all his weaknesses, with no title to special claims, a comparatively insignificant figure or even — in his own eyes — a contemptible one. More terrifying still, he is faced with his conflicts and the hideous fear of being torn to pieces. That this may give him a chance of becoming a much better human being, worth more than all the glory of his idealized image, is a gospel he hears but that for a long time means nothing to him. It is a leap in the dark of which he is afraid.

With so great a subjective value to recommend it, the position of the image would be unassailable if it were not for the huge drawbacks inseparable from it. The whole edifice is in the first place extremely rickety by reason of the fictitious elements involved. A treasure house loaded with dynamite, it makes the individual highly vulnerable. Any questioning or criticism from outside, any awareness of his own failure to measure up to the image, any real insight into the forces operating within him can make it explode or crumble. He must restrict his life lest he be exposed to such dangers. He must avoid situations in which he would not be admired or recognized. He must avoid tasks that he is not certain to master. He may even develop an intense aversion to effort of any kind. To him, the gifted one, the mere vision of a picture he might paint is already the master painting. Any mediocre person can get somewhere by hard work; for him to apply himself like every Tom, Dick, and Harry would be an admission that he is not the mastermind, and so humiliating. Since nothing can actually be achieved without work, he defeats by his attitude the very ends he is driven to attain. And the gap between his idealized image and his real self widens.

He is dependent upon endless affirmation from others in the form of approval, admiration, flattery — none of which, however, can give him any more than temporary reassurance. He may unconsciously hate everyone who is overbearing or who, being better than he in any way — more assertive, more evenly balanced, better informed — threatens to undermine his own notions of himself. The more desperately he clings to the belief that he is his idealized image, the more violent the hatred. Or, if his own arrogance is repressed, he may blindly admire persons who are openly convinced of their importance and show it by arrogant behavior. He loves in them his own image and inevitably runs into severe disappointment when he becomes aware, as he must at some time or other, that the gods he so admires are interested only in themselves, and as far as he is concerned care only for the incense he burns at their altars.

Probably the worst drawback is the ensuing alienation from the self. We cannot suppress or eliminate essential parts of ourselves without becoming estranged from ourselves. It is one of those changes gradually produced by neurotic processes that despite their fundamental nature come about unobserved. The person simply becomes oblivious to what he really feels, likes, rejects, believes — in short, to what he really is. Without knowing it he may live the life of his image. Tommy in J.M. Barrie's *Tommy and Grizel* illuminates this process better than any clinical description. Of course it is not possible to behave so without being inextricably caught in a spider's web of unconscious pretense and rationalization, which makes for precarious living. The person loses interest in life because it is not he who lives it; he cannot make decisions because he does not know what he really wants; if difficulties mount, he may be pervaded by a sense of unreality — an accentuated expression of his permanent condition of being unreal to himself. To understand such a state we must realize that a veil of unreality shrouding the inner world is bound to be extended to the outer. A patient recently epitomized the whole situation by saying: "If it were not for reality, I would be quite all right."

Finally, although the idealized image is created to remove the basic conflict and in a limited way succeeds in doing so, it generates at the same time a new rift in the personality almost more dangerous than the original one. Roughly speaking, a person builds up an idealized image of himself because he cannot tolerate himself as he actually is. The image apparently counteracts this calamity; but having placed himself on a pedestal, he can tolerate his real self still less and starts to rage against it, to despise himself and to chafe under the yoke of his own unattainable demands upon himself. He wavers then between self-adoration and self-contempt, between his idealized image and his despised image, with no solid middle ground to fall back on.

Thus a new conflict is created between compulsive, contradictory strivings on the one hand and a kind of internal dictatorship imposed by the inner disturbance. And he reacts to this inner dictatorship just as a person might react to a comparable political dictatorship: he may identify himself with it, that is, feel that he is as wonderful and ideal as the dictator tells him he is; or he may stand on tiptoe to try to measure up to its demands; or he may rebel against the coercion and refuse to recognize the imposed obligations. If he reacts in the first way, we get the impression of a "narcissistic" individual, inaccessible to criticism; the existing rift, then, is not consciously felt as such. In the second instance we have the perfectionistic person, Freud's superego type. In the third, the person appears not to be accountable to anyone or anything; he tends to become erratic, irresponsible, and negativistic. I speak advisedly of impressions and appearances, because whatever is his reaction, he continues to be fundamentally restive. Even a rebellious type who ordinarily believes he is "free" labors under the enforced standards he is trying to overthrow; though the fact that he is still in the clutches of his idealized image may show only in his swinging those standards as a whip over others.[6] Sometimes a person goes through periods of alternating between one extreme and another. He may, for instance, try for a time to be super-humanly "good" and, getting no comfort from that,swing to the opposite pole of rebelling violently against such standards. Or he may switch from an apparently unreserved self-adoration to perfectionism. More often we find a combination of these variant attitudes. All of which points to the fact — understandable in the light of our theory — that none of the attempts are satisfactory; that they all are doomed to failure; that we must regard them as desperate efforts to get out of an intolerable situation; that as in any other intolerable situation the most dissimilar means are tried — if one fails, another is resorted to.

All these consequences combine to build a mighty barrier against true development. The person cannot learn from his mistakes because he does not see them. In spite of his assertions to the contrary he is actually bound to lose interest in his own growth. What he has in mind when he speaks of growth is an unconscious idea of creating a more perfect idealized image, one that will be without drawbacks.

The task of therapy, therefore, is to make the patient aware of his idealized image in all its details, to assist him in gradually understanding all its functions and subjective values, and to show him the suffering that it inevitably entails. He will then start to wonder whether the price is not too high. But he can relinquish the image only when the needs that have created it are considerably diminished.

[1]Herman Nunberg dealt with this problem of the striving for unity in his paper, "Die Synthetische Funktion des Ich," *Internationale Zeitschrift fur Psychoanalyse,* 1930.
[2]*Cf.* Anne Parish, "All Kneeling," *The Second Woollcott Reader,* Garden City Publishing Co., 1939.
[3]*Cf.* the critical examination of Freud's concept of narcissism, superego, and guilt feelings in Karen Horney, *New Ways in Psychoanalysis,* W.W. Norton, 1938; *cf. also* Erich Fromm, "Selfishness and Self-Love," *Psychiatry,* 1939.
[4]*Cf.* Chapter 12, Sadistic Trends.
[5]In that classic illustration of dual personality, Robert Louis Stevenson's *Dr. Jekyll and Mr. Hyde,* the main idea is built around the possibility of separating the conflicting elements in man. After recognizing how radical is the schism between good and evil within himself, Dr. Jekyll says: "From an early date...I had learned to dwell with pleasure, as a beloved daydream, on the thought of the separation of these elements. If each, I told myself, could but be housed in separate identities, life would be relieved of all that was unbearable."
[6]*Cf.* Chapter 12, Sadistic Trends.

II / The Antecedents of Self-Esteem

If I were to search for the central core of difficulty in people as I have come to know them, it is that in the great majority of cases they despise themselves, regarding themselves as worthless and unlovable.
Carl R. Rogers

No psychological health is possible unless this essential core of the person is fundamentally accepted, loved and respected by others and by himself. . . .
Abraham H. Maslow

Self-Worth: The Pot That Nobody Watches

Virginia Satir

When I was a little girl, I lived on a farm in Wisconsin. On our back porch was a huge black iron pot, which had lovely rounded sides and stood on three legs. My mother made her own soap, so for part of the year the pot was filled with soap. When threshing crews came through in the summer, we filled the pot with stew. At other times my father used it to store manure for my mother's flower beds. We all came to call it the "3-S pot." Whenever anyone wanted to use the pot, he was faced with two questions: What is the pot now full of, and how full is it?

Long afterward, when people would tell me of their feelings of self-worth — whether they felt full or empty, dirty, or even "cracked" — I would think of that old pot. One day several years ago, a family was sitting in my office and its members were tryng to explain to one another how they felt about themselves. I remembered the black pot and told them the story. Soon the members of the family were talking about their own individual "pots," whether they contained feelings of worth or of guilt, shame, or uselessness.

Before long this simple shorthand word was helping many of my families express feelings that had been difficult to talk about before. A father might say, "My pot is high today," and the rest of the family would know that he felt on top of things, full of energy and good spirits, secure in the knowledge that he really mattered. Or a son might say, "I feel low-pot." This told everyone that he felt that he did not matter, that he felt tired or bored or bruised, not particularly lovable. It might even mean that he had always felt he was no good; that he had to take what was handed to him and could not complain.

Pot is a plain word, in this use almost a nonsense word. Incidentally, I had this word long before marijuana became popular, so I lay first claims to it. So many of the words professional people use to talk about human beings sound sterile and lack life-and-breath images. Families seem to find it easier to express themselves in "pot" terms and to understand when other people express themselves that way. They seem suddenly more comfortable, released from our culture's foolish taboo against talking about one's feel-

© Satir, V. PEOPLEMAKING. Palo Alto, California: Science & Behavior Books, 1972. Reprinted by Permission.

ings. A wife, who would hesitate to tell her husband that she feels inadequate, depressed, worthless, can say frankly, "Don't bother me now—my pot is dragging!"

So, in this book when I say "pot," I mean *self-worth* or *self-esteem*. And pot is what we are going to talk about in this chapter.

In my many years of teaching young children, treating families of all economic and social levels, training people from all walks of life — from all the day-to-day experiences of my professional and personal living, I am convinced that the crucial factor in what happens both *inside* people and *between* people is the picture of individual worth that each person carries around with him — his *pot*.

Integrity, honesty, responsibility, compassion, love — all flow easily from the person whose pot is high. He feels that he matters, that the world is a better place because he is here. He has faith in his own competence. He is able to ask others for help, but he believes he can make his own decisions and is his own best resource. Appreciating his own worth, he is ready to see and respect the worth of others. He radiates trust and hope. He doesn't have rules against anything he feels. He accepts all of himself as human.

Vital people feel high-pot most of the time. True, everyone experiences times when he would just as soon chuck it all; when fatigue overwhelms him and the world has dealt him too many disappointments too quickly; when the problems of life suddenly seem more than he can manage. But the vital person treats these temporary low-pot feelings as just what they are — a crisis of the moment from which he can emerge whole and something he can feel uncomfortable about but does not have to hide.

Other people, however, spend most of their lives in a low-pot condition. Because they feel they have little worth, they expect to be cheated, stepped on, deprecated by others. Expecting the worst, they invite it and usually get it. To defend themselves, they hide behind a wall of distrust and sink into the terrible human state of loneliness and isolation. Thus separated from other people, they become apathetic, indifferent toward themselves and those around them. It is hard for them to see, hear, or think clearly, and therefore they are more prone to step on and deprecate others.

Fear is a natural consequence of this distrust and isolation. Fear constricts and blinds you; it keeps you from risking new ways of solving your problems and so gives rise to still more self-defeating behavior. (Fear, incidentally, is always fear of some *future* thing. I have observed that as soon as a person confronts or challenges whatever he is afraid of, the fear vanishes.)

When the perennially low-pot person experiences defeats — the kinds that would make even a vital person feel low-pot for a while — he feels desperate. How can such a worthless person as he cope with such troubles? he asks himself. It is not surprising that occasionally a low-pot person under overwhelming pressure will resort to drugs or suicide or murder. I truly believe that most of the pain, problems, ugliness in life — even wars — are the result of someone's low pot, which he really can't talk straight about.

Can you remember some time recently when your spirits were up? Perhaps the boss had just told you that you had been promoted; or you wore a becoming new dress and received several compliments; or you handled a difficult problem with one of the children and everything turned out happily. Try to go back now and feel again the feelings you had that day. That is what it is like to feel high pot.

Can you remember another occasion, when you made an embarrassing slip, or a costly error; or you were scolded angrily by your boss or your spouse; or you felt helpless in handling a problem with the children? Again, go back and relive the feelings you had, even though it is painful. That is what it is like to feel low pot.

Feeling low is not really the same as low pot. Low pot essentially means that you are experiencing undesirable feelings at the moment and are trying to behave as though those feelings did not exist. It takes a lot of trust to express your low self-esteem feelings. Low pot is a form of lying to yourself and others.

Now relax for a moment, then feel the state of your pot today. Is it high or low? Has something special happened to give you this feeling, or do you feel this way most of the time?

I hope that several members of your family will try this experiment together. Tell one another your feelings. Compare the things that make you feel low pot or high pot. You may find new dimensions to the people you've been living with all these years, and feel closer to one another as a result.

I am convinced that there are no genes to carry the feelings of worth. *It is learned.* And the family is where it is learned. You learned to feel high pot or low pot in the family your parents created. And your children are learning it in your family right now.

An infant coming into the world has no past, no experience in handling himself, no scale on which to judge his own worth. He must rely on the experiences he has with the people around him and the messages they give him about his worth as a person. For the first five or six years, the child's pot is formed by the family almost exclusively. After he starts school, other influences come into play, but the family remains important all through his adolescence. Outside forces tend to reinforce the feelings of worth or worthlessness that he has learned at home: the high-pot child can weather many failures in school or among peers; the low-pot child can experience many successes yet feel gnawing doubt about his own value.

Every word, facial expression, gesture, or action on the part of the parent gives the child some message about his worth. It is sad that so many parents don't realize the effect these messages have on the child, and often don't even realize what messages they are sending. A mother may accpet the bouquet clutched in her three-year-old's hand and say, "Where did you pick these?"—her voice and smile implying "How sweet of you to bring me these! Where do such lovely flowers grow?" This message would strengthen the child's feelings of worth. Or she might say, "—How pretty!" but add, "Did you pick these in Mrs. Randall's garden?"—implying that the child was bad to steal them. This message would make him feel wicked and worthless. Or she might say, "How pretty! Where did you pick them?" but wear a worried expression that added, "Did you steal them from Mrs. Randall's garden?" In this case, she is building low pot but probably does not realize it.

What kind of self-worth is your family building? You can begin to find out with this little experiment.

Tonight, when the family has settled around the table for dinner, try to feel what is happening to your pot each time another member speaks to you. There will be some remarks that have no "pot-content," of course. But you may be surprised to find that even "Pass the potatoes, please" can make you feel valued or deprecated, depending on the tone of voice, the facial expression, the timing (did it interrupt you or serve as a way of ignoring something you said?).

When dinner is about half finished, change the game. Listen to what you are saying to others. Is your remark likely to make the other person feel better about himself? Does his reply or his facial expression fit that prediction? If not, your face or tone or gestures may be communicating some message of which you are not aware. Try to be spontaneous and say what you would have said if you weren't trying this experiment. That won't be easy. Just being aware of what you say will make you tend to say pot-building things. But then that is another value of the experiment.

Tomorrow night explain this little game to the other members of the family. If they are old enough, let them read this chapter before dinner. Then all of you try the experiment at the same time. After dinner, talk together about what you discovered and how you felt.

Feelings of worth can only flourish in an atmosphere where individual differences are appreciated, mistakes are tolerated, communication is open, and rules are flexible—the kind of atmosphere that is found in a nurturing family. It is no accident that the children of these families usually feel good about themselves, or that the children of troubled families so often feel worthless, growing up as they must amid "crooked" communication, inflexible rules, criticism of their differences and punishment for their mistakes.

These same differences in self-worth can be seen in the adults in nurturing and troubled families. But here I think it is not so much that the family affects the adult's pot (although that certainly happens) as that high-pot parents are more likely to create nurturing families, and low-pot parents troubled families.

After years of working with families, I find that I no longer feel like blaming parents, no matter how destructive or foolish their actions. Instead, I try to find ways to raise their pot. This is a good first step to improving the whole family situation.

Happily, it is possible to raise anyone's pot, no matter what his age. Since the feeling of worth has been learned, it can be unlearned, and something new can be learned in its place. The possibility for this learning lasts from birth to death, so it is never too late. At any point in a person's life he can begin to feel better about himself.

I mean this to be the most important message in this book: *there is always hope that your life can change because you can always learn new things.* Human beings can grow and change all their lives. It is a little harder as we grow older, and it takes a little longer. But knowing that change is possible, and wanting to do it, are two first big steps. We may be slow learners, but we are all educable.

I want to close this chapter with a bit of prose which contains my feelings and ideas about self worth.

MY DECLARATION OF SELF-ESTEEM

I am me.

In all the world, there is no one else exactly like me. There are persons who have some parts like me, but no one adds up exactly like me. Therefore, everything that comes out of me is authentically mine because I alone chose it.

I own everything about me — my body, including everything it does; my mind, including all its thoughts and ideas; my eyes, including the images of all they behold; my feelings, whatever they may be — anger, joy, frustration, love, disappointment, excitement; my mouth, and all the words that come out of it, polite, sweet or rough, correct or incorrect; my voice, loud or soft; and all my actions, whether they be to others or to myself.

I own my fantasies, my dreams, my hopes, my fears.

I own all my triumphs and successes, all my failures and mistakes.

Because I own all of me, I can become intimately acquainted with me. By so doing I can love me and be friendly with me in all my parts. I can then make it possible for all of me to work in my best interests.

I know there are aspects about myself that puzzle me, and other aspects that I do not know. But as long as I am friendly and loving to myself, I can courageously and hopefully look for the solutions to the puzzles and for ways to find out more about me.

However I look and sound, whatever I say and do, and whatever I think and feel at a given moment in time is me. This is authentic and represents where I am at that moment in time.

When I review later how I looked and sounded, what I said and did, and how I thought and felt, some parts may turn out to be unfitting. I can discard that which is unfitting, and keep that which proved fitting, and invent something new for that which I discarded.

I can see, hear, feel, think, say, and do. I have the tools to survive, to be close to others, to be productive, and to make sense and order out of the world of people and things outside of me.

I own me, and therefore I can engineer me.

I am me and I am okay.*

*Reprinted by permission of the publisher from V. Satir, "A Goal of Living," ETCETERA, December, 1970.

Polishing Parental Mirrors

Dorothy C. Briggs

SEEING THROUGH FILTERS

Each of us sees our children to some degree through a haze of filters born of our past experiences, personal needs, and cultural values. They all combine to form a network of expectations. And

these expectations become yardsticks by which we measure a child.

Knowing *what* you expect and *why* is the first step toward polishing your parental mirror. Let's look at some common filters and see how they influence your parenting.

INEXPERIENCE

Since each child is different, we all wear the filter of inexperience to some extent. But we usually feel it most keenly with our first child. Mrs. B., for example, explodes when she finds her son's room in shambles after his afternoon rest. She tells him in no uncertain terms that he is a bad boy. A few years later, the wild disorder left by her third son doesn't surprise her. In fact, had she found his room neat, she'd have suspected he was sick. Sheer experience with pre-schoolers and her ability to adapt to reality changed her expectations. She measured her third son's behavior against the yardstick of experience and saw it as normal. Her treatment in both instances resulted from her expectations.

BORROWED STANDARDS

Many of our expectations are borrowed unthinkingly. A popular notion is that a quiet child is a "good" child. And our acceptance varies with his output of noise.

Expectations our parents had for us are heavily relied on as guides. These borrowed images allow us to act without thinking, questioning, or experimenting with the natural ways of children. They conserve energy, but they may take their toll.

Blueprints adopted from our culture are legion. "Boys shouldn't cry"; "Girls should play with dolls, but boys never should"; "Brothers and sisters should always love one another"; "Children should never be angry with parents"; "Boys should be athletes." We continuously measure children by many such pat standards, unrealistic though they may be.

In middle-class America, we parents place high value on rapid scholastic achievement, respect for property, cleanliness, sociability, and sexual control. Desirable as these goals may be, expecting such behavior at the wrong ages, or under all circumstances, or expecting children to learn the first, second, or third time around makes our approval conditional on the impossible. Then, we involve a child in a rat race that undermines self-esteem. *How early* and *how fast* we press for these goals affects each child's view of himself.

HANG-OVER WISHES

Some of our expectations for children are designed to meet our own unmet childhood wishes. One mother tearfully shared this story with her daughter's high school counselor. "I saved for months to give Ginny a matching cashmere sweater and skirt set, only to have her exchange it because none of her friends wore them! I'd have given my eye teeth for those things at her age. Where have I gone wrong to have raised such an ungrateful child?"

An unfulfilled dream made this mother expect gratitude. Her hangover wish kept her from understanding that her daughter's needs differed from hers.

CURRENT HUNGERS

We may treat our children in ways that feed a current hunger in us. Mrs. T., for instance, is starved for approval. She needs it from everyone. If a visiting neighbor is a strict disciplinarian, she becomes a regular dictator with her children. If her visitor is highly permissive, she lets them get away with anything short of murder. Her response to her children—born of her present, unsatisfied hunger—depends on whom she is with.

If we crave status but cannot earn it through our own efforts, we may unconsciously push our child to fill the gap. We may want him to get all "A's," win the lead in the class play, or get elected to office because of the reflected glory. He must harvest distinctions to feed our needs. On the other hand, we may have heaped many honors on ourselves in our own lives. But if we see children as extensions of ourselves, rather than as separate individuals, we may feel the luster of our own star is dulled if they are less than outstanding. Our expectation is that anything coming from us must shine with equal brightness.

Hungers in our marriage relationship make up another set of filters. If we feel unloved or unappreciated by our husbands or wives, we can easily fall into the trap of maneuvering our children to fill these needs. And we dislike them when they fail. The more satisfying your marriage, the freer you are from asking your child to fill in your voids.

UNFINISHED BUSINESS

Expectations for children often help us work out unfinished business from our own childhood. Most of us raise youngsters on the basis of our own needs rather than theirs. An uncomfortable thought, but true.

As a boy, Mr. P. had to do constant battle with an older, dominating brother. He never came to terms with his brother, nor did he lose the urge to get even. Without realizing it, he found a splendid opportunity to even the score, however, with his eldest son. When the older boy dominated the younger one, former memories in him were triggered off. He lashed out at his eldest with exaggerated intensity. He was unaware of why he did this and so was the son who bore the brunt of the unresolved conflict. But the father's unfinished business affected his youngster's self-esteem.

THE IMPACT OF EXPECTATIONS ON SELF-ESTEEM

Your child measures what he can do against your standards. He then draws his own conclusions as to his value by how closely he fits your expectations.

A basic pattern found in the childhood home of the adult alcoholic is expectations too high to meet. Constantly falling short, the person concludes, "I'm worthless." Feeling no worthwhile resources within, he turns to alcohol as an outside crutch to build a sense of adequacy. Strong dependency and low self-esteem start him on a path that is self-defeating in the long run.

Underachievers most frequently come from homes where there is constant pressure to do more and better. The ever-prodding parent indirectly says to his child, "I have little faith in you." And, "You're not measuring up."

Whenever expectations are too high or too rigid to fit a particular child at a *particular* age under *particular* circumstances, we are disappointed too often. And our disappointments act like termites: they eat at the foundations of self-respect, toppling self-esteem.

**Children rarely question our expectations;
instead, they question their personal adequacy.**

Does this mean that to avoid damaging self-esteem, you must throw out expectations lock, stock, and barrel? *Absolutely not!* Just as expectations that are too high make a youngster feel he is a constant failure, so the *lack* of expectations comes through as, "Why expect anything of you? You probably couldn't do it anyway." Such lack of faith wipes out a child's feeling of value.

Your child feels the force of your expectations; they directly affect his view of himself. Robert Rosenthal, a Harvard psychologist, found that children whose teachers had confidence in their ability to learn spurted ahead with IQ gains of fifteen to twenty-seven points. Nonverbal valuing became positive reflections for each child, enabling him to say, "I can do." The teacher's faith became the child's faith. *The fine line lies in realistic expectations coupled with a warm belief in each child.*

Conditional approval—"Fit my blueprints or go unloved"—tears at self-respect. Mike, by his physical makeup, is a quiet, studious boy, but he is alert to his father's preference for an outgoing athlete. To win approval Mike must give up his natural inclinations and struggle to fit his father's image of what a lovable son is like.

A child's belief in himself is the core that allows him to flourish. When he buckles under to fit preconceived expectations that disregard his essential nature, his self-respect is maimed. Being true to himself means maintaining the integrity of his uniqueness; it is the tap root for his stability. Submitting to expectations that run contrary to his nature always causes impairment. Rigid, unrealistic expectations fairly shriek, *"Be as I need you to be. Don't be you!"*

A child's confidence has to be in what *he* truly is, not in someone else's images.

THE TRAGEDY OF THE LOST SELF

An eloquent and tragic example of a youngster faced with the dilemma of fitting his parents' unrealistic expectations or going unloved is seen in this summary from a conseling interview.

A fifteen-year-old boy, living with parents whose standards were rigid, authoritarian, and in no way appropriate to his nature, said, "I'm completely resigned. There's nothing I can do about my parents. I can't get them to change, so I'm going to have to change. Anything I feel or want to be...well, it just means trouble, I really have only one choice; I have to go their way.

"Of course, other kids are completely ruled by their folks, so I won't be the only one. But y'know something? I think something in them kinda dies. You know, I died a long time ago...I guess I died when I was born. The way I really am couldn't please my family or anybody. How do you get rid of what you are?"

This young boy sadly resigned himself to the path he must follow. Never questioning his parents' expectations, he reasoned it was he who was off-base. His is the tragedy of the lost self.

Yet he was poignantly aware that a psychological death occurs when youngsters make this decision. He was willing to commit this "suicide" for the safety of outward acceptance and a veneer of peace. But in his immature naivete he was movingly aware of a profound psychological truth; many children do not psychologically survive the tyranny of the parental image!

When expectations cut across a child's grain, they force him into the dilemma of whether to be or not to be himself. If he chooses to fit our images, he rejects himself; and for as long as he denies his true self, he is a hollow person—a carbon copy of the expectations of others. Then he is robbed of becoming the one person he was created to become—*himself!*

THE DOUBLE DILEMMA

Many a child is pushed into a double dilemma when his parents have different images for the kind of child they could love.

Mr. R.'s picture of an acceptable son is one who is highly outgoing and aggressive. Mrs. R.'s preference is for a son who clings and needs mothering. Their boy stands to lose no matter which image he tries to fit. Meanwhile, the kind of person he innately is may be lost in the shuffle.

RECIPE FOR DEPENDENCY

Imagine that your blueprints are such that your child can fit them, but only with strenuous effort. You churn out the designs for his feelings, attitudes, values, and goals. You know best, and you teach your child *not* to listen to his inner promptings. He becomes a highly dependent puppet, moving as you pull the strings. His reward? Your approval. (Remember, approval is an oxygen line, particularly for the young child.) The youngster then places his psychological center of gravity outside himself. Others have his answers and his own *self*-confidence never has a chance to flourish. Rigid parental images and tightly held expectations put huge hurdles in the way of movement toward genuine selfhood. They are the cause of the "lost self."

Highly dependent children don't suddenly blossom into emotionally mature, confident adults. Our country suffers when a large proportion of our citizens are highly dependent. Democracies need confident adults who have the courage of their own convictions. Children with high self-esteem become adults with such courage. With their energies free for tackling problems outside themselves, they can contribute meaningfully to our nation. And our country cannot afford to lose them.

REALISTIC EXPECTATIONS

If standards that are either too high or too low damage self-respect, how can you know if yours are realistic?

Expectations are more likely to be in line if they are based on the facts of child development, keen observation, and consideration of your child's past and present pressures.

You cannot know what is reasonable to expect unless you are familiar with what children *in general* are like. Young Ted's parents constantly expected a miniature adult instead of a child. They were angry when he couldn't handle long excursions for his benefit or waiting for service in a restaurant. They were distressed when his shoes and pants looked shoddy and moth-eaten in a week's time. They couldn't understand his inability to settle down for sleep on visits to his cousins. Common, insignificant situations—compounded by many more—gave Ted daily doses of negative reflections. It was no one's fault; his parents simply weren't familiar with the ways of youngsters.

Not only do you need to know what children are like, but you must know what developmental job is preoccupying them at each stage of growth. Then, your expectations do not clash with the demands of growth.

Knowing what the average child can and cannot do is, however, not sufficient to make expectations realistic. None of us lives with a child-in-general. (Wouldn't life be simpler if we did!) Each child gives his own special twist to the over-all pattern of growth. And this you *must* attend to. Treating children assembly-line fashion is not respecting individuality. Knowing the basic trend for four-year-olds is helpful, but you must be alert to how Charlie handles this stage. *Close observation is a must.*

Fair expectations always consider past and present pressures. Most of us tend to do this to a large extent.

"Billy's grades fell way down this semester, but he's had a hard time accepting his grandfather's death. They were so close."

"Danny's taken to sucking his thumb, but I'm not surprised since he's adjusting to the new baby."

43

"Agnes is so grouchy lately, but she's under heavy competition in her accelerated class. She's always been the star pupil, but no more. It must be hard on her."

Each of these parents tailors his attitude to consider the pressures on his youngster. *Knowing that behavior is caused* and periodically looking at a child's world from *his* point of view helps you make allowances in what to expect. When inner or outer pressures are strong, we all appreciate some leeway from those we live with.

EXPECTATION INVENTORY

Since your expectations affect the quality of your "mirroring," you need to examine them. By looking inside, you may unearth one of the various filters that affect your behavior toward your child. Then, you can deal with it, rather than reacting blindly with expectations that meet your needs alone.

During the next few days, observe your behavior toward each child. Try to identify your expectations. Write each one down and look at it in the light of these questions:

Why do I have this expectation?
Where did it come from?
What's in it for me?
Is it based on my needs or my child's?
What purpose does it serve?
Does it realistically fit this particular child at his age and with his temperament and background?

An honest inventory may be painful, but it is the forerunner to change. Your child's self-esteem is at stake.

WORKING WITH YOUR INVENTORY

Check each expectation for fairness. How much meaning does it actually have for you and your child?

Perhaps you have been pressing for hearty breakfasts. But your son prefers light ones. When you examine this expectation, you realize he eats well at lunch and dinner and after school. He is rarely ill and his weight is normal. Result? You can toss out a borrowed standard.

Weed out all expectations that you've followed blindly but that have no real meaning for you and your child.

Go through your list again to check for expectations that meet your needs alone. Mr. and Mrs. J., for instance, were both dead-set against their son's flying. They supported any wholesome activity but that. Lloyd's high school teacher told them that of all the boys in his navigation club, none were as interested or talented as their son. After much discussion, they faced the real issue. Their expectation was born of their fear of flying. They decided Lloyd had the right to live his life, unencumbered by their fears. They dropped their objections and went all out to support his genuine talent.

To help children grow strong, you, too, must be able to let go of images that do not fit the uniqueness of your child. Can you drop your dream of an engineer for your animal-loving son? Does Betty have to stay in scouting when she dislikes it? Must Tom study music because *you* think it is a good idea?

Each of us has needs that cannot be dismissed as unimportant, but they must be met through our own efforts. Otherwise, we run the risk of inintentionally asking our children to fill the void.

Ask yourself, "Do I feel loved? Do I have a sense of personal achievement, recognition, and belonging in my relationships with adults?" (This is not to say that children don't provide us with love, a sense of belonging, and achievement. Hopefully, they do. But the point is that they must not be saddled with the burden of being our sole providers.)

Check each expectation to see if it exists to meet your hidden hungers, hang-over wishes or unfinished business. Be careful, for it is easy to camoflage a need in yourself as a need in your child.

Parenthood means *nurturing*; feeding children the "psychological foods" that help them to self-respect. You do a better job when you yourself are not psychologically starved; that is, when your own needs are met through your own efforts.

You nourish from overflow, not from emptiness.

The more fulfilled you are as a person, the less you will use your children as your personal security blankets.

If you find yourself using your children as your major source of satisfaction, you need to change this arrangement. Mere awareness may be enough to spur you to action. If not, professional help can release you.

People used to think of therapy as only for the mentally ill. Today, however, counseling is increasingly seen as an experience that can free people from low self-esteem, rigid expectations, and help them develop their potentials for fuller, richer lives. Individual and group therapy, parent-education and developing personal potential classes are attracting growing numbers of people who are not mentally ill, but who are aware that they have room for growth.

THE STICKY WICKET

Mrs. L. confided in her neighbor, "If that son of mine doesn't start asserting himself, I'm going to explode!"

Her neighbor, who had known Mrs. L. for some time, said, "Give him time, he's only four. But who are you to talk? You let people walk all over you."

"That's just the point. I can't stand it in myself, and I hate to see it in him!"

Our attitudes toward others are inextricably bound by our attitudes toward ourselves. As Frederick Perls said, "You do unto others what you do unto yourself." If you are hard on yourself, you are hard on others. If you accept yourself, you can accept others. When you have come to terms with your own hostilities, you are less threatened by hostility from without. So it is that *your ability to confirm your child hinges in large part on your capacity to confirm yourself.*

MOVING TOWARD SELF-ACCEPTANCE

Because you see others—and particularly your children—in the light of your own self-attitudes, a necessary check on the mirroring you provide involves looking at your own self-esteem. What are your answers to the question, "Who am I?"

Write out your personal feelings about yourself. What kind of person are you? What qualities do you see yourself as having, and how do you feel about them? Do you basically enjoy being yourself or would you rather be someone else?

If you don't like yourself, keep in mind that this attitude is *learned*. Remember: low self-esteem is not a commentary on your value but rather a reflection of the judgments and experiences you have had. *You hold the power of choice* to do something about your low self-esteem.

Just as you cannot afford to ignore the attitudes your child has toward himself, you cannot afford to ignore your attitudes toward yourself. Your own self-image plays a significant part in the quality of the mirroring you do. If you had an insulin or thyroid deficiency, you would doubtless take steps to correct it.

It is even more important to correct a self-image deficiency.

To like yourself, seek people who treat you with respect, for you need experience in being enjoyed. Get involved in activities that give you a feeling of competence and achievement. If your self-concept has become inflexible so that you cannot accept positive evidence about yourself, seek professional help. It can free you from the rigidity of low self-esteem.

Although being around others who enjoy you and having experiences with success will be important to your own personal growth, it is *crucial* that you do not allow others' mirrors to *totally* influence your image of yourself. Every human being will see you to some extent through his own personal filters—his own personal needs. It is vital that you remember that *any one person's view of you* is only *one* of the many reflections coming your way. But that person's view may not always be accurate. In short, the mirrors of others may contain some distortions.

The child uses others to get a picture of himself and tends to believe these reflections. You, as an adult, also cannot see yourself without the mirrors of others. But as an adult, you can and *must keep in mind* that how others see you may in some way be distorted—their mirrors may not be completely accurate.[1]

Hopefully, as more of us become aware of the importance of self-esteem, we will take active steps to strengthen our own self-respect. Our growth pays off, not only for us, but for countless generations to come as our children pass on their self-acceptance to their youngsters and they to theirs. Evolving your own potentials as a human being is a life-long challenge. To be or not to be fully you—that is your life's question.

While you are working to improve your own self-attitudes, your children do not have to go wanting. Expose them to other adults and children who enjoy them as they are. Encourage those activities that bring them success. Positive mirrors they need, but if necessary their self-confirmation can come from sources other than you.

[1] I am indebted to Verne Kallejian for suggesting this inclusion.

III / Self Concept and Effective Behavior

Self-trust is the first secret of success.
Ralph Waldo Emerson

Love of others and love of ourselves are not alternatives. On the contrary, an attitude of love towards themselves will be found in all those who are capable of loving others.
Erich Fromm

"To Be That Self Which One Truly Is"—A Therapist's View of Personal Goals

Carl R. Rogers

In these days most psychologists regard it as an inuslt if they are accused of thinking philosophical thoughts. I do not share this reaction. I cannot help but puzzle over the meaning of what I observe. Some of these meanings seem to have exciting implications for our modern world.

In 1957 Dr. Russell Becker, a friend, former student and colleague of mine, invited me to give a special lecture to an all-college convocation at Wooster College in Ohio. I decided to work out more clearly for myself the meaning of the personal directions which clients seem to take in the free climate of the therapeutic relationship. When the paper was finished I had grave doubts that I had expressed anything which was in any way new or significant. The rather astonishingly long-continued applause of the audience relieved my fears to some degree.

As the passage of time has enabled me to look more objectively at what I said, I feel satisfaction on two counts. I believe it expresses well the observations which for me have crystallized into two important themes: my confidence in the human organism, when it is functioning freely; and the existential quality of satisfying living, a theme presented by some of our most modern philosophers, which was however beautifully expressed more than twenty-five centuries ago by Lao-tzu when he said, "The way to do is to be."

THE QUESTIONS

"What is my goal in life?" "What am I striving for?" "What is my purpose?" These are questions which every individual asks himself at one time or another, sometimes calmly and meditatively, sometimes in agonizing uncertainty or despair. They are old, old questions which have been asked and answered in every century of history. Yet they are also questions which every individual must ask and answer for himself, in his own way. They are questions which I, as a counselor, hear expressed in many differing ways as men and women in personal distress try to learn, or understand, or choose, the directions which their lives are taking.

In one sense there is nothing new which can be said about these questions. Indeed the opening phrase in the title I have chosen for this paper is taken from the writings of a man who wrestled with these questions more than a century ago. Simply to express another personal opinion about this whole issue of goals and purposes would seem presumptuous. But as I have worked for many years with troubled and maladjusted individuals I believe that I can discern a pattern, a trend, a commonality, an orderliness, in the tentative answers to these questions which they have found for themselves. And so I would like to share with you my perception of what human beings appear to be striving for, when they are free to choose.

SOME ANSWERS

Before trying to take you into this world of my own experience with my clients, I would like to remind you that the questions I have mentioned are not pseudo-questions, nor have men in the past or at the present time agreed on the answers. When men in the past have asked themselves the purpose of life, some have answered, in the words of the catechism, that "the chief end of man is to glorify God." Others have thought of life's purpose as being the preparation of oneself for immortality. Others have settled on a much more earthy goal — to enjoy and release and satisfy every sensual desire. Still others — and this applies to many today — regard the purpose of life as being to achieve — to gain material possessions, status, knowledge, power. Some have made it their goal to give themselves completely and devotedly to a cause outside of themselves such as Christianity, or Communism. A Hitler has seen his goal as that of becoming the leader of a master race which would exercise power over all. In sharp contrast, many an Oriental has striven to eliminate all personal desires, to exercise the utmost of control over himself. I mention these widely ranging choices to indicate some of the very different aims men have lived for, to suggest that there are indeed many goals possible.

In a recent important study Charles Morris investigated objectively the pathways of life which were preferred by students in six different countries — India, China, Japan, the United States, Canada, and Norway (5). As one might expect, he found decided differences in goals between these national groups. He also endeavored, through a factor analysis of his data, to determine the underlying dimensions of value which seemed to operate in the thousands of specific individual preferences. Without going into the details of his analysis, we might look at the five dimensions which emerged, and which, combined in various positive and negative ways, appeared to be responsible for the individual choices.

The first such value dimension involves a preference for a responsible, moral, self-restrained participation in life, appreciating and conserving what man has attained.

The second places stress upon delight in vigorous action for the overcoming of obstacles. It involves a confident initiation of change, either in resolving personal and social problems, or in overcoming obstacles in the natural world.

The third dimension stresses the value of a self-sufficient inner life with a rich and heightened self-awareness. Control over persons and things is rejected in favor of a deep and sympathetic insight into self and others.

The fourth underlying dimension values a receptivity to persons and to nature. Inspiration is seen as coming from a source outside the self, and the person lives and develops in devoted responsiveness to this source.

The fifth and final dimension stresses sensuous enjoyment, self-enjoyment. The simple pleasures of life, an abandonment to the moment, a relaxed openness to life, are valued.

This is a significant study, one of the first to measure objectively the answers given in different cultures to the question, what is the purpose of my life? It has added to our knowledge of the answers given. It has also helped to define some of the basic dimensions in terms of which the choice is made. As Morris says, speaking of these dimensions, "it is as if persons in various cultures have in common five major tones in the musical scales on which they compose different melodies." (5, p. 185)

ANOTHER VIEW

I find myself, however, vaguely dissatisfied with this study. None of the "Ways to Live" which Morris put before the students as possible choices, and none of the factor dimensions, seems to contain satisfactorily the goal of life which emerges in my experience with my clients. As I watch person after person struggle in his therapy hours to find a way of life for himself, there seems to be a general pattern emerging, which is not quite captured by any of Morris' descriptions.

The best way I can state this aim of life, as I see it coming to light in my relationship with my clients, is to use the words of Søren Kierkgaard—"to be that self which one truly is" (3, p. 29) I am quite aware that this may sound so simple as to be absurd. To be what one is seems like a statement of obvious fact rather than a goal. What does it mean? What does it imply? I want to devote the remainder of my remarks to those issues. I will simply say at the outset that it seems to mean and imply some strange things. Out of my experiences with my clients, and out of my own self-searching, I find myself arriving at views which would have been very foreign to me ten or fifteen years ago. So I trust you will look at these views with critical scepticism, and accept them only in so far as they ring true in your own experience.

DIRECTIONS TAKEN BY CLIENTS

Let me see if I can draw out and clarify some of the trends and tendencies which I see as I work with clients. In my relationships with these individuals my aim has been to provide a climate which contains as much of safety, of warmth, of empathic understanding, as I can genuinely find in myself to give. I have not found it satisfying or helpful to intervene in the client's experience with diagnostic or interpretative explanations, nor with suggestions and guidance. Hence the trends which I see appear to me to come from the client himself, rather than emanating from me.*

*I cannot close my mind, however, to the possibility that someone might be able to demonstrate that the trends I am about to describe might in some subtle fashion, or to some degree, have been initiated by me. I am describing them as occurring in the client in this safe relationship, because that seems the most likely explanation.

AWAY FROM FACADES

I observe first that characteristically the client shows a tendency to move away, hesitantly and fearfully, from a self that he is *not*. In other words, even though there may be no recognition of what he might be moving toward, he is moving away from something. And of course in so doing he is beginning to define, however negatively, what he *is*.

At first this may be expressed simply as a fear of exposing what he is. Thus one eighteen-year-old boy says, in an early interview: "I know I'm not so hot, and I'm afraid they'll find it out. That's why I do these things...They're going to find out some day that I'm not so hot. I'm just trying to put that day off as long as possible...If you know me as I know myself—. *(Pause)* I'm not going to tell you the person I really think I am. There's only one place I won't cooperate and that's it...It wouldn't help your opinion of me to know what I think of myself."

It will be clear that the very expression of this fear is a part of becoming what he is. Instead of simply *being* a facade, as if it were himself, he is coming closer to being *himself*, namely a frightened person hiding behind a facade because he regards himself as too awful to be seen.

AWAY FROM "OUGHTS"

Another tendency of this sort seems evident in the client's moving away from the compelling image of what he "ought ot be." Some individuals have absorbed so deeply from their parents the concept "I ought to be good," or "I have to be good," that it is only with the greatest of inward struggle that they find themselves moving away from this goal. Thus one young woman, describing her unsatisfactory relationship with her father, tells first how much she wanted his love. "I think in all this feeling I've had about my father, that *really* I *did* very much want a good relationship with him...I wanted so much to have him care for me, and yet didn't seem to get what I really wanted." She always felt she had to meet all of his demands and expectations and it was "just too much. Because once I meet one there's another and another and another, and I never really meet them. It's sort of an endless demand." She feels she has been like her mother, submissive and compliant, trying continually to meet his demands. "And really *not* wanting to be that kind of person. I find it's not a good way to be, but yet I think I've had a sort of belief that that's the way you *have* to be if you intend to be thought a lot of and loved. And yet who would *want* to love somebody who was that sort of wishy washy person?" The counselor responded, "Who really would love a door mat?" She went on, "At least I wouldn't want to be loved by the kind of person who'd love a door mat!"

Thus, though these words convey nothing of the self she might be moving toward, the weariness and disdain in both her voice and her statement make it clear that she is moving away from a self which *has* to be good, which *has* to be submissive.

Curiously enough a number of individuals find that they have felt compelled to regard themselves as bad, and it is this concept of themselves that they find they are moving away from. One young man shows very clearly such a movement. He says: "I don't know how I got this impression that being ashamed of myself was such an *appropriate* way to feel.... Being ashamed of me was the way I just *had* to be. . . .There was a world where being ashamed of myself was the best way to feel. . . .If you are something which is disapproved of very much, then I guess the only way you can have any kind of self-respect is to be ashamed of that part of you which isn't approved of. . . .

"But now I'm adamantly refusing to do things from the old viewpoint. . . .It's as if I'm convinced that someone said, 'The way you will *have* to be is to be *ashamed* of yourself—so *be* that way!" And I accepted it for a long, long time, saying 'OK, that's me!' And now I'm standing up against that somebody, saying, 'I don't care *what* you say. I'm *not* going to feel ashamed of myself!' " Obviously he is abandoning the concept of himself as shameful and bad.

AWAY FROM MEETING EXPECTATIONS

Other clients find themselves moving away from what the culture expects them to be. In our current industrial culture, for example, as Whyte has forcefully pointed out in his recent book (7), there are enormous pressures to become the characteristics which are expected of the "organization man." Thus one should be fully a member of the group, should subordinate his individuality to fit into the group needs, should become "the well-rounded man who can handle well-rounded men."

In a newly completed study of student values in this country Jacob summarizes his findings by saying, "The main overall effect of higher education upon student values is to bring about general acceptance of a body of standards and attitudes characteristic of college-bred men and women in the American community. . . .The impact of the college experience...to *socialize* the individual, to refine, polish, or 'shape up' his values so that he can fit comfortably into the ranks of American college alumni."(1, p. 6)

Over against these pressures for conformity, I find that when clients are free to be any way they wish, they tend to resent and to question the tendency of the organization, the college or the culture to mould them to any given form. One of my clients says with considerable heat: "I've been so long trying to live according to what was meaningful to other people, and what made no sense at *all* to me, really. I somehow felt so much *more* than that, at some level." So he, like others, tends to move away from being what is expected.

AWAY FROM PLEASING OTHERS

I find that many individuals have formed themselves by trying to please others, but again, when they are free, they move away from being this person. So one professional man, looking back at some of the process he has been through, writes, toward the end of therapy: "I finally felt that I simpy *had* to begin doing what I *wanted* to do, not what I thought I *should* do, and regardless of what other people feel I *should* do. This is a complete reversal of my whole life. I've always felt I *had* to do things because they were expected of me, or more important, to make people like me. The hell with it! I think from now on I'm going to just be me — rich or poor, good or bad, rational or irrational, logical or illogical, famous or infamous. So thanks for your part in helping me to rediscover Shakespeare's — 'To thine own *self* be true.' "

So one may say that in a somewhat negative way, clients define their goal, their purpose, by discovering, in the freedom and safety of an understanding relationship, some of the directions they do *not* wish to move. They prefer not to hide themselves and their feelings from themselves, or even from some significant others. They do not wish to be what they "ought" to be, whether that imperative is set by parents, or by the culture, whether it is defined positively or negatively. They do not wish to mould themselves and their behavior into a form which would be merely pleasing to others. They do not, in other words, choose to be anything which is artificial, anything which is imposed, anything which is defined from without. They realize that they do not value such purposes or goals, even though they may have lived by them all their lives up to this point.

TOWARD SELF-DIRECTION

But what is involved positively in the experience of these clients? I shall try to describe a number of the facets I see in the directions in which they move.

First of all, the client moves toward being autonomous. By this I mean that gradually he chooses the goals toward which *he* wants to move. He becomes responsible for himself. He decides what activities and ways of behaving have meaning for him, and what do not. I think this tendency toward self-direction is amply illustrated in the examples I have given.

I would not want to give the impression that my clients move blithely or confidently in this direction. No indeed. Freedom to be oneself is a frighteningly responsible freedom, and an individual moves toward it cautiously, fearfully, and with almost no confidence at first.

Nor would I want to give the impression that he always makes sound choices. To be responsibly self-directing means that one chooses — and then learns from the consequences. So clients find this a sobering but exciting kind of experience. As one client says — "I feel frightened, and vulnerable, and cut loose from support, but I also feel a sort of surging up or force or strength in me." This is a common kind of reaction as the client takes over the self-direction of his own life and behavior.

TOWARD BEING PROCESS

The second observation is difficult to make, because we do not have good words for it. Clients seem to move toward more openly being a process, a fluidity, a changing. They are not disturbed to find that they are not the same from day to day, that they do not always hold the same feelings toward a given experience or person, that they are not always consistent. They are in flux, and seem more content to continue in this flowing current. The striving for conclusions and end states seems to diminish.

One client says, "Things are sure changing, boy, when I can't even predict my own behavior in here anymore. It was something I was able to do before. Now I don't know what I'll say next. Man, it's quite a feeling. . . . I'm just surprised I even said these things. . . . I see something new every time. It's an adventure, that's what it is—into the unknown. . . . I'm beginning to enjoy this now, I'm joyful about it, even about all these old negative things." He is beginning to appreciate himself as a fluid process, at first in the therapy hour, but later he will find this true in life. I cannot help but be reminded of Kierkegaard's description of the individual who really exists. "An existing individual is constantly in process of becoming, ...and translates all his thinking into terms of process. It is with (him)...as it is with a writer and his style; for he only has a style who never has anything finished, but 'moves the waters of the language' every time he begins, so that the most common expression comes into being for him with the freshness of a new birth." (2, p. 79) I find this catches excellently the direction in which clients move, toward being a process of potentialities being born, rather than being or becoming some fixed goal.

TOWARD BEING COMPLEXITY

It also involves being a complexity of process. Perhaps an illustration will help here. One of our counselors, who has himself been much helped by psychotherapy, recently came to me to discuss his relationship with a very difficult and disturbed client. It interested me that he did not wish to discuss the client, except in the briefest terms. Mostly he wanted to be sure that he was clearly aware of the complexity of his own feelings in the relationship — his warm feelings toward the client, his occasional frustration and annoyance, his sympathetic regard for the client's welfare, a degree of fear that the client might become psychotic, his concern as to what others would think if the case did not turn out well. I realized that his overall attitude was that if he could *be,* quite openly and transparently, all of his complex and changing and sometimes contradictory feelings in the relationship, all would go well. If, however, he was only part of his feelings, and partly facade or defense, he was sure the relationship would not be good. I find that this desire to be *all* of oneself in each moment—all the richness and complexity, with nothing hidden from oneself, and nothing feared in oneself — this is a common desire in those who have seemed to show much movement in therapy. I do not need to say that this is a difficult, and in its absolute sense an impossible goal. Yet one of the most evident trends in clients is to move toward becoming all of the complexity of one's changing self in each significant moment.

TOWARD OPENNESS TO EXPERIENCE

"To be that self which one truly is" involves still other components. One which has perhaps been implied already is that the individual moves toward living in an open, friendly, close relationship to his own experience. This does not occur easily. Often as the client senses some new facet of himself, he initially rejects it. Only as he experiences such a hitherto denied aspect of himself in an acceptant climate can he tentatively accept it as a part of himself. As one client says with some shock after experiencing the dependent, small boy aspect of himself, "That's an emotion I've never felt clearly — one that I've never been!" He cannot tolerate the experience of his childish feelings. But gradually he comes to accept and embrace them as a part of himself, to live close to them and in them when they occur.

Another young man, with a very serious stuttering problem, lets himself be open to some of his buried feelings toward the end of his therapy. He says, "Boy, it was a terrible fight. I never realized it. I guess it was too painful to reach that height. I mean I'm just beginning to feel it now. Oh, the *terrible* pain.... It was *terrible* to talk. I mean I wanted to talk, and then I didn't want to.... I'm feeling—I think I know—it's just plain strain—terrible strain—*stress, that's the word, just so much stress* I've been feeling. I'm just beginning to *feel* it now after all these years of it...it's terrible. I can hardly get my breath now too, I'm just all choked up inside, all *tight* inside.... I just feel like I'm *crushed (He begins to cry.)* I never realized that, I never knew that." (6) Here he is opening himself to internal feelings which are clearly not new to him, but which up to this time, he has never been able fully to experience. Now that he can permit himself to experience them, he will find them less terrible, and he will be able to live closer to his own experiencing.

Gradually clients learn that experiencing is a friendly resource, not a frightening enemy. Thus I think of one client who, toward the close of therapy, when puzzled about an issue, would put his head in his hands and say, "Now what *is* it I'm feeling? I want to get next to it. I want to learn what it is." Then he would wait, quietly and patiently, until he could discern the exact flavor of the feelings occurring in him. Often I sense that the client is trying to listen to himself, is trying to hear the messages and meanings which are being communicated by his own physiological reactions. No longer is he so fearful of what he may find. He comes to realize that his own inner reactions and experiences, the messages of his senses and his viscera, are friendly. He comes to want to be close to his inner sources of information rather than closing them off.

Maslow, in his study of what he calls self-actualizing people, has noted this same characteristic. Speaking of these people, he says, "Their ease of penetration to reality, their closer approach to an animal-like or child-like acceptance and spontaneity imply a superior awareness of their own impulses, their own desires, opinions, and subjective reactions in general." (4, p. 210)

This greater openness to what goes on within is associated with a similar openness to experiences of external reality. Maslow might be speaking of clients I have known when he says, "self-actualized people have a wonderful capacity to appreciate again and again, freshly and naively, the basic goods of life with awe, pleasure, wonder, and even ecstasy, however stale these experiences may be for other people." (4, p. 214)

TOWARD ACCEPTANCE OF OTHERS

Closely related to this openness to inner and outer experience in general is an openness to and an acceptance of other individuals. As a client moves toward being able to accept his own experience, he also moves toward the acceptance of the experience of others. He values and appreciates both his own experience and that of others for what it *is*. To quote Maslow again regarding his self-actualizing individuals: "One does not complain about water because it is wet, nor about rocks because they are hard....As the child looks out upon the world with wide, uncritical and innocent eyes, simply noting and observing what is the case, without either arguing the matter or demanding that it be otherwise, so does the self-actualizing person look upon human nature both in himself and in others." (4, p. 207) This acceptant attitude toward that which exists, I find developing in clients in therapy.

TOWARD TRUST OF SELF

Still another way of describing this pattern which I see in each client is to say that increasingly he trusts and values the process which is himself. Watching my clients, I have come to a much better understanding of creative people. El Greco, for example, must have realized as he looked at some of his early work, that "good artists do not paint like that." But somehow he trusted his own experiencing of life, the process of himself, sufficiently that he could go on expressing his own unique perceptions. It was as though he could say, "Good artists do not paint like this, but *I* paint like this." Or to move to another field, Ernest Hemingway was surely aware that "good writers do not write like this." But fortunately he moved toward being Hemingway, being himself, rather than toward some one else's conception of a good writer. Einstein seems to have been unusually oblivious to the fact that good physicists did not think his kind of thoughts. Rather than drawing back because of his inadequate academic preparation in physics, he simply moved toward being Einstein, toward thinking his own thoughts, toward being as truly and deeply himself as he could. This is not a phenomenon which occurs only in the artist or the genius. Time and again in my clients, I have seen simple people become significant and creative in their own spheres, as they have developed more trust of the processes going on within themselves, and have dared to feel their own feelings, live by values which they discover within, and express themselves in their own-unique ways.

THE GENERAL DIRECTION

Let me see if I can state more concisely what is involved in this pattern of movement which I see in clients, the elements of which I have been trying to describe. It seems to mean that the individual moves toward *being,* knowingly and acceptingly, the process which he inwardly and actually *is.* He moves away from being what he is not, from being a facade. He is not trying to be more than he is, with the attendant feelings of insecurity or bombastic defensiveness. He is not trying to be less than he is, with the attendant feelings of guilt or self-depreciation. He is increasingly listening to the deepest recesses of his physiological and emotional being, and finds himself increasingly willing to be, with greater accuracy and depth, that self which he most truly is. One client, as he begins to sense the direction he is taking, asks himself wonderingly and with incredulity in one interivew. "You mean if I'd really be what I feel like being, that that would be all right?" His own further experience, and that of many another client, tends toward an affirmative answer. To be what he truly is, this is the path of life which he appears to value most highly, when he is free to move in any direction. It is not simply an intellectual value choice, but seems to be the best description of the groping, tentative, uncertain behaviors by which he moves exploringly toward what he wants to be.

SOME MISAPPREHENSIONS

To many people, the path of life I have been endeavoring to describe seems like a most unsatisfactory path indeed. To the degree that this involves a real difference in values, I simply respect it as a difference. But I have found that sometimes such an attitude is due to certain misapprehensions. In so far as I can I would like to clear these away.

DOES IT IMPLY FIXITY?

To some it appears that to be what one is, is to remain static. They see such a purpose or value as synonymous with being fixed or unchanging. Nothing could be further from the truth. To be what one is, is to enter fully into being a process. Change is facilitated, probably maximized, when one is willing to be what he truly is. Indeed it is the person who is denying his feelings and his reactions who is the person who tends to come for therapy. He has, often for years, been trying to change, but finds himself fixed in these behaviors which he dislikes. It is only as he can become more of himself, can be more of what he has denied in himself, that there is any prospect of change.

DOES IT IMPLY BEING EVIL?

An even more common reaction to the path of life I have been describing is that to be what one truly is would mean to be bad, uncontrolled, destructive. It would mean to unleash some kind of monster on the world. This is a view which is very well known to me, since I meet it in almost every client. "If I dare to let the feelings flow which are dammed up within me, if by some chance I should live in those feelings, then this would be catastrophe." This is the attitude, spoken or unspoken, of nearly every client as he moves into experiencing of the unknown aspects of himself. But the whole course of his experience in therapy contradicts these fears. He finds that gradually he can be his anger, when anger is his real reaction, but that such accepted or transparent anger is not destructive. He finds that he can be his fear, but that knowingly to be his fear does not dissolve him. He finds that he can be self-pitying, and it is not "bad." He can feel and be his sexual feelings, or his "lazy" feelings, or his hostile feelings, and the roof of the world does not fall in. The reason seems to be that the more he is able to permit these feelings to flow and to be in him, the more they take their appropriate place in a total harmony of his feelings. He discovers that he has other feelings with which these mingle and find a balance. He feels loving and tender and considerate and cooperative, as well as hostile or lustful or angry. He feels interest and zest and curiosity, as well as laziness or apathy. He feels courageous and venturesome, as well as fearful. His feelings, when he lives closely and acceptingly with their complexity, operate in a constructive harmony rather than sweeping him into some uncontrollably evil path. Sometimes people express this concern by saying that if an individual were to be what he truly is, he would be releasing the beast in himself. I feel somewhat amused by this, because I think we might take a closer look at the beasts. The lion is often a symbol of the "ravening beast." But what about him? Unless he has been very much warped by contact with humans, he has a number of the qualities I have been describing. To be sure, he kills when he is hungry, but he does not go on a wild rampage of killing, nor does he overfeed himself. He keeps his handsome figure better than some of us. He is helpless and dependent in his puppyhood, but he moves from that to independence. He does not cling to dependence. He is selfish and self-centered in infancy, but in adulthood he shows a reasonable degree of cooperativeness, and feeds, cares for, and protects his young. He satisfies his sexual desires, but this does not mean that he goes on wild and lustful orgies. His various tendencies and urges have a harmony within him. He is, in some basic sense, a constructive and trustworthy member of the species *felis leo*. And what I am trying to suggest is that when one is truly and deeply a unique member of the human species, this is not something which sould excite horror. It means instead that one lives fully and openly the complex process of being one of the most widely sensitive, responsive, and creative creatures on this planet. Fully to be one's own uniqueness as a human being, is not, in my experience, a process which would be labeled bad. More appropriate words might be that it is a positive, or a constructive, or a realistic, or a trustworthy process.

SOCIAL IMPLICATIONS

Let me turn for a moment to some of the social implications of the path of life I have attempted to describe. I have presented it as a direction which seems to have great meaning for individuals. Does it have, could it have, any meaning or significance for groups or organizations? Would it be a direction which might usefully be chosen by a labor union, a church group, an industrial corporation, a university, a nation? To me it seems that this might be possible. Let us take a look, for example, at the conduct of our own country in its foreign affairs. By and large we find, if we listen to the statements of our leaders during the past several years, and read their documents, that our diplomacy is always based upon high moral purposes; that it is always consistent with the policies we have followed previously; that it involves no selfish desires; and that it has never been mistaken in its judgments and choices. I think perhaps you will agree with me that if we heard an individual speaking in these terms we would recognize at once that this must be a facade, that such statements could not possibly represent the real process going on within himself.

Suppose we speculate for a moment as to how we, as a nation, might present ourselves in our foreign diplomacy if we were openly, knowingly, and acceptingly being what we truly are. I do not know precisely what we are, but I suspect that if we were trying to express ourselves as we are, then our communications with foreign countries would contain elements of this sort.

We as a nation are slowly realizing our enormous strength, and the power and responsibility which go with that strength.

We are moving, somewhat ignorantly and clumsily, toward accepting a position of responsible world leadership.

We make many mistakes. We are often inconsistent.

We are far from perfect.

We are deeply frightened by the strength of Communism, a view of life different from our own.

We feel extremely competitive toward Communism, and we are angry and humiliated when the Russians surpass us in any field.

We have some very selfish foreign interests, such as the oil in the Middle East.

On the other hand, we have no desire to hold dominion over peoples.

We have complex and contradictory feelings toward the freedom and independence and self-determination of individuals and countries: we desire these and are proud of the past support we have given to such tendencies, and yet we are often frightened by what they may mean.

We tend to value and respect the dignity and worth of each individual, yet when we are frightened, we move away from this direction.

Suppose we presented ourselves in some such fashion, openly and transparently, in our foreign relations. We would be attempting to be the nation which we truly are, in all our complexity and even contradictoriness. What would be the results? To me the results would be similar to the experiences of a client when he is more truly that which he is. Let us look at some of the probable outcomes.

We would be much more comfortable, because we would have nothing to hide.

We could focus on the problem at hand, rather than spending our energies to prove that we are moral or consistent.

We could use all of our creative imagination in solving the problem, rather than in defending ourselves.

We could openly advance both our selfish interests, and our sympathetic concern for others, and let these conflicting desires find the balance which is acceptable to us as a people.

We could freely change and grow in our leadership position, because we would not be bound by rigid concepts of what we have been, must be, ought to be.

We would find that we were much less feared, because others would be less inclined to suspect what lies behind the facade.

We would, by our own openness, tend to bring forth openness and realism on the part of others.

We would tend to work out the solutions of world problems on the basis of the real issues involved, rather than in terms of the facades being worn by the negotiating parties.

In short what I am suggesting by this fantasied example is that nations and organizations might discover, as have individuals, that it is a richly rewardng experience to be what one deeply is. I am suggesting that this view contains the seeds of a philosophical approach to all of life, that it is more than a trend observed in the experience of clients.

SUMMARY

I began this talk with the question each individual asks of himself — what is the goal, the purpose of my life? I have tried to tell you what I have learned from my clients, who in the therapeutic relationship, with its freedom from threat and freedom of choice, exemplify in their lives a commonality of direction and goal.

I have pointed out that they tend to move away from self-concealment, away from being the expectations of others. The characteristic movement, I have said, is for the client to permit himself freely to be the changing, fluid process which he is. He moves also toward a friendly openness to what is going on within him — learning to listen sensitively to himself. This means that he is increasingly a harmony of complex sensings and reactions, rather than being the clarity and simplicity of rigidity. It means that as he moves toward acceptance of the "is-ness" of himself, he accepts others increasingly in the same listening, understanding way. He trusts and values the complex inner processes of himself, as they emerge toward expression. He is creatively realistic, and realistically creative. He finds that to be all of himself is to maximize the rate of change and growth in himself. He is continually engaged in discovering that to be all of himself in this fluid sense is not synonymous with being evil or uncontrolled. It is instead to feel a growing pride in being a sensitive, open, realistic, inner-directed member of the human species, adapting with courage and imagination to the complexities of the changing situation. It means taking contnual steps toward being, in awareness and in expression, that which is congruent with one's total organismic reactions. To use Kierkegaard's more aesthetically satisfying terms, it means "to be that self which one truly is." I trust I have made it evident that this is not an easy direction to move, nor one which is ever completed. It is a continuing way of life.

In trying to explore the limits of such a concept, I have suggested that this direction is not a way which is necessarily limited to clients in therapy, nor to individuals seeking to find a purpose in life. It would seem to make the same kind of sense for a group, an organization, or a nation, and would seem to have the same kind of rewarding concomitants.

I recognize quite clearly that this pathway of life which I have outlined is a value choice which is decidedly at variance with the goals usually chosen or behaviorally followed. Yet because it springs from individuals who have more than the usual freedom to choose, and because it seems to express a unified trend in these individuals, I offer it to you for your consideration.

REFERENCES

1. Jacob, P.E. *Changing Values in College*. New Haven: Hazen Foundation, 1956.
2. Kierkegaard, S. *Concluding Unscientific Postscript*. Princeton University Press, 1941.
3. Kierkegaard, S. *The Sickness Unto Death*. Princeton University Press, 1941.
4. Maslow, A.H. *Motivation and Personality*. Harper and Bros., 1954.
5. Morris, C.W. *Varieties of Human Value*. University of Chicago Press, 1956.
6. Seeman, Julius. *The Case of Jim*. Nashville, Tennessee: Educational Testing Bureau, 1957.
7. Whyte, W.H., Jr. *The Organization Man*. Simon & Schuster, 1956.

Selfishness, Self-Love, and Self-Interest[1]

Erich Fromm

> Thou shalt love thy neighbour as thyself.
> —Bible

Modern culture is pervaded by a tabu on selfishness. We are taught that to be selfish is sinful and that to love others is virtuous. To be sure, this doctrine is in flagrant contradiction to the practice of modern society, which holds the doctrine that the most powerful and legitimate drive in man is selfishness and that by following this imperative drive the individual makes his best contribution to the common good. But the doctrine which declares selfishness to be the arch evil and love for others to be the greatest virtue is still powerful. Selfishness is used here almost synonymously with self-love. The alternative is to love others, which is a virtue, or to love oneself, which is a sin.

This principle has found its classic expression in Calvin's theology, according to which man is essentially evil and powerless. Man can achieve absolutely nothing that is good on the basis of his own strength or merit. "We are not our own," says Calvin. "Therefore neither our reason nor our will should predominate in our deliberations and actions. We are not our own; therefore let us not propose it as our end to seek what may be expedient for us according to the flesh. We are not our own; therefore, let us, as far as possible, forget ourselves and all things that are ours. On the contrary, we are God's; for Him, therefore, let us live and die. For, as it is the most devastating pestilence which ruins people if they obey themselves, it is the only haven of salvation not to know or to want anything by oneself but to be guided by God Who walks before us."[2] Man should have not only the conviction of his absolute nothingness but he should do everything to humiliate himself. "For I do not call it humility if you suppose that we have anything left .... we cannot think of ourselves as we ought to think without utterly despising everything that may be supposed an excellence in us. This humility is unfeigned submission of a mind overwhelmed with a weighty sense of its own misery and poverty; for such is the uniform description of it in the word of God."[3]

This emphasis on the nothingness and wickedness of the individual implies that there is nothing he should like and respect about himself. The doctrine is rooted in self-contempt and self-hatred. Calvin makes this point very clear: he speaks of self-love as "a pest."[4] If the individual finds something "on the strength of which he finds pleasure in himself," he betrays this sinful self-love. This fondness for himself will make him sit in judgment over others and despise them. Therefore, to be fond of oneself or to like anything in oneself is one of the greatest sins. It is supposed to exclude love for others[5] and to be identical with selfishness.[6]

The view of man held by Calvin and Luther has been of tremendous influence on the development of modern Western society. They laid the foundation for an attitude in which man's own happiness was not considered to be the aim of life but where he became a means, an adjunct, to ends beyond him, of an all-powerful God, or of the not less powerful secularized authorities and norms, the state, business, success. Kant, who, with regard to the idea that man should be an end in himself and never a means only, was perhaps the most influential ethical thinker of the Enlightenment period, nevertheless had the same condemnation for self-love. According to him, it is a virtue to want happiness for others, but to want one's own happiness is ethically indifferent, since it is something for which the nature of man is striving, and since a natural striving cannot have a positive ethical value.[7] Kant admits that one must not give up one's claims to happiness; under certain circumstances it may even be a duty to be concerned with it, partly because health, wealth, and the like may be means necessary for the fulfillment of one's duty, partly because the lack of happiness—poverty—can prevent one from fulfilling his duty.[8] But love for oneself, striving for one's own happiness, can never be a *virtue*. As an ethical principle, the striving for one's own happiness "is the most objectionable one, not merely because it is false .... but because the springs it provides for morality are such as rather to undermine it and destroy its sublimity ...."[9]

Kant differentiates egotism, self-love, *philautia*—a benevolence for oneself—and arrogance, the pleasure in oneself. But even "rational self-love" must be restricted by ethical principles, the pleasure in oneself must be battered down, and the individual must come to feel humiliated in comparing himself with the sanctity of moral laws.[10] The individual should find supreme happiness in the fulfillment of his duty. The realization of the moral principle—and, therefore, of the individual's happiness—is only possible in the general whole, the nation, the state. But "the welfare of the state"—and *salus rei publicae suprema lex est*—is not identical with the welfare of the citizens and their happiness.[11]

In spite of the fact that Kant shows a greater respect for the integrity of the individual than did Calvin or Luther, he denies the individual's right to rebel even under the most tyrannical government; the rebel must be punished with no less than death if he threatens the sovereign.[12] Kant emphasizes the native propensity for evil in the nature of man,[13] for the suppression of which the moral law, the categorical imperitive, is essential lest man should become a beast and human society end in wild anarchy.

In the philosophy of the Enlightenment period the individual's claims to happiness have been emphasized much more strongly by others than by Kant, for instance, by Helvetius. This trend in modern philosophy has found its most radical expression in Stirner and Nietzsche.[14] But while they take the opposite position to that of Calvin and Kant with regard to the value of selfishness, they agree with them in the assumption that love for others and love for oneself are alternatives. They denounce love for others as weakness and self-sacrifice and postulate egotism, selfishness, and self-love—they too confuse the issue by not clearly differentiating between these last—as virtue. Thus Stirner says: "Here, egoism, selfishness must decide, not the principle of love, not love motives like mercy, gentleness, good-nature, or even justice and equity—for *iustitia* too is a phenomenon of love, a product of love; love knows only sacrifice and demands self-sacrifice."[15]

The kind of love denounced by Stirner is the masochistic dependence by which the individual makes himself a means for achieving the purposes of somebody or something outside himself. Opposing this concept of love, he did not avoid a formulation, which, highly polemical, overstates the point. The positive principle with which Stirner was concerned[16] was opposed to an attitude which had been that of Christian theology for centuries—and which was vivid in German idealism prevalent in his time; namely, to bend the individual so that he submits to, and finds his center in, a power and a principle outside himself. Stirner was not a philosopher of the stature of Kant or Hegel, but he had the courage to rebel radically against that side of idealistic philosophy which negated the concrete individual and thus helped the absolute state to retain its oppressive power over him.

In spite of many differences between *Nietzsche* and *Stirner*, their ideas in this respect are very much the same. Nietzsche too denounces love and altruism as expressions of weakness and self-negation. For Nietzsche, the quest for love is typical of slaves unable to fight for what they want and who therefore try to get it through love. Altruism and love for mankind thus have become a sign of degeneration.[17] For Nietzsche it is the essence of a good and healthy aristocracy that it is ready to sacrifice countless people for its interests without having a guilty conscience. Society should be a "foundation and scaffolding by means of which a select class of beings may be able to elevate themselves to their higher duties, and in general to a higher existence."[18] Many quotations could be added to document this spirit of contempt and egotism. These ideas have often been understood as *the* philosophy of Nietzsche. However, they do not represent the true core of his philosophy.[19]

There are various reasons why Nietzsche expressed himself in the sense noted above. First of all, as with Stirner, his philosophy is a reaction—a rebellion—against the philosophical tradition of subordinating the empirical individual to powers and principles outside himself. His tendency to overstatement shows this reactive quality. Second, there were, in Nietzsche's personality, feelings of insecurity and anxiety that made him emphasize the "strong man" as a reaction formation. Finally, Nietzsche was impressed by the theory of evolution and its emphasis on the "survival of the fittest." This interpretation does not alter the fact that Nietzsche believed that there is a contradiction between love for others and love for oneself; yet his views contain the nucleus from which this false dichotomy can be overcome. The "love" which he attacks is rooted not in one's own strength, but in one's weakness. "Your neighbor-love is your bad love of yourselves. Ye flee unto your neighbor from yourselves and would fain make a virtue thereof! But I fathom your 'unselfishness.' " He states explicitly, "You cannot stand yourselves and you do not love yourselves sufficiently."[20] For Nietzsche the individual has "an enormously great significance,"[21] The "strong" individual is the one who has "true kindness, nobility, greatness of soul, which does not give in order to take, which does not want to excel by being kind;—'waste' as type of true kindness, wealth of the person as a premise."[22] He expresses the same thought also in *Thus Spake Zarathustra:* "The one goeth to his neighbor because he seeketh himself, and the other because he would fain lose himself."[23]

The essence of this view is this: Love is a phenomenon of abundance; its premise is the strength of the individual who can give. Love is affirmation and productiveness, "It seeketh to create what is loved!"[24] To love another person is only a virtue if it springs from this inner strength, but it is a vice if it is the expression of the basic inability to be oneself.[25] However, the fact remains that Nietzsche left the problem of the relationship between self-love and love for others as an unsolved antinomy.

The doctrine that selfishness is the arch-evil and that to love oneself excludes loving others is by no means restricted to theology and philosophy, but it became one of the stock ideas promulgated in home, school, motion pictures, books; indeed in all instruments of social suggestion as well. "Don't be selfish" is a sentence which has been impressed upon millions of children, generation after generation. Its meaning is somewhat vague. Most people would say that it means not to be egotistical, inconsiderate, without any concern for others. Actually, it generally means more than that. Not to be selfish implies not to do what one wishes, to give up one's own wishes for the sake of those in authority. "Don't be selfish," in the last analysis, has the same ambiguity that it has in Calvinism. Aside from its obvious implication, it means, "don't love yourself," "don't be yourself," but submit yourself to something more important than yourself, to an outside power or its internalization, "duty." "Don't be selfish" becomes one of the most powerful ideological tools in suppressing spontaneity and the free development of personality. Under the pressure of this slogan one is asked for every sacrifice and for complete submission: only those acts are "unselfish" which do not serve the individual but somebody or something outside himself.

This picture, we must repeat, is in a certain sense one-sided. For besides the doctrine that one should not be selfish, the opposite is also propagandized in modern society: keep your own advantage in mind, act according to what is best for you; by so doing you will also be acting for the greatest advantage of all others. As a matter of fact, the idea that egotism is the basis of the general welfare is the principle on which competitive society has been built. It is puzzling that two such seemingly contradictory principles could be taught side by side in one culture; of the fact, however, there is no doubt. One result of this contradiction is confusion in the individual. Torn between the two doctrines, he is seriously blocked in the process of integrating his personality. This confusion is one of the most significant sources of the bewilderment and helplessness of modern man.[26]

The doctrine that love for oneself is identical with "selfishness" and an alternative to love for others has pervaded theology, philosophy, and popular thought; the same doctrine has been rationalized in scientific language in *Freud's* theory of narcissism. Freud's concept presupposes a fixed amount of libido. In the infant, all of the libido has the child's own person as its objective, the stage of "primary narcissism," as Freud calls it. During the individual's development, the libido is shifted from one's own person toward other objects. If a person is blocked in his "object-relationships," the libido is withdrawn from the objects and returned to his own person; this is called "secondary narcissism." According to Freud, the more love I turn toward the outside world the less love is left for myself, and vice versa. He thus describes the phenomenon of love as an impoverishment of one's self-love because all libido is turned to an object outside oneself.

These questions arise: Does psychological observation support the theses that there is a basic contradiction and a state of alternation between love for oneself and love for others? Is love for oneself the same phenomenon as selfishness, or are they opposites? Furthermore, is the selfishness of modern man really a *concern for himself* as an individual, with all his intellectual, emotional, and sensual potentialities? Has "he" not become an appendage of his socioeconomic role? *Is his selfishness identical with self-love or is it not caused by the very lack of it?*

Before we start the discussion of the psychological aspect of selfishness and self-love, the logical fallacy in the notion that love for others and love for oneself are mutually exclusive should be stressed. If it is a virtue to love my neighbor as a human being, it must be a virtue—and not a vice—to love myself since I am a human being too. There is no concept of man in which I myself am not included. A doctrine which proclaims such an exclusion proves itself to be intrinsically contradictory. The idea expressed in the Biblical "Love thy neighbor as thyself!" implies that respect for one's own integrity and uniqueness, love for and understanding of one's own self, can not be separated from respect for and love and understanding of another individual. The love for my own self is inseparably connected with the love for any other self.

We have come now to the basic psychological premises on which the conclusions of our argument are built. Generally, these premises are as follows: not only others, but we ourselves are the "object" of our feelings and attitudes; the attitudes toward others and toward ourselves, far from being contradictory, are basically *conjunctive*. With regard to the problem under discussion this means: Love of others and love of ourselves are not alternatives. On the contrary, an attitude of love toward themselves will be found in all those who are capable of loving others. *Love, in principle, is indivisible as far as the connection between "objects" and one's own self is concerned.* Genuine love is an expression of productiveness and implies care, respect, responsibility, and knowledge. It is not an "affect" in the sense of being affected by somebody, but an active striving for the growth and happiness of the loved person, rooted in one's own capacity to love.

To love is an expression of one's power to love, and to love somebody is the actualization and concentration of this power with regard to one person. It is not true, as the idea of romantic love would have it, that there is only *the* one person in the world whom one could love and that it is the great chance of one's life to find that one person. Nor is it true, if that person be found that love for him (or her) results in a withdrawal of love from others.

Love which can only be experienced with regard to one person demonstrates by this very fact that it is not love, but a symbiotic attachment. The basic affirmation contained in love is directed toward the beloved person as an incarnation of essentially human qualities. Love of one person implies love of man as such. The kind of "division of labor" as William James calls it, by which one loves one's family but is without feeling for the "stranger," is a sign of a basic inability to love. Love of man is not, as is frequently supposed, an abstraction coming after the love for a specific person, but it is its premise, although, genetically, it is acquired in loving specific individuals.

From this it follows that my own self, in principle, must be as much an object of my love an another person. *The affirmation of one's own life, happiness, growth, freedom, is rooted in one's capacity to love,* i.e., in care, respect, responsibility, and knowledge. If an individual is able to love productively, he loves himself too; if he can love *only* others, he can not love at all.

Granted that love for oneself and for others in principle is conjunctive, how do we explain selfishness, which obviously excludes any genuine concern for others? The *selfish* person is interested only in himself, wants everything for himself, feels no pleasure in giving, but only in taking. The world outside is looked at only from the standpoint of what he can get out of it; he lacks interest in the needs of others, and respect for their dignity and integrity. He can see nothing but himself; he judges everyone and everything from its usefulness to him; he is basically unable to love. Does not this prove that concern for others and concern for oneself are unavoidable alternatives? This would be so if selfishness and self-love were identical. But that assumption is the very fallacy which has led to so many mistaken conclusions concerning our problem. *Selfishness and self-love, far from being identical, are actually opposites.* The selfish person does not love himself too much but too little; in fact he hates himself. This lack of fondness and care for himself, which is only one expression of his lack of productiveness, leaves him empty and frustrated. He is necessarily unhappy and anxiously concerned to snatch from life the satisfactions which he blocks himself from attaining. He seems to care too much for himself but actually he only makes an unsuccessful attempt to cover up and compensate for his failure to care for his real self. Freud holds that the selfish person is narcissistic, as if he had withdrawn his love from others and turned it toward his own person. *It is true that selfish persons are incapable of loving others, but they are not capable of loving themselves either.*

It is easier to understand selfishness by comparing it with greedy concern for others, as we find it, for instance, in an oversolicitous, dominating mother. While she consciously believes that she is particularly fond of her child, she has actually a deeply repressed hostility toward the object of her concern. she is overconcerned not because she loves the child too much, but because she has to compensate for her lack of capacity to love him at all.

This theory of the nature of selfishness is borne out by psychoanalytic experience with neurotic "unselfishness," a symptom of neurosis observed in not a few people who usually are troubled not by this symptom but by others connected with it, like depression, tiredness, inability to work, failure in love relationships, and so on. Not only is unselfishness not felt as a "symptom"; it is often the one redeeming character trait on which such people pride themselves. The "unselfish" person "does not want anything for himself"; he "lives only for others," is proud that he does not consider himself important. He is puzzled to find that in spite of his unselfishness he is unhappy, and that his relationships to those closest to him are unsatisfactory. He wants to have what he considers are his symptoms removed—but not his unselfishness. Analytic work shows that his unselfishness is not something apart form his other symptoms but one of them; in fact often the most important one; that he is paralyzed in his capacity to love or to enjoy anything; that he is pervaded by hostility against life and that behind the facade of unselfishness a subtle but not less intense self-centeredness is hidden. This person can be cured only if his unselfishness too is interpreted as a symptom along with the others so that his lack of productiveness, which is at the root of both his unselfishness *and* his other troubles, can be corrected.

The nature of unselfishness becomes particularly apparent in its effect on others and most frequently, in our culture, in the effect the "unselfish" mother has on her children. She believes that by her unselfishness her children will experience what it means to be loved and to learn, in turn, what it means to love. The effect of her unselfishness, however, does not at all correspond to her expectations. The children do not show the happiness of persons who are convinced that they are loved; they are anxious, tense, afraid of the mother's disapproval and anxious to live up to her expectations. Usually, they are affected by their mother's hidden hostility against life, which they sense rather than recognize, and eventually become imbued with it themselves. Altogether, the effect of the "unselfish" mother is not too different from that of the selfish one; indeed, it is often worse because the mother's unselfishness prevents the children from criticizing her. They are put under the obligation not to disappoint her; they are taught, under the mask of virtue, dislike for life. If one has a chance to study the effect of a mother with genuine self-love, one can see that there is nothing more conducive to giving a child the experience of what love, joy, and happiness are than being loved by a mother who loves herself.

Having analyzed selfishness and self-love we can now proceed to discuss the concept of *self-interest*, which has become one of the key symbols in modern society. It is even more ambiguous than selfishness or self-love, and this ambiguity can be fully understood only by taking into account the historical development of the concept of self-interest. The problem is what is considered to constitute self-interest and how it can be determined.

There are two fundamentally different approaches to this problem. One is the objectivistic approach most clearly formulated by Spinoza. To him self-interest or the interest "to seek one's profit" is identical with virtue. "The more," he says, "each person strives and is able *to seek his profit*, that is to say, to preserve his being, the more virtue does he possess; on the other hand, in so far as each person neglects his own profit he is impotent."[27] According to this view, the interest of man is to preserve his existence, which is the same as realizing his inherent potentialities. This concept of self-interest is objectivistic inasmuch as "interest" is not conceived in terms of the subjective feeling of what one's interest is but in terms of what the nature of man is, objectively. Man has only one real interest and that is the full development of his potentialities, of himself as a human being. Just as one has to know another person and his real needs in order to love him, one has to know one's own self in order to understand what the interests of this self are and how they can be served. It follows that man can deceive himself about his real self-interest if he is ignorant of his self and its real needs and that the science of man is the basis for determining what constitutes man's self-interest.

In the last three hundred years the concept of self-interest has increasingly been narrowed until it has assumed almost the opposite meaning which it has in Spinoza's thinking. It has become identical with selfishness, with interest in material gains, power, and success; and instead of its being synonymous with virtue, its conquest has become an ethical commandment.

This deterioration was made possible by the change from the objectivistic into the erroneously subjectivistic approach to self-interest. Self-interest was no longer to be determined by the nature of man and his needs; correspondingly, the notion that one could be mistaken about it was relinquished and replaced by the idea that what a person felt represented the interest of his self was necessarily his true self-interest.

The modern concept of self-interest is a strange blend of two contradictory concepts: that of Calvin and Luther on the one hand, and on the other, that of the progressive thinkers since Spinoza. Calvin and Luther had taught that man must suppress his self-interest and consider himself only an instrument for God's purposes. Progressive thinkers, on the contrary, have taught that man ought to be only an end for himself and not a means for any purpose transcending him. What happened was that man has accepted the contents of the Calvinistic doctrine while rejecting its religious formulation. He has made himself an instrument, not of God's will but of the economic machine or the state. He has accepted the role of a tool, not for God but for industrial progress; he has worked and amassed money but essentially not for the pleasure of spending it and of enjoying life but in order to save, to invest, to be successful. Monastic asceticism has been, as Max Weber has pointed out, replaced by an *inner-worldly* asceticism where personal happiness and enjoyment are no longer the real aims of life. But this attitude was increasingly divorced from the one expressed in Calvin's concept and blended with that expressed in the progressive concept of self-interest, which taught that man had the right—and the obligation—to make the pursuit of his self-interest the supreme norm of life. The result is that modern man *lives* according to the principles of self-denial and *thinks* in terms of self-interest. He believes that he is acting in behalf of *his* interest when actually his paramount concern is money and success; he deceives himself about the fact that his most important human potentialities remain unfulfilled and that he loses himself in the process of seeking what is supposed to be best for him.

The deterioration of the meaning of the concept of self-interest is closely related to the change in the concept of self. In the Middle Ages man felt himself to be an intrinsic part of the social and religious community in reference to which he conceived his own self when he as an individual had not yet fully emerged from his group. Since the beginning of the modern era, when man as an individual was faced with the task of experiencing himself as an independent entity, his own identity became a problem. In the eighteenth and nineteenth centuries the concept of self was narrowed down increasingly; the self was felt to be constituted by the property one had. The formula for this concept of self was no longer "I am what I think" but "I am what I have," "what I possess."[28]

In the last few generations, under the growing influence of the market, the concept of self has shifted from meaning "I am what I possess" to meaning "I am as you desire me."[29] Man, living in a market economy, feels himself to be a commodity. He is divorced from himself, as the seller of a commodity is divorced from what he wants to sell. To be sure, he is interested in himself, immensely interested in his success on the market, but "he" is the manager, the employer, the seller—and the commodity. His self-interest turns out to be the interest of "him" as the subject who employs "himself," as the commodity which should obtain the optimal price on the personality market.

The "fallacy of self-interest" in modern man has never been described better than by Ibsen in *Peer Gynt*. Peer Gynt believes that his whole life is devoted to the attainment of the interests of his *self*. He describes this self as:

"The Gyntian Self!
—An army, that, of wishes, appetites, desires.
The Gyntian Self!
It is a sea of fancies, claims and aspirations;
In fact, it's all that swells within my breast
And makes it come about that I am I and live as such."[30]

At the end of his life he recognizes that he had deceived himself; that while following the principle of "self-interest" he had failed to recognize what the interests of his real self were, and had lost the very self he sought to preserve. He is told that he never had been himself and that therefore he is to be thrown back into the melting pot to be dealt with as raw material. He discovers that he has lived according to the Troll principle: "To thyself be enough"—which is the opposite of the human principle: "To thyself be true." He is seized by the horror of nothingness to which he, who has no self, can not help succumbing when the props of pseudo self, success, and possessions are taken away or seriously questioned. He is forced to recognize that in trying to gain all the wealth of the world, in relentlessly pursuing what seemed to be his interest, he had lost his soul—or, as I would rather say, his self.

The deteriorated meaning of the concept of self-interest which pervades modern society has given rise to attacks on democracy from the various types of totalitarian ideologies. These claim that capitalism is *morally* wrong because it is governed by the principle of selfishness, and commend the moral superiority of their own systems by pointing to their principle of the unselfish subordination of the individual to the "higher" purposes of the state, the "race," or the "socialist fatherland." They impress not a few with this criticism because many people feel that there is no happiness in the pursuit of selfish interest, and are imbued with a striving, vague though it may be, for a greater solidarity and mutual responsibility among men.

We need not waste much time arguing against the totalitarian claims.

In the first place, they are insincere since they only disguise the extreme selfishness of an "elite" that wishes to conquer and retain power over the majority of the population. Their ideology of unselfishness has the purpose of deceiving those subject to the control of the elite and of facilitating their exploitation and manipulation. Furthermore, the totalitarian ideologies confuse the issue by making it appear that they represent the principle of unselfishness when they apply to the state as a whole the principle of ruthless pursuit of selfishness. Each citizen ought to be devoted to the common welfare, but the state is permitted to pursue its own interest without regard to the welfare of other nations. But quite aside from the fact that the doctrines of totalitarianism are disguises for the most extreme selfishness, they are a revival—in secular language—of the religious idea of intrinsic human powerlessness and impotence and the resulting need for submission, to overcome which was the essence of modern spiritual and political progress. Not only do the authoritarian ideologies threaten the most precious achievement of Western culture, the respect for the uniqueness and dignity of the individual; they also tend to block the way to constructive criticism of modern society, and thereby to necessary changes. The failure of modern culture lies not in its principle of individualism, not in the idea that moral virtue is the same as the pursuit of self-interest, but in the deterioration of the meaning of self-interest; not in the fact that people are *too much concerned with their self interest,* but that they are *not concerned enough with the interest of their real self; not in the fact that they are too selfish, but that they do not love themselves.*

If the causes for persevering in the pursuit of a fictitious idea of self-interest are as deeply rooted in the contemporary social structure as indicated above, the chances for a change in the meaning of self-interest would seem to be remote indeed, unless one can point to specific factors operating in the direction of change.

Perhaps the most important factor is the inner dissatisfaction of modern man with the results of his pursuit of "self-interest." The religion of success is crumbling and becoming a facade itself. The social "open spaces" grow narrower; the failure of the hopes for a better world after the First World War, the depression at the end of the twenties, the threat of a new and immensely destructive war so shortly after the Second World War, and the boundless insecurity resulting from this threat, shake the faith in the pursuit of this form of self-interest. Aside from these factors, the worship of success itself has failed to satisfy man's ineradicable striving to be himself. Like so many fantasies and daydreams, this one too fulfilled its function only for a time, as long as it was new, as long as the excitement connected with it was strong enough to keep man from considering it soberly. There is an increasing number of people to whom everything they are doing seems futile. They are still under the spell of the slogans which preach faith in the secular paradise of success and glamour. But doubt, the fertile condition of all progress, has begun to beset them and has made them ready to ask what their real self-interest as human beings is.

This inner disillusionment and the readiness for a revaluation of self-interest could hardly become effective unless the economic conditions of our culture permitted it. I have pointed out that while the canalizing of all human energy into work and the striving for success was one of the indispensable conditions of the enormous achievement of modern capitalism, a stage has been reached where the problem of *production* has been virtually solved and where the problem of the *organization* of social life has become the paramount task of mankind. Man has created such sources of mechanical energy that he has freed himself from the task of putting all his human energy into work in order to produce the material conditions for living. He could spend a considerable part of his energy on the task of living itself.

Only if these two conditions, the subjective dissatisfaction with a culturally patterned aim and the socioeconomic basis for a change, are present, can an indispensable third factor, rational insight, become effective. This holds true as a principle of social and psychological change in general and of the change in the meaning of self-interest in particular. The time has come when the anesthetized striving for the pursuit of man's real interest is coming to life again. Once man knows what his self-interest is, the first and the most difficult, step to its realization has been taken.

1. Cf. Erich Fromm. "Selfishness and Self-Love," *Psychiatry* (November, 1939). The following discussion of selfishness and self-love is a partial repetition of the earlier paper.

2. Johannes Calvin, *Institutes of the Christian Religion*, trans. by John Allen (Philadelphia: Presbyterian Board of Christian Education, 1928), in particular Book III, Chap. 7, p. 619. From "For, as it is...." the translation is mine from the Latin original (Johannes Calvini. *Institutio Christianae Religionis. Editionem curavit*, A. Tholuk, Berolini, 1935, par 1, p. 445).

3. *Ibid.*, Chap. 12, par. 6, p. 681.

4. *Ibid.*, Chap. 7, par. 4, p. 622.

5. It should be noted, however, that even love for one's neighbor, while it is one of the fundamental doctrines of the New Testament, has not been given a corresponding weight by Calvin. In blatant contradiction to the New Testament, Calvin says: "For what the schoolmen advance concerning the priority of charity to faith and hope, is a mere reverie of a distempered imagination...."—Chap. 24, par. 1, p. 531.

6. Despite Luther's emphasis on the spiritual freedom of the individual, his theology, different as it is in many ways from Calvin's, is pervaded by the same conviction of man's basic powerlessness and nothingness.

7. Compare Immanuel Kant, *Kant's Critique of Practical Reason and Other Works on the Theory of Ethics*, trans. by Thomas Kingsmill Abbott (New York: Longmans, Green & Co., 1909), Part I, Book I, Chap. I, par. VIII, Remark II, p. 126.

8. *Ibid.*, in particular Part I, Book I, Chap. III, p. 186.

9. *Loc cit., Fundamental Principles of the Metaphysics of Morals;* second section, p. 61.

10. *Loc. cit.*, Part I, Book I, Ch. III, p. 165.

11. Immanuel Kant, *Immanuel Kant's Werke* (Berlin: Cassierer), in particular "Der Rechtslehre Zweiter Teil" I. Abschnitt, par. 49, p. 124. I translate from the German text, since this part is omitted in the English translation of *The Metaphysics of Ethics* by I. W. Semple (Edinburgh: 1871).

12. *Ibid.*, p. 126.

13. Compare Immanuel Kant, *Religion within the Limits of Reason Alone*, trans. by T.M. Greene and H.H. Hudson (Chicago: Open Court, 1934), Book I.

14. In order not to make this chapter too long I discuss only the modern philosophical development. The student of philosophy will know that Aristotle's and Spinoza's ethics consider self-love a virtue, not a vice, in striking contrast to Calvin's standpoint.

15. Max Stirner, *The Ego and His Own*, trans. by S.T. Byington (London: A.C. Fifield, 1912), p. 339.

16. One of his positive formulations, for example, is: "But how does one use life? In using it up like the candle one burns.... Enjoyment of life is using life up." F. Engels has clearly seen the one-sidedness of Stirner's formulations and has attempted to overcome the false alternative between love for oneself and love for others. In a letter to Marx in which he discusses Stirner's book, Engels writes: "If, however, the concrete and real individual is the true basis for our 'human' man, it is self-evident that egotism—of course not only Stirner's egotism of reason, but also the egotism of the heart—is the basis for our love of man."—*Marx-Engels Gesamtausgabe* (Berlin: Marx-Engels Verlag, 1929), p. 6.

17. Friedrich Nietzsche *The Will to Power*, trans. by Anthony M. Ludovici (Edinburgh and London: T.N. Foulis, 1910), stanzas 246, 326, 369, 373, and 728.

18. Friedrich Nietzsche, *Beyond Good and Evil*, trans. by Helen Zimmer (New York: The Macmillan Company, 1907), stanza 258.

19. Cf. G.A. Morgan, *What Nietzsche Means* (Cambridge: Harvard University Press, 1943).

20. Friedrich Nietzsche, *Thus Spake Zarathustra*, trans. by Thomas Common (New York: Modern Library), p. 75.

21. *The Will to Power*, stanza 785.
22. *Ibid.*, stanza 935.
23. *Thus Spake Zarathustra*, p. 76.
24. *Ibid*, p. 102.
25. See Friedrich Nietzsche, *The Twilight of Idols*, trans. by A.M. Ludovici (Edinburgh: T.N. Foulis, 1911), stanza 35; *Ecce Homo*, trans. by A.M. Ludovici (New York: The Macmillan Company, 1911), stanza 2; *Nachlass Nietzsches Werke* (Leipzig: A. Kroener), pp. 63-64.
26. This point has been emphasized by Karen Horney, *The Neurotic Personality of Our Time* (New York: W.W. Norton & Company, 1937), and by Robert S. Lynd, *Knowledge for What?* (Princeton: Princeton University Press, 1939).
27. Spinoza, *Ethics*, IV, Prop. 20.
28. William James expressed this concept very clearly. "To have," he says, "a self that I can care for, Nature must first present me with some object interesting enough to make me instinctively wish to appreciate it for its own sake.... My own body and what ministers to its needs are thus the primitive object, instinctively determined, of my egoistic interests. Other objects may become interesting derivatively, through association with any of these things, either as means or as habitual concomitants; and so, in a thousand ways, the primitive sphere of the egoistic emotions may enlarge and change its boundaries. This sort of interest is really the meaning of the word *mine*. Whatever has it, is, *eo ipso*, a part of me!"—*Principles of Psychology* (New York: Henry Holt and Company, 2 vols., 1896), I, 319, 324. Elsewhere James writes: "It is clear that between what a man calls *me* and what he simply calls *mine*, the line is difficult to draw. We feel and act about certain things that are ours very much as we feel and act about ourselves. Our fame, our children, the work of our hands, may be as dear to us as our bodies are, and arouse the same feelings and the same acts of reprisal if attacked.... In its widest possible sense, however, a man's Self is the sum-total of all that he can call his, not only his body and his psychic powers, but his clothes and his house, his wife and children, his ancestors and friends, his reputation and works, his land and horses and yacht and bank account. All these things give him the same emotions. If they wax or prosper, he feels triumphant, if they dwindle and die away, he feels cast down—not necessarily in the same degree for each thing, but in much the same way for all."—*Ibid.*, I, 291-292.
29. Pirandello in his plays has expressed this concept of self and the self-doubt resulting from it.
30. *Loc cit.*, Act V. Scene I.

IV / Changing One's Self Image

I think there's a difference between being selfish *and being* self-centered. *To me selfish is a very good quality because if you don't love you, you sure as hell can't love anybody else. Being self-centered is a whole different trip. But no, I am all for selfishness. Doing what's good for you is good for everybody.*
Lynn Caine

Self-Concept: Product and Producer of Experience

Arthur W. Combs, Donald L. Avila, and William W. Purkey

The most important single factor affecting behavior is the self-concept. What people do at every moment of their lives is a product of how they see themselves and the situations they are in. While situations may change from moment to moment or place to place, the beliefs that people have about themselves are always present factors in determining their behavior. The self is the star of every performance, the central figure in every act. Persons engaged in the helping professions, therefore, need the broadest possible understandings of the nature, origins, and functions of the self-concept.

WHAT IS THE SELF-CONCEPT?

By the self-concept is meant all those aspects of the perceptual field to which we refer when we say "I" or "me." It is the organization of perceptions about self which seems to the individual to be who he is. It is composed of thousands of perceptions varying in clarity, precision, and importance in the person's peculiar economy. Taken altogether these are described by the perceptual psychologist as the self-concept.

Each of us has literally thousands of ideas or concepts about himself: who he is, what he stands for, where he lives, what he does or does not do, and the like. A particular person might see herself as Mrs. Sally Blanton — wife, mother, part-time social worker; American, white; young; resident of Tampa, Fla.; measurements 34-25-34; good swimmer; poor tennis player. All these and many other perceptions or beliefs about herself make up the personal and unique self-concept of Mrs. Sally Blanton. To be sure, not all the concepts about herself are equally important to Mrs. Blanton. Some concepts of herself may be recognized as transitory. Others, like her concept of herself as a woman and a "Mrs.," are probably extremely important aspects of herself and are difficult to change.

Descriptions like those Mrs. Blanton has of herself serve to distinguish her self as unique from all other selves. But self-description does not stop there. We are seldom content with description alone. Even more important are the values a person places upon his various qualities of self. People do not regard themselves only as fathers or mothers, but as "good" or "bad" fathers and mothers. They see themselves not simply as people, but as attractive or ugly, pleasant or unpleasant, fat or thin, happy or sad, adequate or inadequate people. These, too, are perceptions of self and, taken together with the thousands of other concepts of self, make up the person's self-concept.

The self-concept, it should be understood, is not a thing but an organization of ideas. It is an abstraction, a Gestalt, a peculiar pattern of perceptions of self. Despite being no more than an abstraction, however, these ideas are terribly important for the person who holds them. They may seem only like ideas to outsiders but, for the person himself, they have a feeling of absolute reality. In fact the self-concept is even more important to its owner than the body in which it exists. The body, according to Earl Kelley, is but "the meat house we live in," the vehicle in which the self rides. We recognize the distinction between body and self when we complain that "the spirit is willing but the flesh is weak," or "I would have come to the meeting, Joe, but my old body let me down and I had to stay in bed with the flu."

This distinction between the self-concept and the physical self may be observed in other ways. For example, the self-concept may be defined in such a way as to include matters quite outside the skin. This often happens with respect to one's most cherished possessions. A man may regard his desk as so much a part of him that he treats interference with it as a personal violation. Consequently, his reaction to a secretary who has intruded upon his territory by disturbing things in or on the desk may be so angry and forceful as to bewilder her. She exclaims to the other girls in the office, "You'd think I'd wounded him, or something!" Of course, she had. What appears to be only a piece of furniture to the secretary seems to be an extension of self to the owner of the desk.

The extension of self is observable even more often with respect to persons or groups. Psychologists refer to this experience as a feeling of "identification." By this, they mean the feeling of oneness we have with those persons or groups who have come to have special value for us. The self of a father, for instance, may be extended to include his son or daughter. When they are insulted, he almost literally behaves as though he were himself offended. The feeling of oneness with those we love and cherish has been experienced by almost everyone. Sometimes it may be so very strong, in fact, that awareness of physical separation may be temporarily lost. In the following excerpt from a letter, a young mother describes this feeling with respect to her newborn child:

When they brought my baby to me I unwrapped her and lay for a while in awe examining the marvelous way she was made. Then, after a while, I placed her on my stomach with her head between by breasts and lay there with a curious feeling of triumph and exquisite peace. Now and then I would raise the covers a little and peek down at her. As she lay there I honestly couldn't tell where she began and I left off. I remember I wept a little because I was so happy. I'll never forget the moment as long as I live.

While few of us are privileged to experience the depth of identification felt by this young mother, almost everyone has some feelings of identification with other people somewhere. It is one of those feelings that makes us human.

The expansion of self-concept also extends to feelings about groups. In fact, one of the reasons groups come together in the first place is to have the experience of oneness with each other. In becoming a member of a group, the self-concept is expanded to include the other members. Thereafter the individual begins to behave as though the members are an extension of his self. He speaks of "my gang," "my school," "my friend," "my church," "my neighborhood," "my state," or "my country." Depending upon how strong the identification, he behaves with respect to them as though they were part of self. He may even begin to call the members of his fraternity, church, or racial group "brothers" or "sisters."

THE SELF: CENTER OF THE UNIVERSE

For each person, his self-concept is who he is. It is the center of his universe, the frame of reference from which he makes his observations. It is his personal reality and the vantage point from which all else is observed and comprehended. We speak of things as "right" or "left," "near" or "far," and, of course, we mean from ourselves. The self is also used as a yardstick for making judgments. We regard others as taller, shorter, smarter, more unscrupulous, more handsome, faster, older, or younger than ourselves. As the self changes, furthermore, the yardstick changes and what we believe to be true changes with it. What is considered "old" is likely to be quite differently defined at ages six, eighteen, thirty-six, or sixty.

Generally speaking, we feel quite at home with "what is me." Toward what is "not me," we are likely to be indifferent, even repelled. Allport points out, for example, that when a person cuts his finger he may put it in his mouth and, in doing so, drink his own blood without the slightest concern. Once the finger has been bandaged, however, any dried blood on the bandage is no longer regarded as "me"; a suggestion to lick the blood from the bandage would likely be regarded with revulsion. Similarly, everyone is continuously engaged in swallowing the saliva which collects in his mouth.This same saliva, collected in a glass and offered to the person to drink, is a very different matter indeed! Experiences consistent with the existing self-concept are accepted quite readily. They are treated as though they belong even when accepting them may be painful. A failing grade for a student who already believes he is a failue may not concern him at all. It only represents a further corroboration of what he already believes. It fits. On the other hand, incongruous experiences may produce feelings of great discomfort. When a man who believes he is highly attractive is told in no uncertain terms by a beautiful girl what a heel he really is, the shock to the self is likely to be considerable. Doctors and nurses often find it very difficult to get patients newly diagnosed as "diabetic" to care for themselves properly. Such patients often find it very difficult to accept this new concept of self and the use of insulin and dietary prescriptions they must follow. It takes time to assimilate their new definitions of self. The disturbing effect of inconsistent experiences will occur even if the new thought is something the person would like to believe. This can be observed in the embarrassment a person feels when after long periods of failure, he is told he has done something very well. He may even suspect that the teller is being sarcastic!

SELF-CONCEPT DETERMINES BEHAVIOR

The importance of the self-concept in the economy of the individual goes far beyond providing his basis of reality. Its very existence determines what else he may perceive. The self-concept has a selective effect on perceptions. People tend to perceive what is congruent with their already existing concept of self. People who see themselves as men perceive what is appropriate for men to perceive, while people who see themselves as women see what is appropriate for women to perceive. So it happens that on the way home from a party, Mrs. Adams may say to her husband, "John, did you notice what Helen was wearing?" John is quite likely to reply, "No, I didn't notice that." But, being a man, there were other things he noticed which, almost certainly, his wife will not think to ask him about!

It is notorious how a man's behavior may change when he puts on a uniform and becomes a "soldier." With this self-concept he is free to behave in ways he would dream of as a civilian. Students have been known to fail in school because of unfortunate beliefs about themselves, as in this example reported by Coach Darrel Mudra of Western Illinois University:

What a boy believes about himself is really important. We had a student at Greeley who scored in the 98 percentile on the entrance test, and he thought that he has a 98 IQ. And because he thought he was an average kid, he knew college would be hard for him. He almost failed in his first term. He went home and told his parents, "I don't believe I'm college caliber," and the parents took him back to school and talked with the college counselor. When he found out that 98 percentile score meant that he had a 140 IQ, he was able to do "A" work before the year was over.

Once established, the self-concept thereafter provides a screen through which everything else is seen, heard, evaluated, and understood. Architects do not look at buildings in the same way the rest of us do. Similarly, the view of the world is different as seen by dressmakers, plumbers, house painters, nuclear physicists, or people who see themselves as Russian, Chinese, white, black, Hindu, or Muslim. Each person perceives the world around him filtered through his own self-conceptions; and this occurs whether he is aware of what is happening or not. Even when the businessman goes on vacation, he may find it very difficult to forget his busines. In any vacation resort, men can be observed by the hundreds seeking each other out to discuss the comfortable things of the world they know while their wives equally uncomfortable so far from home, find comfort in talking housewifely things with people they never knew before.

The psychological literature is overflowing with learned articles and research studies dealing with the effects of the self-concept on a great variety of behaviors including farilure in school, levels of aspiration or goal-setting, athletic prowess, mental health, intelligence, delinquency and criminality, ethnic groups, the socially disadvantaged, and industrial productivity. In every aspect of human existence the self-concept exerts its influence upon what people do and how they behave. When we know how a person sees himself, then much of his behavior becomes clear to us and it is often possible to predict with great accuracy what he is likely to do next.

CIRCULAR EFFECT OF THE SELF-CONCEPT

The selective effect of the self-concept has another important result. It corroborates and supports the already existing beliefs about self and so tends to maintain and reinforce its own existence. This circular characteristic of the self-concept may often be observed at work in the problems of children in learning arithmetic, spelling, public speaking, physical education, history, music, or any of the rest of the school subjects. Take the case of reading, for example: It now seems clear that many children who cannot read are unable largely because they *believe* they cannot read. It is comparatively rare these days that the child coming to the reading clinic has anything wrong with his eyes. With modern methods of testing children's health, sight deficiencies are usually discovered routinely. Instead, the youngster who comes to the reading clinic is much more likely to be handicapped because he believes he cannot read. For one reason or another he has developed an idea that he is unable to read. Thereafter, he is caught in a vicious circle which goes something like this: Because he believes he can't read, he avoids it. In this way he avoids the very thing that would be helpful for him. Because he avoids reading, he doesn't get any practice and so he doesn't read very well. Then, when his teacher asks him to read, he reads very poorly and she says, "My goodness, Jimmy, you don't read very well!" This, of course, is what he already believed in the first place! Then, to make matters worse, a report card is often sent home telling his parents how badly he reads and so they, too, join the act confirming the child's belief that he is indeed a very poor reader. In this way a poor reader is frequently surrounded by a veritable conspiracy in which all of his experience points out his deficiency to him. This conspiracy, moreover, is produced for the most part by persons whose intentions were excellent. They *wanted* the child to be a good reader, even though the net effect of their pressures was to prove to him he was not.

The reader himself may be one of those thousands of people who believes he cannot do mathematics, make a speech, or spell. With such a belief, he probably shuns those occasions where it is necessary to use the skill and so avoids the opportunity to practice it. Then, of course, his failure experiences when he is forced to act corroborate what he already firmly believes! Many research studies are now available showing the effects of student beliefs upon achievement in a wide variety of school subjects. There is even evidence to suggest that the self-concept may be a better predictor of a child's success in school than the time-honored IQ score.

The self-perpetuating effect of the self-concept is by no means limited to success or failure in academic subjects. It extends to every aspect of human experience. The same dynamics may be seen at work in all walks of life. The juvenile delinquent, for example, who has come to believe that nobody likes him, wants him, cares about him, and who thinks he is not much good, often comes to the conclusion that other people are his enemies. Thereafter, he may find delight in confounding authority. He builds up his feelings of self-esteem and value by taunting the police, and enjoys finding ingenious ways of frustrating and embarrassing them. Such behavior is hardly likely to endear him to others. Almost certainly, it will cause others to behave toward him in ways which confirm and support his already unhappy views of himself.

Dr. Walter Reckless and his colleagues at Ohio State University carried out a series of studies on the self-concepts of delinquent and non-delinquent boys. Among their findings are the following: The 12-year old "good" boy in a slum area perceives himself as staying out of trouble, of his friends as keeping out of trouble, of himself as going to finish school, as of his family as a good family. The mothers of the "good" boys also had favorable perceptions and prognostications of their sons. On the other hand, the so-called "bad" boy, spotted by his sixth-grade teacher as headed for trouble and for dropout, has the opposite perception of himself. He perceives himself as headed for trouble, of his friends as delinquents, and of his family as a "bum" family. The "bad" boy's mother echoed his perceptions. In a follow-up study at the end of four years, these investigations found that the "good" boy was practically delinquency free, while 40 percent of the "bad" boys were in the juvenile court one to seven times.

Fortunately, the circular effect of the self-concept operates equally well in positive directions. Persons with positive self-concepts are quite likely to behave in ways that cause others to react in corroborative fashion. People who believe they *can,* are more likely to succeed. The very existence of feelings about self creates conditions likely to make them so. The nurse who feels sure of herself behaves with dignity and certainty, expecting positive response from other people. To those with whom she works, this in turn calls forth responses which tend to confirm the beliefs she already holds. So, the circular effect of the self-concept creates a kind of spiral in which "the rich get richer and the poor get poorer." The self-corroborating character of the self-concept gives it a high degree of stability and makes it difficult to change once it has become firmly established.

SELF-CONCEPT AND SOCIAL PROBLEMS

The self-perpetuating characteristic of the self-concept makes it of special concern in attempting to deal with the great social problems of our time. Millions of people everywhere in the world are caught in a vicious circle in which their experience seems always to confirm their unhappy or disastrous concepts of self. "Like mirrors locked face to face, in an infinite corridor of despair," they are trapped in a way of life from which there seems no escape. Having defined themselves in ways that preclude much hope of success, they remain forever victims of their own self-perceptions. Believing they are only X much, that is all the much they do. Other people seeing them do only X much then learn to expect that much from them and describe them as "X much people" which, of course, only confirms what the person felt in the first place! Many Negroes, for example, have been so thoroughly brainwashed by generations of experience into believing that they are unable, incapable, and second-rate citizens that they often continue to behave so, even in conditions where it is no longer appropriate. Poverty-stricken men in Appalachia who have lived too long without jobs or hope for the future eventually give up trying altogether. White men who have grown up with serious doubts about themselves but feeling superior to "niggers" resist with violence ideas of social equality. Their self-concepts are so negative and their world so full of hopelessness that they must have some belief that makes them better than something. How to help these and thousands of other desperate victims of their own perceptions off the treadmill of self-corroboration is one of the great problems faced by our generation.

The self-concept also plays its part in the social and philosophical problems posed by our great international dilemmas. People who see themselves as Americans behave like Americans, while people who see themselves as Russians, Chinese, Japanese, German, British, or Ghanians behave in ways appropriate to their conceptions of themselves. So also, people who see themselves as Buddhists, Taoists, Jews, Moslems, or Christians tend to think and behave in terms of their beliefs. Sometimes diverse ways create differences and misunderstandings where none really exist if it were possible to penetrate to the basic issues beneath the surface of differences. U Thant, as Secretary-General of the United Nations, once expressed this in a description of his own growth and philosophy which had brought him to a point where he could see himself as a "person of the world" rather than a representative of Thailand, his native country. Feeling so, he said that he could watch a wrestling match between a man from his own and a different country and rejoice for whomever won. For most of us, more is the pity, such a "citizen of the world" self-concept is still beyond our experience.

HOW THE SELF-CONCEPT IS LEARNED

The self-concept, we have said, is an organization of beliefs about the self. These concepts are learned in the same fashion in which all other perceptions are acquired — as a consequence of experience. Before a child is born, he has already begun to make differentiations about himself and the world he lives in. This process continues after birth. A very large part of the infant's waking hours are spent in continuous exploration. Everything is smelled, felt, tasted, listened to, and looked at. Very early he begins to distinguish between what is "me" and "not me." With continued exploration, these perceptions in turn become increasingly differentiated into more and more explicit definitions. As language use develops, it soon becomes possible to give "me" a name, and the whole process of differentiation and concept formation is immensely accelerated. Before long the child is in possession of large numbrs of perceptions about himself and his world, and a sense of his identity emerges. He becomes aware of himself as a unique person of many qualities and values all together having a feeling of personness. A new self has come into being. Once established, this self will exert its influence on every behavior for the rest of its owner's life.[1]

Some of the things people learn about self are discovered from interaction with the physical world. From these experiences they learn how big or how little they are, how fast they can walk or swim, or where they are located in the space they live in. They also learn what they can lift or not lift, what they can control, what dangers they must avoid or protect themselves from, what things are good or enhancing, and thousands of other perceptions more or less useful for getting along in the physical world we all live in.

ROLE OF SIGNIFICANT OTHERS

Of much more importance to the growth of the self, however, are the concepts we acquire from interaction with other human beings. Man is primarily a social animal, and it is from experiences with other people that his most crucial concepts of self are derived. People learn who they are and what they are from the ways they are treated by the important poeple in their lives — sometimes called "significant others" by psychologists. From interactions with such people, each of us learns that he is liked or unliked, acceptable or unacceptable, a success or failure, respectable or of no account. We learn very little from unimportant people even if they are called teachers, parents, social workers, counselors, priests, or rabbis. Only the significant people have much effect on the self-concept. The nurse, for example, is not very disturbed by what the casual acquaintance says about her skill. She is very much concerned about what her supervisor or doctor has to say (providing, of course, that she believes they know their business). What is learned about the self is a product of the peculiar experience occurring in the private world of the individual. What he learns from any event may be quite different from the way it appears to the outside observer.

Because the self-concept is primarily learned from experience with significant others, it should not be assumed that this is simply a matter of what one is told by the important people in his life. So much of our daily interaction with one another occurs through verbal communication that it is easy to fall into the belief that what people say to each other has immense importance. Sometimes, of course, it may. The effect of words does not lie in what was said, however, but how it was read by the hearer. Understanding this fact is especially important for persons in the helping professions because so much of these people's work is dependent upon verbal interaction in one form or another. Believing that words are terribly important or that any matter can be solved by talk can result in making the helper ineffective. Certainly, talking is one of the most valuable tools we have at our disposal for influencing the behavior of others, but it is easy to exaggerate its contribution. It is not enough to be told one is loved; it is necessary to *feel* he is loved, and by someone who matters. One need only remind himself how seldom he takes "good advice" from others. Telling may be a way of affecting a change in another's self-concept. It is by no means infallible and is often vastly overrated.

From whatever source the self-concept is acquired, what is learned is a matter of the individual's own experience, not what seems to some outsider to be happening to him. A parent who scolds a child for not doing well in school may do so with the best of intentions, hoping to motivate his child to greater effort. To the child the meaning of this event may only be that he is stupid, unacceptable, or not much good. This kind of unintended learning is called "incidental learning" by psychologists and is often far more important in determining behavior than what the counselor or teacher or social worker expected to convey. Children learn about themselves, for example, from the atmosphere of the classroom, from the moods of teachers, and from the overt or covert indications of success or failure implied by approval or disapproval of teachers and classmates. This unplanned learning is likely to be much more significant and permanent than what the teacher taught. The child in fifth grade who is reading at second-grade level has a daily diet of failure imposed upon him by the rigidity of a system which insists on teaching all children at a given level as though they were alike. In the face of this daily experience, telling him he is a "good boy" is like a drop of water in a dry lake bed. Or, trying too hard to teach the young mother all she should know to care for her sick child may result in convincing her how inadequate she really is.

PLACE OF TRAUMA IN THE GROWTH OF SELF

Many people believe the self-concept is primarily a product of the dramatic events occurring to the child in the process of growing up. This idea has come about very largely because of the concepts introduced to our thinking by Sigmund Freud and his students. As he listened to his patients retrace the steps of their growth and development in the course of psychoanalysis, Freud found them repeatedly bringing to light shocking events which had happened to them in the past. It was natural to assume that these events had had deep and powerful influences on the formation of personality and the creation of the problems his patients carried into adult years. This impression was further confirmed by the patients themselves, who frequently spoke of these events as having had a critical effect upon them.

In more recent years we have come to see the role of early trauma in a different way. We now understand that the most important changes in the self-concept come about only as a consequence of many experiences repeated over long periods of time. It is the little day to day things repeatedly chipping away at an individual's feelings about himself that produce the most permanent, pervasive effects on the self. A child learns that his is acceptable or unacceptable—not so much from the dramatic events as from the thousands of little every day nuances of attitude and feeling picked up from those around him, often so subtle and indistinct at the time they occurred as to make it quite impossible in later life for the grownup to put his finger upon the particular event which produced his current feeling.

If the self-concept is learned only slowly as a consequence of many experiences, why should we have the feeling that dramatic events in the past have so deeply influenced us? The reason seems to be that dramatic events are easier to recall and become symbols which crystallize and bring into clear figure the essence of a particular feeling. The event has tremendous significance, not because the experience was that crucial in its own right but because the experience became symbolic making explicit many implicit feelings developed over a long period of time. Many a child has known the death of a grandfather with little or no feeling of loss, and many are quite unable in later days to remember the event at all. For the lonely, rejected child whose grandfather was an island of care and concern, the same event has a far different meaning. Looking backward down the years of our growth, dramatic events provide the hooks on which we can hang accumulated meanings. As a consequence the adult may recall how shy he was as a child and how devastated he was the day in third grade "when all the children laughed at me!" What makes the difference in human personality is not the trauma itself, but the multitude of other experiences which hammered and molded its meaning into being.

STABILITY OF THE SELF-CONCEPT

We have described the self-concept as composed of thousands of concepts of self varying in importance to the person. We have also observed that the core of the self-concept has a high degree of permanence and stability once it has become established. Unimportant aspects of the self can c f·en be acquired or changed fairly quickly. These are generally peripheral aspects of the self, or matters of comparatively little concern. Thus, it may be possible to teach a person a game so that he comes to think of himself as a person who knows how to play that game. By taking a person for a ride in an airplane, we may produce a change in his self-concept to "one who has been in a plane." While these kinds of changes are comparatively simple to bring about, they are seldom enough to produce imortant changes in personality. Most of the truly important changes in the self-concept, such as those related to values, attitudes, or basic beliefs, occur much more slowly and sometimes only after very long periods of time. This is often very frustrating to those who like to help people quickly or easily. Frustrating as it is, however, we need to remind ourselves that this same resistance to change is also our very best guarantee against being taken over by a demagogue. It is a good thing people do not change easily!

Generally speaking, the more important the aspect of self in the economy of the individual, the more experience will be required to establish it and the more difficult it will be to change it. Fritz Redl once illustrated this slow development of individual feelings about self in the course of a lecture on juvenile delinquency. Delinquents, he pointed out, are not made by any one thing:

It takes fourteen years to make a good delinquent. Before that you can't really be sure you have one. To make a good delinquent everything has to go wrong, not once, but over and over again. The home has to go wrong, the school has to go wrong, the church has to go wrong, the community has to go wrong, his friends have to let him down, not once, but over and over again. They have to make a habit of it! Then, after 14 years of that you may have a good dellinquent.[2]

After fourteen years of such experience it is also understandable why it takes time to change such a child's beliefs about himself and the world.

SELF-CONCEPT AND SELF-REPORT

If the self-concept plays as important a role in the determination of behavior as modern psychologists believe, then members of the helping professions must become sensitive to the self-concepts of their students, clients, or patients, and must be skillful in helping them make changes in their concepts of self. At first glance, understanding someone's self-concept would seem like an easy proposition; if you would like to know how someone sees himself, why not just ask him? That seems obvious and straightforward enough. Unfortunately, it is not that simple. How a person perceives himself is a very private matter, and what he is able to tell you about himself will depend upon his willingness to reveal himself to you. Even if he is willing, there is still a question as to whether he can describe himself accurately to you on demand. It is important for members of the helping professions to have a clear understanding of the differences between a person's self-report and his self-concept.[3]

The self-concept is what a person perceives himself to be; it is what he *believes* about himself. The self-report, on the other hand, is what a person is willing or able to divulge, or what he can be tricked into *saying* about himself when asked to do so. The self-report is a behavior; the self-concept is a system of beliefs. Clearly, these matters are not the same.

All behavior is affected in one way or another by the self-concept including what a person says about himself. This does not mean, however, that the relationship exists as one to one or that the self-report can be accepted without question as an accurate description of the self-concept. What a person says about himself may or may not be what he truly feels. Even with the very best of intentions, he may be unable to give an accurate description of himself because other perceptions interfere and create a measure of distraction or distortion. Few of us, for example, are ever free from social expectancy. What we say about ourselves is affected by our awareness of what we are "supposed" to say. Little boys, for instance, must insist they hate school even though they would give their eyeteeth to go back the week after it is over. Adults are not completely free to express their true feelings about self because our society disapproves of immodesty. It is regarded as very bad taste to go around telling people how great you are! Some aspects of self may be unreportable simply because they are so threatening that they cannot be openly admitted even though they may be clearly apparent to others. Who has not seen such a person stoutly denying what all of his friends and acquaintances quite clearly know to be true? The healthiest of people do not always feel safe enough to reveal their deepest feelings to other people even under the warmest and friendliest of conditions with their sweethearts, wives, or psychotherapists. If these constraints on accurate reporting of self do not exist, there remain the further difficulties of lack of language to express feelings accurately and the willingness of the reporter to cooperate on demand. Requests for information which seem impertinent or "nosy" to the recipient are quite unlikely to produce accurate self-descriptions.

What people say of themselves may be accepted as interesting and informative data but not, without question, as an indication of the self-concept directly. This was clearly demonstrated in several researches carried out at the University of Florida. In one of these studies, sixth-grade children were asked to describe themselves. Without knowing what the children said of themselves, a group of trained observers were asked to rate the children with respect to the very same self-concept items. When the children's self-reports were compared with the self-concept inferences made by the trained observers, no significant correlation could be found between the two. In another experiment, teachers were asked to pick which of two descriptions best fitted each child in their classes. One of these descriptions was the child's self-report; the other was a self-concept description made by trained observers. The teachers overwhelmingly chose the trained observer's descriptions as most like the children they knew.

Because it exists inside the person, the self-concept is not open to direct examination by any means currently known to us. It can, however, be understood indirectly through a process of inference from some form of observed behavior, as was done in the experiments mentioned above. The rationale is as follows: If it is true that behavior is a product of the individual's perceptual field, then it should be possible, by a process of reading behavior backward, to infer from observed behavior the nature of the perceptions which produced it. This is, in fact, what all of us do with people who are important to us. We deduce what it is they are thinking and feeling from the ways we see them behave. The psychologist in his research and the helper in his professional role do exactly the same thing although perhaps with greater control and precision than the man in the street.

The question may legitimately be raised as to why inferences about the self-concept, made from observed behavior, are more acceptable indicators of the self-concept than a person's own self-report. First, the inferred self-concept is more accurate on theoretical grounds; it approaches the self-concept as an organization of *perceptions* which *produce* behavior rather than accepting the person's behavior as synonymous with self-perception. Second, it recognizes the existence of distorting factors in the self-report and attempts to eliminate as many of these as practicable. Among the distortions mentioned above, for example, making inferences about the self-concept can eliminate or reduce errors introduced by social expectancy, lack of cooperation of the subject, lack of adequate language, or the subject's feelings of threat. It may, of course, be true that the inference procedure introduces other errors in the perceptions of the observer, but that is a problem in every human observation which scientists must deal with no matter what the nature of the observations. It is incumbent on the scientist to approach his problem with maximum awareness of the factors involved and scrupulous attention to their effects.

A person's *real self*, of course, is measured precisely neither by the inferred self-concept nor the self-report. The question is, Which of these provides the closest approximation for the purposes we have in mind? Despite criticism of the self-report as a measure of self-concept, the self-report has value in its own right. What a person has to say about himself is valuable data. It is observable behavior. Like any other behavior, it is an expression of the subject's perceptual field at the moment of acting. Because of its symbolic character and the uses the behaver makes of it for self-expression, it has more than ordinary value for helping us understand another person. Employed as behavioral data, it may provide valuable clues to the nature of the self-concept which produced it when subjected to processes of inference. Often the self-report, despite its distortions, may be quite sufficient data for the citizen operating in daily life. The scientist, student of behavior, or practitioner in the helping professions, however, will generally need descriptions of self that are more carefully and more rigorously obtained.

SELF-CONCEPT AND THE HELPING PROFESSIONS

Any aspect of human personality which affects behavior so fundamentally as the self-concept must be of vital concern to workers in the helping professions. It is, in fact, their primary subject matter in whatever arena they practice their arts. Counselors, teachers, social workers, and priests are in the business of helping students, clients, and parishioners to explore and discover better, more effective relationships between themselves and the world they live in. Whether or not they are successful in the practice of their professions will depend upon the effects they have on the self-concepts of those who seek their help, for major principles of human personality structures cannot be set aside because they are inconvenient for helpers. If the self-concept has the central importance suggested by modern psychology, then those whose responsibilities require that they work with people can ignore it only at the risk of making themselves ineffective.

People do not leave their self-concepts at the door. They bring them right in with them everywhere they go. While signing papers for his relief check the poverty-stricken head of a family is learning about himself. The child in school may be discovering more about himself in a given class hour than about the arithmetic lesson his teacher thinks she is presenting. What persons in the helping professions do or do not do, affects the helpee's self-concept whether or not helpers are aware of their impact and regardless of what they might wish.

In a fascinating experiment in New South Wales, J.W. Staines found marked differences in the sensitivities of teachers to the self-concepts of children. This sensitivity was accompanied by greater evidence of growth in the children they worked with. What is more, Staines found that the self-concepts of children were affected whether the teacher was consciously attending to their self-concepts or not. In the conclusion of his experiment he says:

> The educational significance of the self is reaffirmed when it is realized that changes in the self picture are an inevitable part of both outcomes and conditions of learning in every classroom, whether or not the teacher is aware of them or aiming for them. They occur, as in A's class where the teacher deliberately included them in his teaching goals and adopted them in his methods accordingly, and they occur in B's class where the teacher aimed at orthodox goals and was ignorant of these correlative factors. Since both classes were reasonably typical and both teachers recognized by their headmasters as competent teachers, it is reasonable to generalize and expect such factors to operate in all classrooms. (Staines, 1958)

Persons in the helping professions who ignore the importance of the role of self-concept in their patients, clients, students, or parishioners are in grave danger of defeating themselves. People's self-concepts will not go away because we wish it. To ignore the self-concept and its impact upon behavior seriously handicaps the helper's effectiveness. His position is as ridiculous as the man who says, "I know my car needs a carburetor, but I think I'll run mine without one!" Or the rocket launcher who says, "I recognize that gravity is a factor which affects our procedures, but let us launch this rocket without taking it into account!"

The self-concept is important to helpers for another reason. Students, clients, and patients judge the value of their experience with helpers from the frame of reference of the self-concept. What affects the self-concept seems relevant; what appears remote from the self seems irrelevant. If the time the student or client or patient spends with the counselor or teacher does not seem relevant to his self, it can safely be ignored. If the helper continually misses the subject's self, what he has to say or do only seems irrelevant to the helpee who sooner or later concludes that the relationship is a waste of time and, one way or another, physically or mentally departs the scene. People do not listen long to those who have no significant message. They also evaluate helpers in terms of this significance and report their-findings to anyone else who may ask their opinion. Thus, the helper who ignores the self-concept and his effect upon it is quite likely to fail to help his client; he also creates a poor reputation for himself in the bargain.

CHANGING THE SELF-CONCEPT

Because the self-concept is learned, it can be taught. This fact provides the theoretical basis upon which the helping professions depend. The purpose of these occupations is to assist other people in exploring and discovering more effective relationships between themselves and the world. The subject brings his self to the relationship. Thereafter, whether anything of importance occurs will be dependent upon the kinds of experiences the helper is able to bring into being for his clients, students, and patients. Whether they are aware of it or not, helpers are engaged in a subtle process of teaching. Since new concepts of self are learned as a consequence of interactions with the helper, effective helpers must be significant people. They cannot be nonentities. One cannot interact with a shadow. The helping relationship is an active one, and a completely passive helper is unlikely to teach his client anything but his own futility. The personality of the helper must play a vital part in any helping relationship. It is the helper's use of his self which makes the interaction whatever it is to become. If a helper's self is to have such a significance, it must be involved in the dialogue.

Helping requires patience. A major task of persons in the helping professions is the facilitation of change in the self. A proper prospective of the dynamics and limitations of these changes can contribute much to the helper's own mental health and to the probabilities of his successful practice. For example, while peripheral and less crucial aspects of the self-concept like "I can't ride a bicycle" or "I am broke" can often be changed fairly quickly, important concepts of self like "I am a man" or "I am unwanted by everyone" are likely to change only very slowly, if at all. Generally speaking, the more basic and more fundamental or important the aspect of self we hope to change, the longer it is likely to take. Appreciation of this fact can forestall the setting of impractical goals and inevitable disappointment for the helper. On the one hand, it will make it possible for the helper to be far more patient and understanding. On the other hand, it can avoid almost certain frustration and despair over the outcomes of his efforts. The man in the street often assumes he can change others by doing or saying some simple thing and that will make all the difference; but helpers should know better.

Failure to appreciate the slowness of change in self may destroy the very thing which helpers seek. This is especially true in the case of those most deeply hurt and in need of assistance. Persons who have been deeply deprived, for example, have a great void within which requires filling. Helping them is something like trying to help a person who has fallen deeply into debt. For a very long time all the money he makes must go just to keep himself solvent from day to day. All his efforts are spent in just trying to balance his budget. Until that is done, little can be used to get ahead. The matter is made more difficult by interest charges upon the old debts or additional withdrawals made from his account to meet new emergencies. It may take a long time to help such a person recover to the point where he can take some positive action on his own, and helpers may become discouraged and give up the effort. One may have to believe his efforts are worthwhile despite no tangible evidence for a considerable period of time. With deeply deprived persons, a single experience is rarely sufficient to make much difference.

Central aspects of self require time to change. Failure to recognize this fact may do more than simply make helping relationships ineffective. Because of the self-perpetuating character of the self-concept, the impatient helper may begin his task intending to help and end by making his client worse! Let us take one of the tough delinquents Fritz Redl tells us it takes fourteen years to produce.

Here he is—surly, angry about the world, feeling as a result of his long experience, "Nobody likes me. Nobody wants me. Nobody cares about me. Well, I don't care about nobody neither!" Now comes the well-meaning social worker who, with the best of intentions, says to him, "Eddie, I like you." Much to her dismay her friendly words may be met with a stream of profanity. The inexperienced social worker may be deeply hurt by this rejection and outraged by the violence of the child's reply. Why should the child behave in this way? He does so because from his point of view, "you simply can't trust people who talk like that." All his past experience has taught him so. The social worker's words seem a mockery to the child. They appear like outright lies or, worse still, someone is making fun of him. Small wonder that he lashes out at his attacker and let's her have "what she deserves." Unless the social worker knows what she is about and possesses "the patience of Job," she may succumb to the "natural" thing and slap him across the mouth. This, of course, only serves to prove what the youngster felt in the first place—"You can't trust people who talk like that!" So, what started out as an attempt to help becomes shipwrecked by the helper's own lack of perspective about the self-concept, ends in disaster, and confirms the child's beliefs more deeply than ever before. Worse still, the experience may serve to increase his distrust of persons in the helping professions generally.

HELPING IS NEVER IN VAIN

A proper perspective on the nature of the self-concept and its capacities for change will do much more for the helper than keep him from errors of impatience. It can provide him with faith in his processes and protect him from unwarranted feelings of futility. Despite the high degree of permanence characteristic of its central aspects, the self-concept can be changed. Throughout life it is continually changing. This change, to be sure, is more rapid in the peripheral and less important aspects of self; but learning goes on continuously and even the central aspects of the self-concept may change as a consequence of experience over the years. One example of this is the change in feeling about self which occurs from childhood to adolescence, to maturity and finally old age. Even very old people in retirement may sometimes make considerable changes in self-concept, for example, albeit not so easily as they did in their youth.

The more open an individual is to his experience the greater is the possibility for him to learn new self-definitions. This openness is likely to be greatest in childhood when there is less clearly differentiated organization in the individual's field and the self-concept is less set in exerting its selecting effect on new experience. This is one of the reasons why a heavy concentration of our efforts to improve the lot of the poor and the culturally disadvantaged must be directed at programs for the very young whose self-concepts are only beginning the process of definition and crystallization.

The importance of the helper in the life of his client is never entirely without meaning unless the helper makes it so. Life is not reversible; every experience a person has, he has had forever. One cannot unexperience what has happened to him! Every experience of significant interaction must have its impact upon those who were involved in it. For some this may have major importance; for others very little. Any meaningful experience or series of experiences may not be sufficient to produce the changes we hope for. But they are always important!

Persons in the helping professions may often be heard to complain that there is little they can do because they do not have control of the outside lives of their clients, students, or patients. They complain that their good offices are spoiled by the unhappy experiences visited upon their clients by bosses, parents, or society in general. As a matter of fact, even a holding operation may make a very important contribution. When everything in a child's life outside of school is teaching him that he is unliked, unwanted, and unable, a loving teacher, skilled in providing experiences of success, may make a world of difference. She may not be able to turn the tide of events completely. If she does no more than help such a child keep his head above water, however, the effect expended is surely not wasted. Teachers rarely get credit for this kind of help, but it probably occurs with far more frequency than any of us realize. Similarly, the social worker who helps a young delinquent stay only "as bad as he is" when everything else in his world is pushing him downhill can make a contribution of tremendous importance—even if he does not succeed in making him over in a more socially approved image.

Even when it is not possible to provide all that is required, helpers must not fall into the trap of thinking their efforts are futile lest they contribute further to the inadequacies of their clients and students. After all, because a child is rejected at home is no good reason to reject him in school as well! What happens to an individual outside the sphere of influence of the helper may operate in directions opposed to those sought by the helper. This does not mean that what the helper does for his client may help his client change his world as well. Take the case of the child whose family is exerting hurtful influences directly contrary to what his teacher is trying to do for him at school. These conditions may seem so bad to his teacher that she exclaims, "What can you do with a child from a home like that?" It seems to her that all her hard won gains are negated by what happens to the child in his family setting. Such an attitude is most unfortunate. It overlooks the fact that a family is a dynamic unit in which each person interacts with all the others. What happens to any one member must have its effects upon everyone else. Let us take, for example, the hypothetical case of George Anderson who is driving his mother to distraction by his hostile behavior. Let us now suppose this child is fortunate enough in school to have a teacher who provides him some feeling of warmth, friendship, and experiences of success. When George goes home from school these days he feels better than he did when school was a more unhappy place. As a consequence he doesn't upset his mother, Mrs. Anderson, quite so much. In turn, Mr. Anderson, coming home tired from work, discovers his wife is easier to live with and his home is a more restful place. When Judith Anderson, George's little sister, claims her father's attention while he is trying to read the paper, instead of pushing her gruffly away, he makes room for her to climb in his lap and so Judith gains from her father a greater measure of the love and care she needs. Because of this, she feels better too. As a result, she feels less need to nag her brother George, as she usually does, and so we have come full circle! Every good thing a helper does for a client, student, or patient, he has done forever. It may not be enough, but it is never futile. There is always the possibility that someone else may contribute something elsewhere, and such cumulative experiences may in time be sufficient to provide the help which is needed.

The self-concept, we have said in this chapter, is the most important single factor affecting human behavior. In so little space we have had time only to outline the major principles involved in this vital concept. The self-concept and its functions lie at the very heart of the helping process. One can be of help to other people knowing nothing about this important aspect of human personality. A proper knowledge of the self-concept and of its dynamics in the production of human behavior and misbehavior, however, can add immeasurably to understanding people in need of help. It can do much more. It can provide the guidelines by which persons in the helping professions may direct their own behavior more effectively and efficiently, and so contribute with greater certainty to the health and growth of their clients.

1. The full story of concept development and the growth of the self is a fascinating field of exploration far beyond the treatment possible here. Interested readers are referred to references listed at the end of this chapter for further introduction to this important field of study.

2. From notes taken at Dr. Redl's lecture by A.W. of this chapter for further introduction to this important field of study.

2. From notes taken at Dr. Redl's lecture by A.W. Combs. Since Dr. Redl was speaking ex tempore, the accuracy of the quotation cannot be checked. The illustration, however, is superb.

3. This is a matter currently in great confusion in the psychological literature. Most of the studies presented in the literature as researches on the self-concept, when reviewed by the present authors through 1968, turn out, on closer examination, to be in reality studies of the self-report. Purporting to be researches on the self-concept, they have utilized measures of the self-report as though these concepts were identical. The undiscriminating use of these terms is a great pity. Treating them as though they were synonymous has immensely complicated the literature, and serious students need to be keenly aware of this state of affairs in interpreting research findings.

SELECTED READINGS

Starred entries indicate appearance in whole or in part in Donald L. Avila, Arthur W. Combs, and William W. Purkey, *The Helping Relationship Sourcebook* (Boston: Allyn & Bacon, 1971).

Allport, G.W. Is the concept of self necessary? In Allport, G.W. (Ed.) *Becoming*, New Haven, Conn.: Yale University Press, 1955, 36-56.

Beard, R.M. *An outline of Piaget's developmental psychology for students and teachers*. New York: Basic Books, 1969.

Combs, A.W. & Snygg, D. *Individual behavior: A perceptual approach to behavior*. (2nd ed.) New York; Harper & Brothers, 1959.

Combs, A.W. & Soper, D.W. The self, its derivative terms and research. *Journal of Individual Psychology*. 1957, **12**, 134-145(b).

Coopersmith, S. *The anecdotes of self esteem*. San Francisco: Freeman Press, 1967.

Gordon, C. & Gergen, K.J. *The self in social interaction. Vol. I: Classic and contemporary perspectives*. New York: Wiley, 1968.

Maehr, M.L., Menking, J. & Nafeger, S. Concept of self and the reaction of others. *Sociometry*, 1962, **25**, 353-357.

Parker, J. The relationship of self respect to inferred self concept. *Educational and Psychological Measurement*, 1966, **26**, 691-700.

* Patterson, C.H. The self in recent Rogerian theory. *Journal of Individual Psychology*, 1961, **17**, 5-11.

*Purkey, W. W. *Self concept and school achievement*. Englewood Cliffs, N.J.: Prentice-Hall, 1970.

Purkey, W. W. *The search for self: Evaluating student self concepts*. Florida Educational Research and Development Council Bulletin, University of Florida, Gainesville, Fla., 1968.

Staines, J.W. The self picture as a factor in the classroom *British Journal of Educational Psychology*, 1958, **28**, 87-111.

Toward Developing
a Healthy Self-Image

Don E. Hamachek

The voluminous literature related to the idea of the self and self-concept leaves little doubt but that mental health and personal adjustment depends deeply on each individual's basic feelings of personal adequacy. Just as each of us must maintain a healthy orientation to objective reality, so, too, must we learn to think of ourselves in healthy ways. Feelings of personal inadequacy, helplessness, inferiority, insecurity, or worthlessness tend to erode and weaken, sometimes to the point of collapse, the main pillars of one's self-structure. The growth of an adequate self-concept, free of neurotic pride, unrealistic fears, and the tyranny of irrational demands of conscience, is a critically important first step toward developing a healthy self-image. In the daily struggle to cope with the requirements of self and of reality and to deal firmly with threats, frustrations, and conflicts, we must have a firm grip on our own identity. Indeed, the admonition to "Know thyself" has been passed down through the ages as the criterion of wisdom and peace of mind until our present day where it has emerged from a religious-philosophical notion into a slogan for better mental health.

Attaining a healthy self-image with its concommitant feelings of adequacy, ableness, personal worth, and confidence is not some lofty goal beyond mortal reach, standing as a kind of poetic ideal. It is an attitude or cluster of attitudes which are learned and acquired, which means that sometimes "bad" (negative, destructive, self-defeating) attitudes must be replaced by healthier attitudes. Most people seem to want to move forward toward higher levels of physical and psychological health, although we would have to admit that there are those odd personalities who seem to get a perverse pleasure out of *un*health and suffering because it is the chief way of knowing they're alive. Sometimes a person says he would like to change his neurotic ways and have healthier attitudes about himself and others, but then says he can't change because, after all, his unfortunate childhood experiences made him the way he is. So busy is he contriving new defenses, inventing new excuses, and enjoying his own self-pity that he seldom has any energy left over for considering more constructive avenues for living. Along these lines, Maslow has suggested that:

From Freud we learned that the past exists *now* in the person. Now we must learn, from growth theory and self-actualization theory, that the future also *now* exists in the person in the form of ideals, hopes, goals, unrealized potentials, mission, fate, destiny, etc. One for whom no future exists is reduced to the concrete, to helplessness, to emptiness. For him, time must be endlessly "filled." Striving, the usual organizer of most activity, when lost, leaves the person unorganized and unintegrated.[1]

As noted in Chapter Two, there is little doubt but that past experiences can have a vast influence on current behavior. However, even though we cannot change what happened yesterday, we can change how we feel about it today. We cannot change past experiences, but we can change our feelings *about* those experiences, which is one step in moving toward a healthy self-image.

SELF-OTHER UNDERSTANDING AS A GOAL

Sometimes it is assumed that one gets to know himself by learning about man in the abstract, i.e., man as a psychological, social, biological, economic, and religious being. Necessarily, then, the "knowledgeable person" winds up knowing about a fictional man fabricated from theories, research, and other people's experiences, not the man who lives and breathes, nor the one to whom the personal pronouns "I" and "me" apply. Indeed, it is possible to major in psychology and to end up knowing a very great deal about psychology, but very little about one's self. For instance, a man may have no idea whatsoever that his fear, let's say, of getting too "involved" with a woman is related to a basically bad relationship with his mother, even though he may be very well versed in the field of psychology and able to discuss at length other men's problems and hangups with women. Clearly, such information is not wisdom, nor does it bring peace of mind, nor does positive mental health commence and prevail because of it. Self-other understanding appears to be specific knowledge about how one's unique individuality grows in an interpersonal social context. How can one arrive at a deeper understanding of himself and others as unique individuals?

A maxim of Goethe may help here. "If you want to know yourself, observe what your neighbors are doing," he said. "If you want to understand others, probe within yourself." Most of us are inclined to do exactly the opposite. We observe the other person in order to understand him, and we probe within ourselves in order to understand ourselves better. Seems obvious enough, but it doesn't often work quite that simply. Why? Normally we look at the other person objectively, but look at ourselves subjectively. We see others with the 20-20 vison of sanity and realism—no myopia here — we behold their flaws, weaknesses, self-deceptions, and even recognize their prejudices masquerading as principles.

However, when we probe within ourselves, we are not inclined to see the same personal distortions. Indeed, most of us "see" only our good intentions, our fondest dreams and hopes, our secret fears and deepest needs, and our unremitting calls for love and recognition. If we persist in distorting our self-perceptions, then we can never change anything about us which may, in the interests of a healthier more accurate self-image, need correcting. There are, however, ways to see ourselves more accurately and to know ourselves, as Goethe suggests, through "observing what our neighbors are doing."

SOCIAL FEELING AS AN AID

Adler's[2] concept of social feeling provides us with a useful conceptual tool for developing a healthy self-image. What does social feeling mean? Basically, it is a notion which refers to a person's ability to empathize with another; to see, hear, and feel with him. The usefulness of this concept lies in the fact that it combines the idea of social, which is an objective reference to common experiences, with the idea of feeling, which is a subjective reference to private experiences. The synthesis of the objective "social" with the subjective "feeling" is one way of bridging the gap between "you" and "me."

Self-other understanding involves, strangely enough, self-transcendence, which calls for one to go beyond his own private motives and thoughts in order to better understand and share another person's needs and goals. Social feeling is an attempt to understand one's self through the understanding of others. It is becoming less involved with one's own hopes, fears, shame, and doubt in order to become more in tune to how the other person thinks and feels. Erich Fromm,[3] for example, has observed: "I discover that I am everybody, and that I discover myself in discovering my fellow man, and vice versa."Self-other understanding through the process of social feeling means to see one's self (insight) by participating and sharing mutual concerns with another, or more succinctly, being an "I" for a "thou" as Buber[4] would say.

How can one practice social feeling and thereby understand himself and others better? Let's look at some ways.

HONESTY AS A WAY OF FACILITATING
SELF-OTHER UNDERSTANDING

This does not mean being brutally and indiscriminately frank, but it does mean showing some of yourself to another person, exhibiting some of your own feelings and attitudes. This isn't particularly easy because from early childhood most people learn to play roles which mask their feelings, as if being honest about them would only hurt others and destroy relationships. Actually, the inevitable consequence of exposing and sharing feelings is usually greater interpersonal closeness. If I am honest with you, this encourages you to be more honest with me. If you are honest with me, I am free to be more honest with you. And so the cycle goes. Consider an example.

Suppose a teacher has put in a relatively sleepless night and goes to class irritable, cranky, and short-tempered. He has two alternatives for handling his feelings. One, he can say nothing to the class and end up snapping at innocent students all day as if they were the cause of his sleepless night. Or, two, he could frankly admit to his irritable feelings, why they exist, and thereby give his students a chance to respond to his honesty. Once they know that his lack of patience and irritability is for a reason, then they will have less need to be defensive and irritable themselves. Furthermore, once the students learn that their teacher has *feelings,* not all of which are pleasant or good, then they are more apt to face up to and *admit feelings within themselves* which might otherwise have remained buried. If a teacher is honest with his students, shares with them some of his personal self, he can be much more assured of his students giving him honest feedback about the conductg of the course, its content, and him as a teacher. Carl Rogers, discussing his way of facilitating or "teaching" a class, puts it this way:

> For me, trust is *the* important ingredient which the facilitator provides. He will, I hope, participate with his own feelings (owned as *his* feelings, not projected on another person). He may risk himself in expressing his problems and weaknesses....The trust is something which cannot be faked. It is not a technique...if it is real and complete, even in a narrow area, it will have a facilitating effect upon the process of the group.[5]

In sum, honesty is one way of facilitating social feeling and healthy self-other understanding because it encourages greater freedom and openness of interpersonal exchange, the medium in which the self-knowledge begins.

EMPATHIC LISTENING AS A WAY OF FACILITATING SELF-OTHER UNDERSTANDING

Another response which may be useful in developing a healthy self-other attitude is to listen. This doesn't mean merely to wait for a person to finish talking (and to spend our listening time preparing what we are going to say), but to try to see how the world is viewed by this person and to communicate this understanding to him. The sort of "total" listening we're talking about here is the kind that responds to the person's *feelings* as well as his *words*. It implies no evaluation, no judgment, no agreement (or disagreement). It simply conveys an effort to understand what the person is feeling and trying to communicate. It is an effort to communicate to the other person that we can accept the notion that his feelings and ideas are valid for *him,* if not for us.

One reason behind being a poor listener lies in the fact that it is difficult to do. We can test this out. For example, try establishing in any group discussion the ground rule that no person may present his own view until he has first satisfied the one who has just spoken that he fully comprehended what this person meant to communicate. That is, he must rephrase in his own words the total meaning of the other person's message and obtain that person's agreement that that was indeed what he said. In doing this we may find out that: (1) it is extremely difficult to get agreement between what was said and what was heard ("listened" to); (2) we frequently are remiss in our good intentions to listen; (3) when we do listen carefuly, we have a hard time remembering what it was that we were going to say, and when we do remember, we find that it is a little off the subject; (4) much argument and irrational emotionality is absent from such a discussion because we spend less time responding to what we *thought* we hear or *wanted* to hear and more time responding to what was actually said, particularly when our misconceptions, if any, are cleared away.

Poor listeners are typically so preoccupied with their own sense of self importance that they leave little room for expanding the range of their self-other knowledge. A person, whether a parent, a teacher, or a friend, who talks a lot *could* have much that was meaningful to say, or he could be protecting himself from running the risk of having to change if he listened too carefully to another person's point of view.

Self-understanding is enhanced through understanding others. Understanding others is a function of one's capacity for social feeling. This capacity is both developed and encouraged by honest communication and good listening. Indeed, most of us know from personal experience that some of our most significant self-other discoveries have resulted from being in the company of persons characterized not only by their total honesty, but also by their lack of preconceptions about how they expect us to behave.

Self-other understanding, then, can be one step toward developing a healthy and accurate self-picture.

SELF-ACCEPTANCE: OUTCOMES AND CONSEQUENCES

While no single definition of self-acceptance is likely to be accepted by all who use the term, it generally has reference to the extent which a person's self-concept is congruent with his description of his "ideal" self. Many self-concept studies, for example, in addition to asking subjects for *self-perceptions* also ask the subjects to go through the same set of items again and indicate how he would like to be *ideally*. Since most of us would like to be "better" than we are, the *ideal* self is usually judged to be at least as good as and almost always better than the perceived or "actual" self. The differences between the scores for the perceived self and ideal self is the *discrepancy* score, which is obtained by subtracting the score of the perceived self from the score representing the ideal self. The larger this discrepancy score the more dissatisfied with himself and less accepting the person is presumed to be.

McCandless reviewed twelve studies designed to investigate the psychological consequences of discrepancies between the perceived self and the ideal self and concluded with the following:

> In summary, most research evidence indicates that people who are highly self-critical — that is, who show a large discrepancy between the way they actually see themselves and the way they would ideally like to be — are less well-adjusted than those who are at least moderately satisfied with themselves. Evidence indicates that highly self-critical children and adults are more anxious, more insecure, and possibly more cynical and depressed than self-accepting people. They *may* be more ambitious and driving, however. At least some evidence indicates that people experience conflict about the traits on which they have the greatest self-ideal discrepancy, and that this conflict is sharp enough to interfere with learning involving such areas....There is some question whether the topic of self-ideal discrepancy is really different from the topic of positive and negative self-concepts.[6]

As you can see, research suggests that self-accepting persons are likely to have smaller self-ideal discrepancies than less self-accepting persons.

SELF-ACCEPTANCE AND ACCEPTANCE OF OTHERS

The notion that people who are self-accepting are accepting of others has considerable practical importance, particularly in light of the evidence suggesting that personal adjustment or maladjustment is socially learned. The self-rejecting person, if he also rejects others, is likely to be rejected by them in turn, with the inevitable consequence of reinforcing the original maladjustment. If, in counseling or psychotherapy, the self-concept can be improved and if this improvement results in increased acceptance of and by other people, then personal improvement is likely to occur. Raimy,[7] for example, has demonstrated that successful cases in psychotherapy enabled patients to acquire a more favorable view of themselves, whereas unsuccessful cases did not.

The overwhelming evidence from Wylie's[8] monumental review of the literature related to the self suggested that self-acceptance was related to adjustment. Generally, a high regard for one's self is reflected in a high level of personal adjustment. Moreover, there is evidence to show that people who are *self-accepting are more accepting of others.*[9][10][11] This means that if an individual thinks well of himself he is likely to think well of others, and that if he disapproves of himself he is likely to disapprove of others. Rogers[12] has noted that "when the individual perceives and accepts into one consistent and integrated system all his sensory and visceral experiences, then he is necessarily more understanding of others and is more accepting of others as separate individuals." A person who carries around a store of suppressed anger is more likely to feel hostile toward other people whose behavior, in his eyes, represents his own suppressed feelings than a person who is more open to his anger and willing to admit that his anger does exist. Or as another example, sometimes a person who feels threatened by his sexual impulses may be the first to criticize and moralize others whom he perceives as behaving in sexual ways. On the other hand, if he accepts his *own* sexual feelings he is usually more tolerant of sexual expression by others.

SELF-ACCEPTANCE AS RELATED TO POPULARITY

We have seen that self-acceptance is related to acceptance of others, but how is acceptance *by* others related to self-acceptance? Fey[13] made a rather interesting study of this and his research may help us answer that question. Using a group of fifty-eight third-year medical students, he obtained: (1) measures of self-acceptance, (2) acceptance of others, (3) each subject's judgment of how well he was accepted by others, and (4) an estimate of actual acceptability or popularity. Among other things, he found that the high self-accepting (positive self-concept) men were more accepting of others, estimated their own popularity higher than did the less self-accepting men, but were not *actually* any more popular.

Fey then split his subjects into groups of men who markedly overestimated their popularity (strong self-enhancing tendencies) and men who grossly underestimated their popularity (strong self-derogatory tendencies). Interestingly, he found the self-derogatory group to be significantly more popular than the self-enhancing group with an average of 6 friendly mentions each to the self-enhancers' 1.5. Fey speculated that individuals who are very self-accepting but who reject others are likely to have "defensive organized" attitudes of superiority, are insensitive to their actual group social status, tend to depreciate others, and are consequently rejected because they threaten the security of people. On the other hand, it was found that men who have low acceptance of themselves, along with high acceptance of others, are seen as nonthreatening and therefore are more well-liked. Fey went on to speculate that the "prototypic well-adjusted person" (that is, the one with high self-other acceptance) "may not appear to 'need' friendships or to repay it...his very psychological robustness is resented, or perhaps it is perceived and rejected as a Pollyanna-like facade."[14] As you may have seen already, there is a striking similarity between Fey's research findings and Maslow's[15] clinical speculations discussed in Chapter One about why it is that some of us are inclined to lose our aplomb, and self-possession, even grow uneasy, anxious, and feel a bit inferior in the company of persons we regard as superior in one way or other.

In sum, self-acceptance, which we could say is a lack of cynicism about the self, appears to be associated with accepting other people. This indicates that the self-accepting person views the world as a more congenial place than the self-rejector and is less defensive toward others and about himself because of it. On the other hand, self-disparaging or self-effacing persons, particularly those who are obviously successful, are better accepted and more popular than the "prototypic well-adjusted person." There is no pat answer for why this seems to be so, but one speculation is that they pose less threat and more actively seek to please others.

Self-acceptance is an important step toward a healthy self-image. What happens, though, if one does not feel as adequate as others? Let's examine this question in greater detail.

THE INFERIORITY COMPLEX: EXPRESSIONS AND OUTCOMES

Allport[16] has defined an inferiority complex as a "strong and persistent tension arising from a somewhat morbid emotional attitude toward one's felt deficiency in his personal equipment." What this refers to is an attitude which a person may have about feeling less able than others. Closely allied to, but not to be confused with, inferiority, is the feeling or conviction of inadequacy. However, where inferiority, whether conscious or unconscious, implies unfavorable comparison with others, inadequacy suggests personal inability to meet the demands of the situation.

The feeling of inferiority is no stranger to most people. For example, one study found that less that 12 percent of a group of college students report that they do *not* know what it is to suffer from gnawing feelings of inferiority.[17] Consider the data presented in Table One.

As you can see, there seems to be four main types. On the whole, women appear to be worse off than men. However, when we consider that women in our culture, from the time they are little girls, are taught to be more socially sensitive than men, this is not surprising. That is, the more sensitive one is about himself in relation to the world around him, the more likely he is to spot qualities in himself which are less well developed or executed than what he may see in other people.

Table 1
College Men and Women Reporting Inferiority Feelings

Type of Inferiority Feeling	Percentage Reporting Persistent Inferiority Feelings	
	MEN	WOMEN
Physical	39	50
Social	52	57
Intellectual	29	61
Moral	16	15
None at all	12	10

Feelings of inferiority cannot be taken as an index of actual inferiority. A feeling of inferiority is a purely subjective affect related to the self, and is measured by the ration between one's *success* and *aspirations* in a given direction. Objective facts seem to make little difference in determining whether a person feels inferior or not. The highest ranking student, or the funniest comedian, or the beauty contest winner may each suffer from a deep-seated sense of inferiority. On the other hand, the lowest student, the "unfunniest" man, or the plainest girl may not feel inferior at all. What one does or has or how one looks is far less important than how he feels about those things and what he aspires to be. For example, if a pretty girl aspires to be an excellent student, but falls short of that goal, being pretty is not likely to compensate for feeling academically inferior.

Important for us to understand is the fact that a sense of *inferiority is developmental or learned, rather than organic or innate.* This means that inferiority is in no sense necessary, and with insight into its causes and consequences, it can be handled, coped with, and in many instances, dispelled. Inferiority feelings are the result of too many failure experiences and frustrations; they are learned reactions that, if not corrected early, may eventually lead to the growth of deeply rooted attitudes of inferiority. Attitudes of this sort can dominate and condition a person to the point where he is left with a general feeling of not being able to do anything very well.

SYMPTOMS OF INFERIORITY

There are at least seven symptoms of inferiority feelings which we can be sensitive to in spotting its existence in others, or, for that matter, in ourselves.

1. *Sensitivity to criticism:* An inferiority-ridden person does not like his weaknesses pointed out to him. Criticism, as viewed by him, is further proof of his inferiority and serves only to accentuate the pain associated with it.

2. *Overresponse to flattery:* The inferior-feeling person grabs at straws, particularly those constructed from praise and flattery because they help him stand more secure against his feelings of uncertainty and insecurity. The other response to flattery or praise, of course, is to stand in red-skinned embarrassment wondering, "How could anyone say anything good about me? Me, of all people!"

3. *Hypercritical attitude:* This is a frequent defense and serves the purpose of re-directing attention away from one's own limitations. Whereas overresponse to flattery is defensive in character, hypercriticism takes the

offensive and is used as a way of actively warding off the implications of inferiority. For example, if I feel inferior about the quality of something I've done in relation to yours and aggressively criticize your effort, you may become so busy defending what you've done that you won't notice the flaws in *my* effort. In other words, hypercriticalness creates the illusion of superiority and relies on this illusion to belie inferiority.

4. *Tendency toward blaming:* Whenever personal weaknesses and failures are projected into others, it is relatively easy to find in them the cause of one's own failures, leading directly to the response of blaming. Indeed, some persons operate a kind of psychological "pulley system" in the sense of being able to feel normal or adequate only if they are pulling other people *down* and themselves *up* in the process. Unless others are made to appear inferior, some persons cannot feel even normal.

5. *Feelings of persecutions:* It is only a short step away from blaming others for one's personal misfortune to the position that they are actively seeking his downfall. For example, if you fail me in a course and I can believe that you failed me because you don't like me or are against me, then I am spared the pain of having to consider that I alone am responsible. In this way, not only do I blame you for my failure but I assign you a motive for doing it — you're out to get me.

6. *Negative feelings about competition:* An inferiority-ridden person is as anxious to win in competition as anyone else, but far less optimistic about winning. He is inclined to react to competition as would a person who knows that he lacks the skills or knowledge for successful competition about the breaks, his opponents' good luck, or favoritism. In some instances, the attitude toward competition is so extreme that he refuses to participate in any competitive situation and tends to shy away in a fearful and hesitant manner.

7. *Tendency toward seclusiveness, shyness and timidity:* Inferiority feelings are usually accompanied by a certain degree of fear, particularly in situations involving other people. Inferior-feeling persons prefer the cloak of anonymity, feeling that if they are neither seen nor heard their shortcomings (real or imagined) will less likely be seen. Not infrequently, students who feel less able than their peers sit near the back of the classroom because of the protection this offers. (If I'm not so easily seen, perhaps I will not so easily be called upon.)[18]

These are not mutually exclusive symptoms, but overlapping in expression and character. For example, timidity leads to avoidance of competition and also to greater sensitivity to criticism. At the same time, sensitivity to criticism can lead to blaming others or overresponding to flattery. All of these symptoms spring from a basic sense of inferiority and any one of them can serve as the catalytic agent, triggering a chain-reaction of defensive and generally self-destructive behavior.

There is still another, albeit distorted, expression of a sense of inferiority worth our consideration.

SELF-CONTEMPT AS A SUBSTITUTE FOR SELF-WORTH

A person who has almost, but not quite, lost his feeling of personal worth sometimes feels a strong need to condemn himself. ("I'm no good."

"I can't do anything." "Others are better than me." "Look how stupid I am, etc.,") Rollo May,[19] a practicing psychoanalyst, has noted that self-condemnation may not be so much an expression of self-punishment as it is a technique to get a quick substitute for a sense of worth. It is as though the person were saying to himself, "I must be important that I am so worth condemning," or "Look how good I am — I have such high ideals that I am ashamed of myself for falling so short of them." Allport has observed:

> The very nature of the neurotic disorder is tied to pride. If the sufferer is hypersensitive, resentful, captious, he may be indicating a fear that he will not appear to advantage in competitive situations where he wants to show his worth.... If he is over-scrupulous and self-critical, he may be endeavoring to show how praiseworthy he really is.[20]

Self-condemnation is not so much an honest statement of one's short-comings as it is a cloak for arrogance. This mechanism of self-condemnation can be observed in various states of psychological depression. The student, for example, who does poorly on a test can always say, generally to himself, "If I had studied more, if I had really wanted to do well on this test, I could have." Or the child who feels he is not loved by his parents can always say to himself something like, "If I were different, if I were not bad, they would love me." In the case of both the student and the child, self-condemnation is a means of avoiding a head-on confrontation with the possibility that he is not intellectually capable, in the first instance, and not loved in the other. The dynamics of self-condemnation works in such a way as to protect a person from the pain of feeling worthless. For he can always say, "If it were not for such and such a defeat, or bad habit, or lack of motivation, I would be as good as anyone else." The student who says, "I could've passed that test if I had studied harder," is really saying, "I'm really not that inadequate and furthermore it hurts to consider the possibility that I might be." An observation by Rollo May may help us understand better the hidden meaning behind self-condemnation:

> ...the emphasis upon self-condemnation is like whipping a dead horse: it achieves a temporary life, but it hastens the eventual collapse of the dignity of a person. The self-condemning substitute for self-worth provides the individual with a method of avoiding an open and honest confronting of his problems of isolation and worthlessness, and makes for a pseudo-humility rather than the honest humility of one who seeks to face his situation realistically and do what he can constructively. Furthermore, the self-condemning substitute provides the individual with a rationalization for his self-hate, and thus reinforces the tendencies toward hating himself. And, inasmuch as one's attitude toward other selves generally parallels one's attitude toward one's self, one's covert tendency to hate others is also rationalized and reinforced. The steps are not big from the feelings of worthlessness of one's self to self-hatred to hatred for others.[21]

STRATEGIES FOR MAINTAINING AND ENHANCING A POSITIVE SELF-IMAGE

What can one do with inferiority feelings besides suffer? Feelings of inferiority are usually deeply rooted and not easily eradicated. Projection ("It's not really my fault I did this poorly on the exam — The teacher was unfair.") and rationalization ("I could have done better on the exam if I had really wanted to and studied harder.'') are two frequently used mechanisms to defend against feeling inferior and have been discussed more fully in Chapter One. There is still another and it has a variety of forms and expressions.

COMPENSATION

Several types can be distinguished. *Direct action* is one kind and occurs when a person persistently attacks the *source* of an actual inferiority and attempts to remove it. When the original weakness or shortcoming is not only removed by turned into a source of strength, we think of this as *overcompensation*. For example, Demosthenes, so the story goes, not only overcame his stammer to become a normal speaker, but a great orator. Theodore Roosevelt built up his small physique, conquered his early childhood frailty, and went on to become a daredevil Rough Rider and fine lion hunter.

We speak of *substitute* compensation when a person cannot remove his handicap or shortcoming but develops other satisfactions. A Helen Keller may compensate for lack of sight and hearing through extraordinary development of tactile and intellectual ability. A physically small boy may work very hard to become a swift and elusive halfback or perhaps he excels in his studies. The somewhat unattractive woman may become an outstanding leader in social movements. The point is, in every walk of life, there are personal opportunities which do not involve setting up unreachable goals, unwisely selected activities, or the cessation of effort and hope. There are legitimate, wholesome, and necessary compensations that can add zest and meaning to any person's life.

Compensatory behavior can be a very effective means for maintaining and enhancing a positive self-image. There are, however, both *constructive* and *destructive* compensations and it may help us to be aware of the differences between the two.[22]

CONSTRUCTIVE COMPENSATORY BEHAVIOR

1. Selection of satisfying and useful fields of occupational endeavor which reflect one's strengths and interests, e.g., "I am poor with numbers, so I'll do something which enables me to use my abilities in reading and writing as in being a writer, copy-editor, or English teacher."
2. Stimulation of ambition expressed in concrete effort, e.g., "I will work very hard to develop the skills and interests I have rather than fret unduly about those things I cannot do well."
3. Attractiveness of personality if the inferiority is not excessive, e.g., "I will work on developing my interpersonal relationship skills, which may help me feel more adequate."
4. An effort to appreciate the relative advantages of one's position in life, e.g., "I'll try to appreciate those things that I have which are positive rather than worry so about those things I have which are negative."

DESTRUCTIVE COMPENSATORY BEHAVIOR

1. Decided superiority reactions, e.g., "I am bigger, or better, or more

important than most." (It might be worthwhile noting here that a sense of self-inflation and conceit does not usually come from greater feelings of self-worth. In fact, it may signal just the opposite. Self-inflation, conceit, and pompous behavior are generally signs of inner emptiness and self-doubt; a strutting display of superiority is one of the most common covers of inferiority feelings.)

2. Goals placed beyond reasonable possibility of attainment, e.g., "My below average grades in biochemistry, physics, and math aren't really that important — I still intend to go to medical school."

3. Occupation selected on a personal basis without regard to personal fitness and limitations, e.g., "So what if I've had some kind of heart problems? I've always wanted to be a physical education teacher and, besides, I like kids."

4. Excessive daydreaming and fantasy living, e.g., "Boy, things would be different if I were only a little bigger," or "If I only had more money then things would be different."

5. Cessation of effort; paralysis of activity, e.g., "Why try? Nothing works for me anyway."

As you can see, the ultimate effectiveness of any form of compensatory behavior is in the impact it has on our conduct.

SELECTION OF PERSONAL VALUES AS RELATED TO POSITIVE SELF-ESTEEM

To know that someone considers himself inferior with respect to some particular quality is insufficient information to tell us what he thinks of himself. We must also have some idea of how much he *values* this quality. What is the mechanism which determines what a person will *value* in his life? Let's see if we can understand this better.

Some years ago, Allport and Odbert[23] gathered a list of over 17,000 adjectives by which objects could be characterized. Not all of them were applicable to individuals, but an enormous number were. There is pratically no end to the types of qualities an individual may consider important in evaluating himself. For example, he may consider it important to be good-looking, or non-conforming, or daring, or ruthless, or imaginative, or thoughtful, and so on and on.

Given this number of choices, which does a person choose? Why? On the whole, a person is inclined to value those things he considers himself good at and to devalue those qualities at which he considers himself poor. As an illustration of this, the quality of "good at working with your hands" was chosen by 68 percent among those who felt they possessed this skill and by only 6 percent of those who felt they lacked this quality. Self-values, we see, tend to be selected in a way that enables an individual to maintain a congenial self-picture. Rosenberg notes that:

> If people are reasonably free to choose their own values, we are led to an interesting paradox of social life: almost everyone can consider himself superior to almost everyone else, as long as he can choose *his own* basis for judgment. Take four boys. One is a good scholar, the second a good athlete, the third very handsome, and the fourth a good musician. As long as each focuses upon the quality at which he excels, each is superior to the rest. At the

same time, each person may blithely acknowledge the superiority of the others with regard to qualities to which he himself is relatively indifferent.[24] One of the outcomes of a healthy, integrated self-concept is the evidence of a wise sense of values. When a problem arises, a careful, thoughtful person considers various possible avenues of action, considers the consequences of each, and then chooses the course most likely to lead to results which are most probable and most important. The discriminating person will evaluate an issue in terms of degrees rather than absolutes and will recognize that some values, for him at least, are more important than others.

SELECTIVE INTERPRETATION OF THE "FACTS" AS RELATED TO POSITIVE SELF-ESTEEM

In judging oneself, one must take account of the "facts." However, as we discussed in Chapter Two, "facts" are highly susceptible to the personal meanings we assign to them. Take a stranger who, in the face of a roaring fire, rushes into a burning house and leads to safety two previously trapped people. What he has done is certainly an objective fact. But how shall we interpret it? Does it mean that he is a fearless, courageous man so unselfish as to take little note of his own welfare? Or does it mean that he is simply too stupid and blind to recognize obvious danger when it stares him in the face? The act was clear, but whether it reflects "courage" or "foolhardiness" is a matter of interpretation.

Whenever there is sufficient lack of clarity about what a "fact" or "set of facts" mean, there is always room for a person to salvage a certain amount of self-esteem. Consider, for example, the matter of grades. One study found that although most people agree that grades are a good indication of whether they are good students, they are by no means convinced that grades indicate much about whether they are "clear-thinking and clever" or "imaginative and original."[25] In fact, it was found that nearly three-fourths of the students with D and F averages considered themselves very likely or fairly likely to be imaginative and original and to have good sense and sound judgment.

This is not a denial of reality. A "D" or "F" student *knows* that he has poor grades. There are, however, many expressions of intelligence and there is nothing in his "objective" grades to compel him to believe that he is less "clear-thinking" or "clever" than students with higher grades.

Another factor which makes it easy (or at least easier) to interpret the "facts" to fit our personal needs and thereby maintain and enhance our self-esteem is the nature of the language used to describe personal traits. For example, if one person says we are sensitive observers about human behavior and another says we are a nosey busybody, are they really describing anything different? If someone says we are ingenious and resourceful and another observes that we are cunning and cagey, is there really any difference between the two? Indeed, both you and your critic may agree that you are "too tough and aggressive," terms he engages to condemn qualities in which you may take the utmost pride. Even though you and your critic may agree on the evidence, you do not necessarily agree on the meaning.

The point is, there is scarcely any behavior which we cannot interpret as admirable in some way. In the seclusion of our mind's eye, generally free of the intrusion of alternative interpretations, we are free to review and weigh the evidence (the "facts") as our biases dictate, to shift our personal perceptions until a congenial one emerges, and to eventually settle for one which is self-enhancing.

Just as selectivity of the "facts" influences the interpretation of the meaning of evidence pertaining to the self, so too does it influence the *choice* of evidence. The type of evidence relevant to a given characteristic is widely varied. For example, by what criteria shall a person judge whether or not he is a sociable person — did he speak to a stranger? has he gone to a party with friends? Is he among the first to speak in a crowd? Does he have many close friends but few casual acquaintances? Does he have one close friend but many casual acquaintances? Does he smile when passing someone on the street? He is not obliged to consider *all* these criteria: he can choose one, any one he wants, any one that *fits*. And he is right — the quality of, in this instance, being sociable is so ambiguous that there is no way to prove him wrong. By his choice of criteria he may be a very friendly person. By your choice he may fall short. And the same is true of the vast range of personal characteristics that reflect a person's behavior.

SELECTION OF PERSONAL STANDARDS AS RELATED TO POSITIVE SELF-ESTEEM

The validity of this observation is apparent in the fact that it is not simply how good a person *thinks* he is with regard to some quality, but how good he *wants to be* that counts. When you think about it, people have a wide range of options in setting standards for themselves. For example a man can aspire to the very pinnacle of achievement, to a high level of performance, to a good level of performance, to moderate accomplishment, or even to modest success. A man may aspire to be the superintendent of a school system or to be a competent teacher within that system. The principle is all the more true of nonoccupational goals. One individual may aspire to love and care for "all mankind," whereas another is satisfied to love and care for just a few individuals he knows well. There is obviously a wide choice available in the setting of personal standards of performance in the immense sweep of areas pertaining to the self.

Given these alternatives, what personal standards do people select for themselves? We have already seen from our discussion in Chapter One that, as a general rule, a person is apt to set higher standards in those areas in which he *backs* himself to be good, or competent, or above average.[26] In Chapter Six we noted that children who experience more failures than successes were unpredictable in setting personal standards; that is, they established standards for performance which were either too high or too low.[27] On the whole, however, research evidence suggests that most people tend to set goals that they interpret as falling within reasonable range of their potential accomplishments.[28]

Surveys of occupational aspirations tend to confirm laboratory findings related to the selection of personal standards. For example, in a study by Rosenberg[29] of college students' values, a sample of respondents was asked: "What business or profession would you *most like* to go into?" and "What business or profession do you realistically think you are *most apt* to go into?" It was found that most students had scaled down their aspirations to correspond to what they considered within their ability to fulfill. In general, a person tends to select goals (standards, level of performance, aspirations) in accord with his assessment of his qualities. This selectivity enables him to achieve his personal goals, to consider himself "good enough," and to maintain a favorable self-image.

As pointed out by Hyman,[30] the occupational attainments of people of working-class origins are lower than those raised in the middle-class environment. Does lower occupational "attainment" or "achievement" result in lower self-esteem? Not necessarily, because level of personal standards is a relative matter. For example, if a boy aspires to be a master plumber and makes it, this can be as self-enhancing for him as the boy who aspires to be a lawyer and makes it. What is important is not so much the *kind* of goal one sets, but its achievement. Accomplishment of a personal goal, whether in a physical, or intellectual, or social realm, can be a self-enhancing experience to the extent that it is personally meaningful and not too easily won.

INTERPERSONAL SELECTIVITY AS RELATED TO POSITIVE SELF-ESTEEM

One of the most consistent findings in mass communications research is that *people tend to relate to other people with whom they agree.*[31] A fundamental principle of social interaciton is the idea that people, when given the choice, will tend to associate with those who think well of them and to avoid those who dislike them, thereby biasing the communications about themselves to which they are exposed in a favorable direction.

The outstanding case in point is *friendship,* which is, perhaps, the purest example of selectively choosing one's propaganda. Characteristically, not only do we like our friend, but he likes us. Indeed, it is possible that we may like him *because* he likes us. And of course friends are inclined to say friendly things, which increases the likelihood of hearing more of what we like to hear about ourselves. Friendship is at least to some extent a "mutual admiration unit," whereby each party helps to sustain the desired self-image of the other.

Indeed, one of the most important props of romantic love is the remarkable intensity of the mutual admiration. To discover that someone considers us the most wonderful girl in the world or the most talented boy is the kind of communication that we very much like to hear.

What is true for friends and lovers is equally true of groups. The persistent search for social acceptance is a major enterprise of both young and old and is apparent in our active involvement in groups that accept and approve of us, thereby enhancing our self-esteem.

It is important to note, however, that interpersonal selectivity which is too cautious, too careful, and too defensive may serve to stunt personal growth. For example, the loner who has no friends, or the suspicious soul who avoids friends who might be "too honest" about him both limit the possibility of feedback which might, in fact, spur them to greater insights into themselves and their behavior. Inasmuch as the self grows best in an interpersonal stream of reflected appraisals, the opportunity for this kind of nurturance is severely curtailed when the selectivity is too guarded. *The point is, if we interact only with those who agree with us and seldom challenge us, then we are seldom forced into the position of having to reevaluate ourselves and our positions on different issues.* Perhaps the best kind of friend is one who can, when it seems appropriate, challenge our most cherished beliefs without being threatened by the possibility of being rejected if he does.

Taking into consideration one's selective interpretation of the "facts," his selective interpretation of personal standards, and his selection of interpersonal relationships, Rosenberg has observed from his research that:

> The communications about ourselves are thus either biased in a generally favorable direction or are so ambiguous that our own biases are free to operate. That this is the case is suggested by the responses of our adolescent subjects to the question: "What do most people think of you?" Nearly 97 percent said that most people thought well or fairly well of them, and only 3 percent said fairly poorly or very poorly. Even two-thirds of those with low self-esteem attributed such benevolent attitudes toward others. They may, of course, be right. It is possible that a vast wave of mutual love and good will engulfs the world. One cannot, however, evade the suspicion that, with the ambiguity inherent in determining another's attitudes, a great many people are giving themselves the benefit of the doubt.[32]

SITUATIONAL SELECTIVITY AS RELATED TO POSITIVE SELF-ESTEEM

In a society as complex as ours, a person is not always able to *create* his environment, but he is often able to *select* his environment. A primary motivation in this selectivity is an ever-present desire to maintain a congenial self-image. For the most part, we tend to expose ourselves to experiences in which we have a fair chance of success rather than those in which we may be found wanting. Occupational selectivity is a good illustration of situational selectivity. For example, one study found that, given a choice, most people naturally gravitate toward occupational situations in which their skills are likely to find expression and their talents appreciated.[33]

Situational selectivity is reflected in many areas of everyday life. For example, if a person is witty rather than deep, he may be inclined to go to parties or social gatherings rather than to lectures or discussions. If he is closed-minded rather than open-minded, he may prefer to press his own point of view rather than consider someone's else's. If he is insecure rather than secure, he may choose friends who are more nurturant than challenging. If he is good at bowling, but a poor bridge player, he will usually prefer to socialize in a bowling alley where his skill is more obvious. Similarly, it is well known that college students tend to elect subjects in which they are strong and avoid those in which they are weak. This is an effective way to avoid failure, to be sure, but it can also be detrimental to the development of a healthy self-concept. The psychology of success is such that it means little if the threat of failure is virtually absent. Winning which is guaranteed or an "A" grade with no effort contributes little to an individual's sense of personal accomplishment and self-esteem. The willingness to gamble, to "take a risk" now and then can be a healthy activity for anyone. For it is in the accomplishment of those things we were not sure we could do in the first place that the foundation for a healthy, positive self-image is laid.

And so it goes — selection of standards, friends, a spouse, an occupation, and so on are a pervasive and central outgrowth of each person's need to maintain and enhance his self-image. The maintenance of a positive self-image is thus a highly constant and ubiquitous aspect of determination of our longer-range goals and aspirations. There are, however, certain restrictions on selectivity which we should take into account.

RESTRICTIONS ON SELECTIVITY

The mechanism of selectivity is such that it operates to help shape our self-attitudes in accord with our desires and in line with our strengths. A reasonable question, then, is why all people do not have favorable self-attitudes. Some people have mild doubts about themselves, others more serious doubts, and still others have doubts so serious as to be convinced beyond question that they are worthless.

This does not mean that the principle of selectivity is wrong, but it does suggest that there are given conditions of human experience which are characterized by a narrow range of alternatives. It is in the interpersonal realm that the range of options is most severely limited. For example, while we are relatively free to choose who our friends will be, the same is not true of our parents, teachers, or classmates. If our parents reject us, or our teachers berate us, or our classmates laugh at us, we are largely deprived of the option of avoiding their company or their criticism. When looked at from the point of view of interpersonal selectivity, it is not difficult to see why it is that some children run away from home, or drop out of school, or become social isolates.

Psychological research clearly shows that the self-attitudes that are the easiest to change, modify, or form are those which are least structured.[34] [35] And it is precisely in childhood that the self-image is most unstructured and unformed. Until a youngster reaches the age of about sixteen or so, his range of interpersonal alternatives is somewhat restricted by virtue of being the offspring of a particular set of parents. He must abide by *their* rules, listen to *their* appraisals, and relate as he can to such friends as there are in *their* neighborhood. These are his parents' choices, not his; of course, with no options there can be no selectivity. Hence, with parents holding a virtual monopoly on the options, the selections parents make have a particularly powerful influence on a youngster's self-esteem. For better or for worse, a child is stuck with his parents. If they choose wise options, if they love him, then he may have a substantial foundation for thinking well of himself. If they do *not* make wise selections; if they, say, live in a neighborhood where there are few children for their child to play with, he may be slow in developing social confidence; if they indulge and overprotect him, he may grow anxious and insecure; if they disparage or reject him, he may feel insignificant or unworthy.

The relative absence of interpersonal options for a growing child is not less serious than the restrictions on his situational selectivity. That is, a child's environment is largely fixed and there is not much he can do about it. For example, a bright child with intellectual potential, in a family which values things and not ideas, cannot choose to move into a family happy to answer his questions and encourage his curiosities. Similarly, there is no guarantee that one's personal whims and interests will meet the norms of the neighborhood peer group. If a child gains no recognition and applause for talents disdained by the group, he is powerless to select a different school or neighborhood.[36]

As we discussed in Chapter Five, we once again can see the enormous impact that childhood experiences and parents can have on a child's later feelings about himself. Despite the generality and power of the principle of selectivity, it is easy to see why many people *do* have low or moderate self-esteem. All in all, the evidence is consistent in suggesting that people *want* to have favorable opinions of themselves and that compensation (not to mention the other defense mechanisms described and discussed in Chapter One) and the various mechanisms of psychological selectivity are some of the strategies we use, consciously and unconsciously, to maintain and enhance positive self-attitudes.

SIGNS OF A HEALTHY, POSITIVE SELF-IMAGE

Since this chapter is devoted to a discussion of ways and means for moving toward a healthy self-image, it seems altogether appropriate that we end it on a positive note.

Increasing literature and research devoted to the problem of self-concept leaves little doubt but that mental health depends deeply on the quality of a person's feelings about himself. Just as an individual must maintain a healthy view of the world around him, so must he learn to perceive himself in positive ways. A person who has a strong, self-accepting attitude presents a behavioral picture very much the opposite of one who feels inadequate and inferior. Although there are certainly variations from one individual to another and for the same individual between situations, generally speaking, a person who has a healthy self-image can be characterized in the following ways:

1. He has certain values and principles he believes in strongly and is willing to defend them even in the face of strong group opinion; however, he feels personally secure enough to modify them if new experience and evidence suggest he is in error. (An insecure person finds it difficult to change his position for fear that it may be interpreted as weakness, or lack of ability, or competency. "You may be right, but I'm not wrong.")

2. He is capable of acting on his own best judgment without feeling excessively guilty or regretting his actions if others disapprove of what he's done. When he does feel guilty, he is not overwhelmed by the guilt. He can say, "I made a mistake — I'll have to improve," rather than "I made a mistake — how terrible I am."

3. He does not spend undue time worrying about what is coming tomorrow, or being upset by today's experience, or fussing over yesterday's mistakes. I remember a little poem which used to hang on the wall in my grandparents' living room. It goes like this:

It's easy enough to be pleasant
When Life flows along like a song.
But the man worth while

Is the man who can smile
When everything goes dead wrong.

4. He retains confidence in his ability to deal with problems, even in the face of failures and setbacks. He does not conclude, "Because I failed I am a failure," but is more likely to say, "I failed. I'll have to work harder."

5. He feels equal to others *as a person* — not superior or inferior — irrespective of the differences in specific abilities, family backgrounds, or attitudes of others toward him. He is able to say, "You are more skilled than I, but I am as much a person as you," which is different from thinking, "You are more skilled than I, therefore you are a better person." He is able to see that another individual's skills or abilities neither devalues nor elevates his own status as a person.

6. He is able to take it more or less for granted that he is a person of interest and value to others — at least to those with whom he chooses to associate. Another way of saying this is that he is not paralyzed by self-consciousness when in the company of other people.

7. He can accept praise without the pretense of false modesty ("Well, gosh, *anyone* could have done it."), and compliments without feeling guilty ("Thanks, but I *really* don't deserve it.")

8. He is inclined to resist the efforts of others to dominate him, especially those who are his peers. The resistance, in effect, is a way of saying, "I am as good as you — therefore there is no reason why I should be dominated by you."

9. He is able to accept the idea (and admit to others) that he is capable of feeling a wide range of impulses and desires, ranging all the way from being very angry to being very loving, from being very sad to being very happy, from feeling deep resentment to feeling great acceptance. It does not follow, however, that he *acts* on all his feelings and desires.

10. He is able to genuinely enjoy himself in a wide variety of activities involving work, play, creative self-expression, companionship, or, of all things, just plain loafing. An unknown author — a very wise man, no doubt — has expressed this idea in the following manner:

> A master in the art of living draws no sharp distinction between his work and his play, his labour and his leisure, his mind and his body, his education and his recreation. He hardly knows which is which. He simply pursues his vision of excellence through whatever he is doing and leaves others to determine whether he is working or playing. To himself he always seems to be doing both.

11. He is sensitive to the needs of others, to accepted social customs and particularly to the idea that he cannot, willy-nilly, go about "self-actualizing" himself at the expense of everyone around him.

Perhaps we would do well to keep in mind that these are not destinations that only a fortunate few have passage to, or end states arrived at by a select number, but, rather, possibilities which any person desiring to better himself can hold as goals within his reach. Usually, motivation is more effective, and happiness more attainable, if a person concentrates on improvement rather than perfection.

IN PERSPECTIVE

Healthy people, research shows, see themselves as liked, wanted, acceptable, able, and worthy. Not only do they feel that they are people of dignity and worth, but they *behave* as though they were. Indeed, it is in this factor of how a person sees himself that we are likely to find the most outstanding differences between high and low self-image people. It is not the people who feel that they are liked and wanted and acceptable and able who fill our prisons and mental hospitals. Rather, it is those who feel deeply inadequate, unliked, unwanted, unacceptable, and unable.

Self and self-other understanding are not mystical ideals standing some place "out there" as unreachable goals. Social feeling, empathic listening, honesty, and an understanding of how we use our defense mechanisms are all ways to assist in the development of greater self-awareness and self-understanding.

A person's feelings about himself are *learned* responses. Sometimes bad feelings have to be unlearned and new feelings acquired. This is not always easy, but it is possible. Sometimes this means "taking stock" of oneself — a kind of personal inventory. Or it may mean baring one's self to another person — a friend or therapist — so that the possibility for honest evaluation and feedback is more probable. And for certain, it means changing those things which one can and accepting those which one cannot.

For most persons, a positive, healthy self-image is quite within reach if they are willing to accept the risks and responsibilities for mature living.

If, as parents or as professional persons, we have a basic understanding of how a healthy self is developed and the conditions and interpersonal relations which nurture it, then we are in a position to move actively in the direction of *creating* those conditions and interpersonal relationships most conducive to positive mental health.

Perhaps the best place to begin is with ourselves.

[1] A.H. Maslow, "Some Basic Propositions of a Growth and Self-Actualization Psychology," in A.W. Combs (Ed.), *Perceiving, Behaving, Becoming*. Association for Supervision and Curriculum Development Year Book. Washington, D.C.: National Education Association, 1962, p. 48.

[2] A. Adler, *The Individual Psychology of Alfred Adler*. New York: Basic Books, Inc., 1956, pp. 135-136.

[3] E. Fromm, *Beyond the Chains of Illusion*. New York: Pocket Books, 1962, p. 186.

[4] M. Buber, *I and Thou*. New York: Charles Scribner's Sons, 1958.

[5] Carl R. Rogers, *Freedom To Learn*. Columbus, Ohio: Charles E. Merrill Books, Inc., 1969, p. 75.

[6] B.R. McCandless, *Children: Behavior and Development* (2nd ed.), New York: Holt, Rinehart and Winston, Inc., 1967, p. 280.

[7] V.C. Raimy, "Self-Reference in Counseling Interviews," *Journal of Consulting Psychology*. 1948, 12: 153-163.

[8] Ruth C. Wylie, *The Self Concept*. Lincoln, Neb.: University of Nebraska Press, 1961.

[9] Ruth C. Wylie, "Some Relationships between Defensiveness and Self-Concept Discrepancies," *Journal of Personality*. 1957, 25: 600-616.

[10] R.W. Levanway, "The Effect of Stress on Expressed Attitudes toward Self and Others," *Journal of Abnormal and Social Psychology*. 1955, 50: 225-226.

[11] E.L. Phillips, "Attitudes toward Self and Others: A Brief Questionnaire Report," *Journal of Consulting Psychology*. 1951, 15: 79-81.

[12] Carl R. Rogers, *Client-Centered Therapy: Its Current Practice, Implications, and Theory*. Boston: Houghton Mifflin Company, 1951, p. 520.

[13] W.F. Fey, "Acceptance by Others and Its Relation to Acceptance of Self and Others, A Re-evaluation," *Journal of Abnormal and Social Psychology*. 1955, 50: 274-276.

[14] Fey, p. 275.

[15] A.H. Maslow, "The Jonah Complex." *Humanitas*. 1967.

[16] G.W. Allport, *Patterns and Growth in Personality*. New York: Holt, Rinehart and Winston Inc. 1961, p. 130.

115

[17] Allport, pp. 130-131.
[18] A.A. Schneiders, *Personality Dynamics and Mental Health*. New York: Holt, Rinehart and Winston, Inc., 1965, pp. 227-228.
[19] Rollo May, *Man's Search for Himself*. New York: W.W. Norton and Company, 1953, pp. 98-101.
[20] G.W. Allport, *The Individual and His Religion*. New York: Crowell-Collier and Macmillan, Inc., 1950, p. 95.
[21] May, p. 100.
[22] E.A. Strecker, K.E. Appel, and J.W. Appel, *Discovering Ourselves* (3rd ed.). New York: Crowell-Collier and Macmillan, Inc., 1958, p. 249.
[23] G.W. Allport and H.S. Odbert, "Trait-Names: A Psycho-Lexical Study," *Psychological Monographs*. 1936, No. 211.
[24] M. Rosenberg, "Psychological Selectivity in Self-Esteem Formation," in C.W. Sherif and M. Sherif (Eds.), *Attitudes Ego-Involvement and Change*. New York: John Wiley & Sons, Inc., 1967, pp. 28-29.
[25] Rosenberg, pp. 26-50.
[26] William James, *Psychology: The Briefer Course*. New York: Harper & Row, Publishers, 1961, pp. 43-83.
[27] P.S. Sears, "Levels of Aspiration in Academically Successful and Unsuccessful School Children," *Journal of Abnormal and Social Psychology*. 1940, 35: 498-536.
[28] Rosenberg, p. 41.
[29] M. Rosenberg, *Occupations and Values*. New York: The Free Press, 1957.
[30] H.H. Hyman, "The Value Systems of Different Classes: A Social Psychological Contribution to the Analysis of Stratification," in R. Bendix and S.M. Lipset (Eds.), *Class, Status and Power*. New York: The Free Press, 1953, pp. 426-442.
[31] D. Cartwright and A. Zander, *Group Dynamics: Research and Theory*. New York: Harper & Row, Publishers, 1968, pp. 45-62.
[32] Rosenberg (1967), p. 47.
[33] E. Ginzberg, S.W. Ginsburg, S. Axelrad, and J.L. Herma, *Occupational Choice*. New York: Columbia University Press, 1951.
[34] M. Sherif and C.W. Sherif, *An Outline of Social Psychology* (rev. ed.). New York: Harper & Row, Publishers, 1956.
[35] B. Berelson, "Communication and Public Opinion," in B. Berelson and M. Janowitz, *Public Opinion and Communication*. New York: The Free Press, 1950, pp. 448-462.
[36] Rosenberg (1967), p. 48.

References of Related Interest

Aronson, E., "Who Likes Whom and Why," *Psychology Today*. August 1970, 48-50, 74.

Babladelis, G., and S. Adams (Eds.), *The Shaping of Personality*. Englewood Cliffs, N.J.: Prentice-Hall, Inc., 1967.

Bugental, J.F.T. (Ed.), *Challenges of Humanistic Psychology*. New York: McGraw-Hill, Inc., 1967.

Clarizio, H.F. (Ed.), *Mental Health and the Educative Process*. Skokie, Ill.: Rand McNally & Company, 1969.

Grebstein, Lawrence C. (Ed.), *Toward Self-Understanding*. Glenview, Ill.: Scott, Foresman and Company, 1969.

Grossack, Martin M., *You Are Not Alone*. Boston: Christopher Publishing House, 1965.

Hamachek, Don E. (Ed.), *The Self in Growth, Teaching, and Learning*. Englewood Cliffs, N.J.: Prentice-Hall Inc., 1965, Parts V, IX.

Hamachek, Don E. (Ed.), *Human Dynamics in Psychology and Education*. Boston: Allyn and Bacon, Inc., 1968, Chap. 11-13.

Maslow, A.H., *Toward A Psychology of Being* (2nd ed.). Princeton, N.J.: D. Van Nostrand Company, 1968.

Matson, F.W. (Ed.), *Being, Becoming, and Behavior*. New York: George Braziller, 1967.

McNeil, E.B., *Human Socialization*. Belmont, Calif.: Brooks/Cole, 1969.

Moustakes, C.E., *The Self: Explorations in Personal Growth*. New York: Harper & Row, Publishers, 1956.

Rogers, C.R., *Being, Becoming, and Behavior*. Boston: Houghton Mifflin Company, 1961.

Sanford, N., *Self and Society*. New York: Atherton Press, 1966.

Shapiro, D., *Neurotic Styles*. New York: Basic Books, Inc., 1965.

Shostrom, E.L., *Man, the Manipulator*. New York: Abingdon Press, 1967.

Southwell, E.A., and M. Merbaum (Eds.), *Personality: Readings in Theory and Research*. Belmont, Calif: Brooks/Cole, 1964.

Stein, M.R., A. J. Vidich, and D.M. White (Eds.), *Identity and Anxiety*. New York: The Free Press, 1960.

Smith, H.C., *Sensitivity to People*. New York: McGraw-Hill, Inc., 1966.

Stoodley, B.H. (Ed.), *Society and Self*. New York: The Free Press, 1962.

White, R.W., *The Abnormal Personality* (3rd ed.). New York: The Ronald Press Company, 1964.

Stretching the Self Concept

Joseph Zinker

My theory of polarities dictates that I do not allow myself to be unkind, I will never be genuinely kind. If I am in touch with my own unkindness and stretch that part of myself, when my kindness emerges it will be richer, fuller, more complete. If I do not allow myself to be in touch with my femininity, then my masculinity will be exaggerated, even perverse—I will be a hard, tough guy. Many of my clients have said to me, "Your're a man, but you're different; you're soft and that's nice." When one side of the polarity gets stretched, it is almost automatic that at some point the other side also stretches. I call this the "around the world" phenomenon: If you keep flying north long enough, you'll eventually be heading south.

In order to grow as a person and have more productive conflict experiences with others, I have to stretch my self concept. I have to teach myself to invade that part of me which I do not approve of. There are various techniques involved in this process. First, I must uncover that part of myself which is disowned. Second, I need to come into contact with the disowned part of myself. This is the preliminary step—getting in touch with how I keep secrets from myself. I might put a part of me on the couch, representing my secretive self, and that part might say: "I am mysterious and I am interesting. You should appreciate me because I keep you from exposing your tenderness and I protect you." And the other part, sitting in a chair, might say, "Yes, but don't we pay a price for that?" Then I go back to the couch and say, "Yes, a lot of the time I find myself alone when I don't want to be alone, and I stew in my secretiveness."

Once I feel kinder toward and more fully understanding of my secret self, I can relate to another person who tries to penetrate that inner territory or threatens that part of me. I call this whole process stretching the self-concept, creating more room in one's picture of the self. The more broadly I know myself, the more comfortable I am with myself.

One of my clients experiences severe anxiety, falling victim to a part of himself that says: "You are not worth living. You are a bad person; your life is bad. There isn't anything good about you." He cannot take ownership of this mean, sadistic attitude as part of his own character. He always

Reprinted by permission from Joseph Zinker, CREATIVE PROCESS IN GESTALT THERAPY, pp. 202-206, © Brunner/Mazel, Publishers, 1977.

experiences "it" as suddenly accosting him, as if "it" came from outer space. As he is working with me, he realizes that the "bad" part of him developed very early in his life. As a child, every time he left his house the other kids kicked, beat and teased him. Slowly, he began to identify with these children, and after a while they taught him to be his own critic, his own enemy. Now, as an adult, he doesn't need his angry friends. He does the job himself, kicking himself in the ass every day.

Once he was able to come in contact with this introjected critic-sadist, he could feel more sympathetic toward this unacceptable part of himself. Now when he feels self-critical, he can address himself to the critic: "Hey, you have really suffered. You are part of me that was beaten. I am sorry you took this job on for yourself. Isn't it time you stopped being so hard on me? After all, you know I am a decent human being."

One may think that if this man accepts the reality of his criticism and sadism, he will become a sadist. This is a fallacy. The more this man accepts his punitive, sadistic self, the less the possibility that he will act on his sadism in the future. The curious result of the stretching process is that the polarities of the critic will become more evident, more solidified. Thus, if for him the polarity of critic and sadist is acceptor and healer, then his acceptance and healing qualities will become more genuine and real with others, as well as with himself.

On the other hand, the less aware he is of these negative aspects of himself, the more he will find himself acting out these parts. I remember a young man who came to see me because he was horrified by his behavior. When I inquired further, he said, "I don't know what got into me, but I hit my baby boy so hard I broke his leg. And yesterday I threw the cat against the wall." This young father had no contact whatsoever with is own sadism. It was totally disowned. "It" popped out of him like a foreign object, beyond his control.

A person who is always considerate and kind may not be in touch with his resentment or anger, or with his sorrow about the pain which was inflicted on him. It is very difficult for such a person to accept his rage. Sometimes the only way he can handle rage is to be a better human being to others than anyone has ever been to him. He does not handle the consequences of being a victim, and it is inconceivable to him to identify with the victimizer.

Let me give you another example. We cannot agree to do something fully unless we have a choice to say, "No." A woman complains because she's agreed to give her time to sôlicit for a worthy cause when she doesn't have the extra time, or when she feels that she's done it so many times before that someone else should do it this time. She can't say "No" because she knows someone should do it, or maybe because she won't look good if she refuses. So she says "Yes" and feels resentful or makes a martr of herself. She's not doing the job because she really wants to. It would be better for the woman to say, "Look, I know this is a worthy cause and I understand your problem in getting volunteers, but I've done this many times before, and I'm tired and busy, and I will not do it this time." If she could learn how to say "I won't" genuinely, she would have much more pleasure saying "I will" when she does accept the job another time. The "I won't" stretches the fullness of the "I will."

V / Building Self-Esteem Through Affirmation

My own vineyard I have not tended.
Song of Songs 1:6

The courage to be is the ethical act in which a man affirms his own being in spite of elements of his existence which conflict with his essential affirmation.
Paul Tillich

New Light on the Human Potential

Herbert A. Otto

William James once estimated that the healthy human being is functioning at less than 10 per cent of his capacity. It took more than half a century before this idea found acceptance among a small proportion of
behavioral scientists. In 1954, the highly respected and widely known
psychologist Gardner Murphy published his pioneering volume *Human
Potentialities*. The early Sixties saw the beginnings of the human potentialities research project at the University of Utah and the organization of
Esalen Institute in California, the first of a series of "Growth Centers" that
were later to be referred to as the Human Potential Movement.

Today, many well-known scientists such as Abraham Maslow,
Margaret Mead, Gardner Murphy, O. Spurgeon English, and Carl Rogers
subscribe to the hypothesis that man is using a very small fraction of his
capacities. Margaret Mead quotes a 6 per cent figure, and my own estimate
is 5 per cent or less. Commitment to the hypothesis is not restricted to the
United States. Scientists in the U.S.S.R. and other countries are also at
work. Surprisingly, the so-called human potentialities hypothesis is still
largely unknown.

What are the dimensions of the human potential? The knowledge we
do have about man is minimal and has not as yet been brought together with
the human potentialities hypothesis as an organizing force and synthesizing
element. Of course, we know more about man today than we did fifty years
ago, but this is like the very small part of the iceberg we see above the water.
Man essentially remains a mystery. From the depths of this mystery there
are numerous indicators of the human potential.

Certain indicators of man's potential are revealed to us in childhood.
They become "lost" or submerged as we succumb to the imprinting of the
cultural mold in the "growing up" process. Do you remember when you
were a child and it rained after a dry spell and there was a very particular,
intensive earthy smell in the air? Do you recall the brilliant colors of leaves,
flowers, grass, and even brick surfaces and lighted signs that you experienced as a child? Furthermore, do you recall that when father and mother
stepped into the room you *knew* how they felt about themselves, about life,
and about you—at that moment.

Reprinted by permission from Herbert A. Otto, "New Light on the Human Potential," © SATURDAY
REVIEW, December 20, 1969, pp. 14-17.

Today we know that man's sense of smell, one of the most powerful and primitive senses, is highly developed. In the average man this capacity has been suppressed except for very occasional use. Some scientists claim that man's sense of smell is almost as keen as a hunting dog's. Some connoisseurs of wines, for example, can tell by the bouquet not only the type of grape and locality where they were grown but even the vintage year and vineyard. Perfume mixers can often detect fantastically minute amounts in mixed essences; finally there are considerable data on odor discrimination from the laboratory. It is also clear that, since the air has become an overcrowded garbage dump for industrial wastes and the internal combustion engine, it is easier to turn off our sense of smell than to keep it functioning. The capacity to experience the environment more fully through our olfactory organs remains a potential.

It is possible to regain these capacities through training. In a similar manner, sensory and other capacities, including visual, kinesthetic, and tactile abilities, have become stunted and dulled. We perceive less clearly, and as a result we feel less—we use our dulled senses to close ourselves off from both our physical and interpersonal environments. Today we also dull our perceptions of how other people feel and we consistently shut off awareness of our own feelings. For many who put their senses to sleep it is a sleep that lasts until death. Again, through sensory and other training the doors of perception can be cleansed (to use Blake's words) and our capacities reawakened. Anthropological research abounds with reports of primitive tribes that have developed exceptional sensory and perceptive abilities as a result of training. Utilization of these capacities by modern man for life-enrichment purposes awaits the future.

Neurological research has shed new light on man's potential. Work at the UCLA Brain Research Institute points to enormous abilities latent in everyone by suggesting an incredible hypothesis: The ultimate creative capacity of the human brain may be, for all practical purposes, infinite. To use the computer analogy, man is a vast storehouse of data, but we have not learned how to program ourselves to utilize these data for problem-solving purposes. Recall of experiential data is extremely spotty and selective for most adults. My own research has convinced me that the recall of experiences can be vastly improved by use of certain simple training techniques, provided sufficient motivation is present.

Under emergency conditions, man is capable of prodigious feats of physical strength. For example, a middle-aged California woman with various ailments lifted a car just enough to let her son roll out from under it after it had collapsed on him. According to newspaper reports the car weighed in excess of 2,000 pounds. There are numerous similar accounts indicating that every person has vast physical reserve capacities that can be tapped. Similarly, the extraordinary feats of athletes and acrobats—involving the conscious and specialized development of certain parts of the human organism as a result of consistent application and a high degree of motivation—point to the fantastic plasticity and capabilities of the human being.

Until World War II, the field of hypnosis was not regarded as respectable by many scientists and was associated with stage performances and charlatanism. Since that time hypnosis has attained a measure of scientific respectibility. Medical and therapeutic applications of hypnosis include the use of this technique in surgery and anesthesiology (hypnoanesthesis for major and minor surgery), gynecology (infertility, frigidity, menopausal conditions), pediatrics (enuresis, tics, asthma in children, etc.), and in dentistry. Scores of texts on medical and dental hypnosis are available. Dr. William S. Kroger, one of the specialists in the field and author of the well-known text *Clinical and Experimental Hypnosis*, writes that hypnotherapy is "directed to the patient's needs and is a methodology to tap the 'forgotten assets' of the *hidden potentials* of behavior and response that so often lead to new learnings and understanding." (My italics.) As far as we know now, the possibilities opened by hypnosis for the potential functioning of the human organism are not brought about by the hypnotist. Changes are induced by the subject, utilizing his belief-structure, with the hypnotist operating as an "enabler," making it possible for the subject to tap some of his unrealized potential.

The whole area of parapsychology that deals with extrasensory perception (ESP), "mental telepathy," and other paranormal phenomena, and that owes much of its development to the work of Dr. J. B. Rhine and others is still regarded by much of the scientific establishment with the same measure of suspicion accorded hypnosis in the pre-World War II days. It is of interest that a number of laboratories in the U.S.S.R. are devoted to the study of telepathy as a physical phenomenon, with research conducted under the heading "cerebral radio-communication" and "bioelectronics." The work is supported by the Soviet government. The reluctance to accept findings from this field of research is perhaps best summarized by an observation of Carl C. Jung's in 1958:

> (Some) people deny the findings of parapsychology outright, either for philosophical reasons or from intellectual laziness. This can hardly be considered a scientifically responsible attitude, even though it is a popular way out of quite extraordinary intellectual difficulty.

Although the intensive study of creativity had its beginnings in fairly recent times, much of value has been discovered about man's creative potential. There is evidence that every person has creative abilities that can be developed. A considerable number of studies indicate that much in our educational system—including conformity pressures exerted by teachers, emphasis on memory development, and rote learning, plus the overcrowding of classrooms—militates against the development of creative capacities. Research has established that children between the ages of two and three can learn to read, tape record a story, and type it as it is played back. Hundreds of children between the ages of four and six have been taught by the Japanese pedagogue Suzuki to play violin concertos. Japanese research with infants and small children also suggests the value of early "maximum input" (music, color, verbal, tactile stimuli) in the personality development of infants. My own observations tend to confirm this. We have consistently underestimated the child's capacity to learn and his ability to realize his potential while *enjoying* both the play elements and the discipline involved in this process.

In contrast to the Japanese work, much recent Russian research appears to be concentrated in the area of mentation, with special emphasis on extending and enlarging man's mental processes and his capacity for learning. As early as 1964 the following appeared in *Soviet Life Today*, a U.S.S.R. English language magazine:

The latest findings in anthropology, psychology, logic, and physiology show that the potential of the human mind is very great indeed. "As soon as modern science gave us some understanding of the structure and work of the human brain, we were struck with its enormous reserve capacity," writes Yefremov (Ivan Yefremov, eminent Soviet scholar and writer). "Man, under average conditions of work and life, uses only a small part of his thinking equipment.... If we were able to force our brain to work at only half its capacity, we could, without any difficulty whatever, learn forty languages, memorize the large Soviet Encyclopedia from cover to cover, and complete the required courses of dozens of colleges."

The statement is hardly an exaggeration. It is the generally accepted theoretical view of man's mental potentialities.

How can we tap this gigantic potential? It is a big and very complex problem with many ramifications.

Another signpost of man's potential is what I have come to call the "Grandma Moses effect." This artist's experience indicates that artistic talents can be discovered and brought to full flowering in the latter part of the life cycle. In every retirement community there can be found similar examples of residents who did not use latent artistic abilities or other talents until after retirement. In many instances the presence of a talent is suspected or known but allowed to remain fallow for the best part of a lifetime.

Reasons why well-functioning mature adults do not use specific abilities are complex. Studies conducted at the University of Utah as a part of the Human Potentialities Research Project revealed that unconscious blocks are often present. In a number of instances a person with definite evidence that he has a specific talent (let's say he won a state-wide contest in sculpture while in high school) may not wish to realize this talent at a later time because he feels this would introduce a change in life-style. Sometimes fear of the passion of creation is another roadblock in self-actualization. On the basis of work at Utah it became clear that persons who live close to their capacity, who continue to activate their potential, have a pronounced sense of well-being and considerable energy and see themselves as leading purposeful and creative lives.

Most people are unaware of their strengths and potentialities. If a person with some college background is handed a form and asked to write out his personality strengths, he will list, on an average, five or six strengths. Asked to to the same thing for his weaknesses, the list will be two to three times as long. There are a number or reasons for this low self-assessment. Many participants in my classes and marathon group weekends have pointed out that "listing your strengths feels like bragging about yourself. It's something that just isn't done." Paradoxically, in a group, people feel more comfortable about sharing problem areas and hang-ups than they do about personality resources and latent abilities. This is traceable to the fact that we are members of a pathology-oriented culture. Psychological and psychiatric jargon dealing with emotional dysfunction and mental illness has become the parlance of the man in the street. In addition, from early childhood in our educational system we learn largely by our mistakes—by having them pointed out to us repeatedly. All this results in early "negative conditioning" and influences our attitude and perception of ourselves and other people. An attitudinal climate has become established which is continually fed and reinforced.

As a part of this negative conditioning there is the heavy emphasis by communications media on violence in television programs and motion pictures. The current American news format of radio, televison, and newspapers—the widely prevalent idea of what constitutes news—results from a narrow, brutalizing concept thirty or forty years behind the times and is inimical to the development of human potential.

The news media give much time and prominent space to violence and consistently underplay "good" news. This gives the consumer the impression that important things that happen are various types of destructive activities. Consistent and repeated emphasis on bad news not only creates anxiety and tension but instills the belief that there is little except violence, disasters, accidents, and mayhem abroad in the world. As a consequence, the consumer of such news gradually experiences a shift in his outlook about the world leading to the formation of feelings of alienation and separation. The world is increasingly perceived as a threat, as the viewer becomes anxious that violence and mayhem may be perpetrated on him from somewhere out of the strange and unpredictable environment in which he lives. There slowly grows a conviction that it is safer to withdraw from such a world, to isolate himself from its struggles, and to let others make the decisions and become involved.

As a result of the steady diet of violence in the media, an even more fundamental and insidious erosion in man's self-system takes place. The erosion affects what I call the "trust factor." If we have been given a certain amount of affection, love, and understanding in our formative years, we are able to place a certain amount of trust in our fellow man. Trust is one of the most important elements in today's society although we tend to minimize its importance. *We basically trust people.* For example, we place an enormous amount of trust in our fellow man when driving on a freeway or in an express lane. We trust those with whom we are associated to fulfill their obligations and responsibilities. The element of trust is the basic rule in human relations. When we distrust people, they usually sense our attitude and reciprocate in kind.

The consistent emphasis in the news on criminal violence, burglarizing, and assault makes slow but pervasive inroads into our reservoir of trust. As we hear and read much about the acts of violence and injury men perpetrate upon one another, year after year, with so little emphasis placed on the loving, caring, and humanitarian acts of man, we begin to trust our fellow man less, and we thereby diminish ourselves. It is my conclusion the media's excessive emphasis on violence, like the drop of water on the stone, erodes and wears away the trust factor in man. By undermining the trust factor in man, media contribute to man's estrangement from man and prevent the full flourishing and deeper development of a sense of community and communion with all men.

Our self-concept, how we feel about ourselves and our fellow man and the world, is determined to a considerable extent by the inputs from the physical and interpersonal environment to which we are exposed. In the physical environment, there are the irritants in the air, i.e., air pollution plus the ugliness and noise of megapolis. Our interpersonal environment is characterized by estrangement and distance from others (and self), and by the artificiality and superficiality of our social encounters and the resultant violation of authenticity. Existing in a setting that provides as consistent inputs multiple irritants, ugliness and violence, and lack of close and meaningful relationships, man is in danger of becoming increasingly irritated, ugly, and violent.

As work in the area of human potentialities progressed, it has become ever clearer that personality, to a much greater degree than previously suspected, functions in response to the environment. This is additional confirmation of what field theorists and proponents of the holistic approach to the study of man have long suspected.

Perhaps the most important task facing us today is the regeneration of our environment and institutional structures such as school, government, church, etc. With increasing sophistication has come the recognition that institutions are not sacrosanct and that they have but one purpose and function—to serve as a framework for the actualization of human potential. It is possible to evaluate both the institution and the contribution of the institution by asking this question: "To what extent does the function of the institution foster the realization of human potential?"

Experimental groups consistently have found that the more a person's environment can be involved in the process of realizing potential, the greater the gains. It is understandable why scientists concerned with the study of personality have been reluctant to consider the importance of here-and-now inputs in relation to personality functioning. To do so would open a Pandora's box of possibilities and complex forces that until fairly recently were considered to be the exclusive domain of the social scientist. Many scientists and professionals, particularly psychotherapists, feel they have acquired a certain familiarity with the topography of "intra-psychic forces" and are reluctant to admit the reality of additional complex factors in the functioning of the personality.

It is significant that an increasing number of psychologists, psychiatrists, and social workers now realize that over and beyond keeping up with developments in their respective fields, the best way to acquire additional professional competence is through group experiences designed for personal growth and that focus on the unfolding of individual possibilities. From this group of aware professionals and others came much of the initial support and interest in Esalen Institute and similar "Growth Centers" later referred to as the Human Potentialities Movement.

Esalen Institute in Big Sur, California, was organized in 1962 by Michael Murphy and his partner, Dick Price. Under their imaginative management the institute experienced a phenomenal growth, established a branch in San Francisco, and is now famous for its seminars and weekend experiences offered by pioneering professionals. Since 1962 more than 100,000 persons have enrolled for one of these activities.

The past three years have seen a rapid mushrooming of Growth Centers. There are more than fifty such organizations ranging from Esalen and Kairos Institutes in California to Oasis in Chicago and Aureon Institute in New York. The experiences offered at these Growth Centers are based on several hypotheses: 1) that the average healthy person functions at a fraction of his capacity; 2) that man's most exciting life-long adventure is actualizing his potential; 3) that the group environment is one of the best settings in which to achieve growth; and 4) that personality growth can be achieved by anyone willing to invest himself in this process.

Human potentialities is rapidly emerging as a discrete field of scientific inquiry. Exploring the human potential can become the meeting ground for a wide range of disciplines, offering a dynamic synthesis for seemingly divergent areas of research. It is possible that the field of human potentialities offers an answer to the long search for a synthesizing and organizing principle which will unify the sciences. The explosive growth of the Human Potentialities Movement is indicative of a growing public interest. Although there exist a considerable number of methods—work on assessment or evaluation of these methods has in most instances not progressed beyond field testing and informal feedback of results. The need for research in the area of human potentialities has never been more pressing. The National Center for the Exploration of Human Potential in La Jolla, California, has recently been organized for this purpose. A nonprofit organization, the center will act as a clearing house of information for current and past approaches that have been successful in fostering personal growth. One of the main purposes of the center will be to conduct and coordinate basic and applied research concerning the expansion of human potential.

Among the many fascinating questions posed by researchers are some of the following: What is the relationship of body-rhythms, biorhythms, and the expansion of sensory awareness to the uncovering of human potential? What are the applications of methods and approaches from other cultures such as yoga techniques, Sufi methods, types of meditation, etc.? What is the role of ecstasy and play vis-a-vis the realizing of human possibilities? The exploration of these and similar questions can help us create a society truly devoted to the full development of human capacities—particularly the capacities for love, joy, creativity, spiritual experiencing. This is the challenge and promise of our lifetime.

How to Accept
and Own Praise -

Sally Wendkos Olds

On Monday I receive a phone call from an old college classmate who asks my advice about a writing workshop she wants to give. When she hears that I have been doing free-lance writing for magazines, she exclaims, "Oh, Dr. Bozorth (our creative-writing professor at the University of Pennsylvania) would be so proud of you! You are such a success!" Her words put me off, and I am immediately wary of her motives.

On Wednesday I meet a neighbor in the supermarket. "I love your new hairstyle!" she cries.

"Do you?" I ask, quickly adding, "Oh, but it really needs a trim. And you've done something different to *your* hair. It's so becoming."

The exchange at the fruit counter leaves me clumsily selecting ripe bananas and wishing I'd worn a hat. I don't like her hairdo at all. What made me say I did? Well, I rationalize, she probably didn't like mine either.

Why am I so discomfited by a compliment? According to a recent sociological study, I am, in fact, very typical. Praise seems to make most of us uneasy.

Compliments are a common enough staple of everyday life. We are constantly telling others that we like their clothes, their hairstyle, their jewelry, or their pipe tobacco. We convey our approval of the way they conduct a meeting, present a report, host a dinner party, or run a business. We laud their possessions—their pets, cars, homes, works of art.

When questioned, many of us say we hate insincere flattery—but we love genuine praise. And yet, even though most of us want, need, and regularly fish for compliments, once we get them we don't know what to do with them.

This point was brought home to Charles Edgley, Ph.D., and Ronny E. Turner, Ph.D., when they were graduate students in sociology at the State University of New York at Buffalo. A classmate of theirs showed great discomfort when his professor congratulated him for having done well on his doctoral exams. His uneasiness struck a common chord in both Turner and Edgley—who decided to take a closer look at the phenomenon of praise.

Dr. Turner, now associate professor of sociology at Colorado State

University,and Dr. Edgley, associate professor of sociology at Oklahoma Baptist University and Oklahoma State University, led a research team of 10 undergraduates who listened in on campus conversations. Whenever the researchers overheard a compliment, they stuck around long enough to interview the recipient. Their recently published findings show that of the 245 people praised, 159, or 65 percent, acknowledged feeling uneasy, even when they viewed the compliments as sincere.

Why do so many of us accept a gift-wrapped word as gingerly as we might a beribboned time bomb? Usually, say Professors Turner and Edgley, for one of six reasons: the felt obligation to return the compliment; the need to keep up a modest front and avoid seeming conceited by agreeing with the praise; suspicion of ulterior motives; fear that commendation is but a prelude to criticism; resentment at being evaluated at all by someone else; or worry that we won't be able to keep up whatever we're being praised for at the moment.

Reciprocity is a fact of social life. Just as we feel obliged to "return" a dinner invitation or a Christmas card, the Turner-Edgley study shows that most people feel they must return a compliment. In fact, 8 out of 10 people praised told the interviewers that they planned to commend their praisers in the near future. In a follow-up study, two-thirds of those praised actually did return compliments within three days after receiving them, and most of the others intended to requite but hadn't gotten around to it yet. Some reciprocated nonverbally at the time with a show of affection—a smile or a kiss—or later, with a present.

Many respondents felt extreme anxiety about returning kind words; some felt the very relationship depended upon it. Most however, didn't like the feeling that they were "beholden" to their complimenters and wanted to even out the relationship as soon as possible.

Sidney B. Simon, Ed.D., professor of education at the University of Massachusetts, calls this rush toward reciprocation the "compliment-flick" syndrome. "Many people get rid of a compliment as fast as they can by giving one back," he says. "They just can't stand hearing themselves praised. That's because so many of us have been trained from an early age to be humble and modest and not to toot our own horns. We can't even enjoy hearing anyone else toot them, either, because that might imply that we think something of ourselves."

Recently, at a party, I talked with folk singer Jean Ritchie, who told me about her childhood in Kentucky. "My mother would set out a grand spread of all kinds of good food for company," she recalled. "Then she would apologize to our guests, 'I'm sorry but this is all we have.' That's how we were taught to act—that whatever we had or whatever we were really wasn't very much.

"So when I first began to sing and people would come backstage to say how much they enjoyed the concert, I couldn't accept what they said, because that would have been like agreeing with them that I *was* able to give a good performance," Ms. Ritchie explained. "I was afraid of seeming too bigheaded."

Such modesty, I learned from Turner and Edgley's study, is not only common, it is also *expected*. After my 12-year-old daughter, Dorie, had mastered a new gymnastics move, a friend commended her by saying, "That was a really good glide kip." When Dorie said, "Thanks," her friend looked stunned and asked, "Aren't you even going to deny it?"

Once the word "compliment" meant a tip, a gratuity, or "something one person pays another to acknowledge inferiority." The very act of giving a compliment implies that the praiser is—at least momentarily—sitting in judgment on the recipient. One high-school principal, recognizing this, bridles every time he gets a good report from the teachers' union representative in his school, "because complimenting me today implies that he has the right to criticize me tomorrow."

In their research, Turner and Edgley found that superiors are more likely to laud their subordinates than the reverse, since it seems presumptuous to judge someone of higher status—and since compliments help to keep people "in their place." An army sergeant comments, "Your quarters are A-1, Private Jones." "You're playing a pretty good game of tennis today," says a cocksure husband to his wife.

One out of five people praised told the interviewers that they wondered about the ulterior motives of people who praised them. Kind words between men and women are generally considered sexual overtures, the study revealed. In business, compliments are usually seen as ways to "grease a sale" or guarantee continued patronage.

Compliments can also become standard-setters for future behavior—and therefore cause great anxiety about performance. Thus the advertising man whose client says, "That campaign of yours was really great for business," may panic at the thought that his next campaign may not draw as well. For this reason, even celebrities often dread acclaim.

When we get compliments from some people, we keep waiting for the other shoe to drop. "You are so smart. How come you're flunking algebra?" or "You usually have such good taste in clothes. That outfit sure doesn't fit your image."

The late Haim Ginott, Ph.D., observed: "It is easier and less confusing to cope with honest praise, or honest criticism, than with a dishonest mixture of them." Dr. Ginott, a child psychologist, contended that, "direct praise of personality, like direct sunlight, is uncomfortable and blinding." In his books and lectures he advised parents to describe what their children have done rather than what they are. For example, instead of saying, "You are a wonderful child," Ginott would urge a mother to say something like, "That card you sent me in the hospital was so funny that it cheered me up all day." Or instead of a father's saying, "You are strong," he could make the same point by telling a child, "It takes a lot of strength to move that heavy workbench."

Alice Ginott, Ph.D., also a psychologist, espouses the same philosophy as her late husband and applies the principle to adults. In a recent newspaper column, she wrote, "Description, not adjectives, constitutes praise. Adjectives are not digestible: "You're great; you're wonderful; you're beautiful; you're creative.' What are we to do with such statements? We can either accept them or reject them, but we cannot assimilate them; we cannot take delight in them; they do not spur us on to bigger and better efforts."

On a recent speaking tour, Dr. Ginott expressed her personal appreciation to a very helpful public relations representative by saying, "Jane, I'm aware of the effort and ingenuity that must have gone into making such a tight schedule work so efficiently. You managed to keep every appointment, and we still had time for a quiet lunch. We didn't even miss the plane. Thank you." Such praise is usually easier to accept than a blanket "I could never have done it without you!" because people have trouble accepting compliments that seem excessive, or that don't fit in with their picture of themselves.

However, even descriptive praise has to be tempered by reality. Says one carpenter's apprentice. "I love compliments about things I make—but only when *I* think they're terrific."

Roger Severson, Ph.D., associate professor of psychology at the University of Wisconsin, says, "When you compliment someone, you can't exceed that person's tolerance level for positive feedback. If you pour on too much, the person you're praising will say, 'That's not really me. I don't want you to say I'm that good because that makes me feel like a phony.' People will also question your sincerity if what you say doesn't jibe with the way they see themselves."

Attitudes toward praise tend to be specific to a situation. I know a writer who practically melts when people praise his books—but turns wary when they praise his golf game. "Maybe I'm a better golfer than the one who's complimenting me, but I know how far I am from being a really good player," he explains.

As situations change, our responses change, too. The stunning 42-year-old executive of a cosmetics firm says, "As a young girl, I didn't like being told I was pretty. It was no compliment to me, because I hadn't had anything to do with the way I looked—it was just the way I happened to get my shuffle of genes. But now that I'm actively *doing* something with makeup and lotions and creams, I can take some personal credit for my face."

Some people think so little of themselves that they reject all praise. Betsy, an eight-year-old girl who was doing poorly in school, couldn't stand being told that her work was good—or even that an answer was right. She would invariably counter with, "No, it's not." Dr. Severson placed Betsy in a program in the psycho-educational clinic at the University of Wisconsin—in order to help the child overcome both her learning problem and her constant negative attitude.

Betsy's tutor at the clinic selected an unusual way to praise her, without sparking her negative retort. She would spin a white card whenever Betsy correctly answered a question. Betsy made no objection to this, and soon she learned to spin the card herself. As the program progressed, the tutor rang a bell when the card was spun. Eventually she spoke a low-intensity word—"correct"—when the bell rang. Then stronger words, such as "right," were gradually introduced, until the child could happily hear that her work was "good."

At the opposite extreme from Betsy are those people who become so habituated to praise that they virtually live from compliment to compliment. Some of these people have grown up to the tune of extravagant praise until, in later years, they cannot live without it.

Capable and attractive Alisa had been surfeited with compliments all her life—from her parents, her teachers, the men she dated. Now that she has been married for five years, her husband has been feeding her fewer compliments. As a senior partner in a law firm, she is seen as a rival by her male colleagues, who are chary with their commendations. Without the steady diet of praise she had been used to ingesting, she began to feel the pangs of an identity crisis.

Now in therapy with Ruth Moulton, M.D., a New York psychiatrist, Alisa is learning to understand why she became so dependent on the approval of others, so that she will not crave it so much.

"People shouldn't have to get this constant reaffirmation from the outside," says Dr. Moulton, who believes we need to become aware of our own assets and liabilities so that we can accurately appraise ourselves.

But, nonetheless, we all need a good dose of outside approval. "I don't know anyone who works around suffering from too much validation," Dr. Sidney Simon told a group at a workshop I attended in Rochester, New York. "Most of us have been corrected and criticized so much that when someone does give us a compliment, we can't believe it. We think, 'If they really knew me, they wouldn't be saying those nice things about me.' " Dr. Simon teaches people how to overcome this "red-pencil mentality" and learn to accept a little positive reinforcement every now and then.

Perhaps the most important clue to enjoying a compliment lies in knowing how to respond to one. Most of the time, a simple "thank you" is the most gracious answer—even if you have to bite back the urge to say, "Oh—this dress? I picked it up for $10 at a thrift shop." Sometimes you may even be comfortable agreeing with a word of praise. Says one artist, "I never used to know what to say when people admired my work. Now if I'm pleased with a painting myself, I can say, 'Thank you—I'm happy with the way that turned out.' And when I'm not so pleased, I just say 'thank you'—and accept the fact that my standards are higher than some other people's."

Finally, praise isn't all bad. Cicero described it as "the sweetest of all sounds." After all, spontaneous, sincere admiration for the things we have done can encourage and inspire us—or simply make us feel good.

Avoiding the put-down

by Lou Benson

A mother suddenly falls into a mood of deep depression shortly after her young child misbehaves in public. A young man attempts suicide when he hears his wife expressing her love for their newborn son. A businessman has to declare bankruptcy in a certain venture and, a week later, is found in a strange city suffering from amnesia.

Although they may not appear related on the surface, all these events have something in common. Clinical analysis of these and similar cases shows that the people were the victims of what is commonly called "the put-down." The put-down as it is used in everyday speech refers to an insult, slight, humiliation, or snub. It is often said to result in "hurt feelings," "ego deflation," or "feelings of worthlessness." For our purposes we may define the put-down as *any attack upon the PR personality*. It is any statement, deed, or innuendo seen by a person as a *deflation of his public image*. It can have extremely important consequences.

An important thing to notice about this syndrome is that the put-down is a perception by the victim and may not be seen by others in the same way. A completely innocent statement, act, or event may be perceived as an insult, when in fact there was no such intent on the part of anyone. On the other hand, sometime the intent to insult may be real, but the "victim" may not perceive it as such. In that case the put-down fails to materialize.

Although this phenomenon is very important phychologically, it has not always received the attention it deserves. In fact, there is no technical term by which this syndrome is designated. The closest we come to some kind of identification of it is through the use of such terms as rejection, stigma (Goffman, 1963), ego deflation, and insult. But each of these terms has a slightly different shade of meaning.

The concept of the put-down really refers to two related things. The first is the action of one person toward another. To put someone down means to insult, humiliate, deride, ridicule, and so on. The second meaning is the feeling of the *victim* when he is belittled, derogated, spurned, and repudiated. For both of these meanings we shall use the term *disparagement*.

Disparagement, when perceived as such by the victim, always results in a feeling of self-derogation. The person comes to acknowledge the fact that some part of his PR personality has become transparent. However, this

From Lou Benson, IMAGES, HEROES, & SELF-PERCEPTIONS: The Struggle for Identity—from Mask-Wearing to Authenticity, © 1974, pp. 45-75. Reprinted by permission of Prentice-Hall, Inc., Englewood Cliffs, NJ.

phenomenon may not always be perceived in the same light by others. This is demonstrated by the examples given above.

In the first case, the woman became depressed after her child misbehaved. Ordinarily, we might be inclined to attribute her response to disappointment in her child's behavior. But an analysis of this particular woman's behavior showed that she had a self-image which involved a picture of herself as a good and efficient parent, whose children were "very well behaved in public." It was not the misbehavior but the fact that it occurred where her friends and others could see it that so distressed her. For it revealed, she thought, her inadequacy as a parent. Her depression was a symptomatic reaction to her feeling of inadequacy in a role that she considered important to her.

The second case concerned a young man who after observing his wife expressing her love for their newborn son, suddenly became terribly unhappy. This turned out to be the case of a very immature young man, who was generally unsure of his wife's love. They had been married only a year and had just had their first child. The girl, also immature, did not know how to express her feelings toward her husband and when she did talk about love, it was without much fervor. However, when the young man heard her talking to the infant, she was rapturous. Such phrases as "more than anyone else in the world" and "the only love of my life" stuck in his mind. He was overwhelmed by a feeling of emptiness and worthlessness and tried to end his life.

In the third example, the put-down may seem more obvious. However, here again, the surface reaction does not tell the whole story. The man did not disappear because he had lost a great deal of money but because he had lost a great deal of prestige. He was an extremely wealthy man and the money lost in this particular venture made little difference in his standing. But he had placed his reputation on the line and had publicly predicted success. When the enterprise failed, he was revealed, so he thought, as a failure (rather than as the infallable success he wanted to be) and his symptoms followed.

All these cases represent situations in which self-devaluation has a profound effect. This, of course, is not rare. Such circumstances in milder form occur every day to all of us. Our reactions, however, depend upon a great many variables. Not all of us develop neurotic symptoms when our egos come under attack. Nevertheless, the victim of a disparaging experience is always made uncomfortable (and defensive) *if he has a stake in that particular segment of his PR personality.*

DISPARAGEMENT AS DE-HERO-IZATION

If it is true that we all try to wear the mask of the hero, then disparagement has the effect of de-hero-izing us. It pierces the armor, so to speak. We are left vulnerable to the view of others and we believe that they can see our imperfections. Disparagement, therefore, reveals us to the world as someone who is unheroic. A person can, for example, be completely destroyed if someone casts an aspersion on his health. And, in fact, nurses and doctors can testify to the fact that just being ill can often be such a blow to a person's ego that it can precipitate serious emotional problems. Worse still, any derogatory allusion to one's mental health is considered a great insult. If fact, the whole family is stigmatized when one of its members is "mentally ill."

Any uncomplimentary reference about one's physical appearance is also a form of disparagement. Any statement regarding one's looks, attire, breath, body scent, hairdo, cosmetics, and so on, when negative, is a great source of humiliation. For we must remember that the hero and heroine are handsome, clean, fashionable, and sweet smelling. They are also extremely virtuous and therefore any innuendo concerning immorality or unethical behavior (except in business where such things are natural) is met with the same feeling of chagrin.

The male, of course, is put down if he cannot fight, or even worse, if he *will* not fight; if he is not good at some sports, and later in life if he can't succeed with girls. The female suffers a similar fate if she is not pretty, chic, capable of performing such "feminine" tasks as sewing or cooking, and if she is not popular with boys. Any of these "shortcomings" therefore takes a person out of the category of the hero or heroine and casts him into another role.

THE NONHERO

Since there are at least two other major types of characters in our folklore, we must fall into either of these categories. We can either be the villain or the plain guy.

The villain, as we have briefly pointed out, is not really the opposite of the hero. He has, in fact, a number of attributes of the hero. He has power; he may be wealthy. He has a certain kind of attractiveness, even fascination. He is at least the second fastest gun in the West and trying (although by foul means) to become the first. He is ambitious, violent, persuasive, strong, and healthy. Note that health is as important for the villain as for the hero. Imagine how it would look if the hero defeated a sick man. You can't chase a man who has gout, punch someone who has a toothache, run a sword through a person suffering from appendicitis, or slay a tubercular dragon. So the villain must be on a par with the hero in many areas or he is not a fit opponent for him.

The opposite of the hero, therefore, is not the villain, but the plain, ordinary, nondescript, plain guy. He is the nonhero. He is the kind of man who will whimper and beg for mercy when being tortured. He will "break" instantly even before the threat of any pain. And if he has no information, he will make some up. Sometimes he has pimples or long hair or merely skin of a different color. He is part of the supporting cast but he goes largely unnoticed as an individual. His personality is bland at best and repulsive at worst. He is the character admired and emulated by no one. If the hero is the model for the PR personality, the nonhero is the model for disparagement.

A distinction should be made here between the nonhero and what is called the "antihero" or the "hero of the absurd." In some ways the nonhero superficially resembles the antihero or the "absurd" hero of some modern fiction. Like Camus' protagonist in *The Stranger* (1946), the nonhero is an unglamorous nobody. His life is usually drab, and the events in it appear to have no meaning. He is, in effect, an unimportant person living an unimportant life. Like Sisyphus in another book by Camus (1960), he is entrapped in an endless, exhausting, and seemingly meaningless routine. He is not smooth in his endeavors. When he tries to seduce a girl, he is awkward or comical. He fails more often than he succeeds. He seldom has a "noble" mission and is sometimes childish rather than "manly."

But the similarities between the hero of the absurd and what we have been describing as the nonhero are only apparent. For in many instances the absurd hero is *really* heroic in the most profound sense. He is a man in collision with his culture. He is one who has examined his society and found it wanting. And he has decided that he will not participate in it. His heroism lies in the fact that very often it is through *his vision* (in the arts, sciences, and so on) that important new human values arise. It is true that he is an outcast. But it is often his own doing. He rejects society because of its shallowness, hypocrisy, or inhumanity and he is rejected in return for his "eccentricity."

The hero of the absurd is often cast in a humanistic mold. As Galloway says in discussing some of the most prominent American novelists, "For however unconventional the environments and 'heroes' of whom they treat, their work is part of a recognizable humanistic tradition" (Galloway, 1966). And later he clarifies the meaning of humanism for these authors. Their heroes, he explains, are rebels, but "the call to revolt is a call to humanize, to transform the inhumanity of the world."

But the nonhero is not a rebel. He is, as we shall see, an authoritarian personality and, as such, he accepts his value system without seriously questioning it. Whatever he believes, he believes because it has been enunciated for him by someone else.

The absurd hero described by Galloway is attempting to question the underlying assumptions of his society and to arrive at a system of values in which he himself can believe. Sometimes his values are in accord with the conventional wisdom, but more often they are not. When the latter is the case, he is perceived by those of a more orthodox persuasion as a troublemaker, a boat rocker, or a dangerous lunatic. It is precisely because of this fact that most of us do not have the courage to *be* the absurd hero. To do so we would "have to go it alone." We would have to disagree with the conventional wisdom where we saw it to be wrong. And we would have to suffer for our beliefs. And the price for most of us would be too dear. For we would have to face one of the most potent put-downs, ostracism.

OSTRACISM AS THE ULTIMATE FORM OF REJECTION

At West Point and the Naval Academy when someone does something that violates some part of the code of behavior, his fellow students sometimes resort to a punishment called "the silent treatment." The silent treatment means that no one may speak to the offending cadet at any time except where absolutely necessary for the performance of duty. This punishment is so harsh to some that it can have devastating consequences.

The young men who are subjected to the silent treatment vary to some extent in their reaction to it. But almost all of them feel a great deal of pressure and anxiety even from the beginning. And if the situation continues for any length of time, it becomes, for some, an agonizing ordeal. The subjective feeling for the victim of this tactic is often one of complete despair. Day after day his friends continue to go about their tasks without a word. When they pass they sometimes avert their eyes, or look right through him. People engaged in happy conversation suddenly stop when he comes into view. Their expressions become grave and their voices become muffled. He comes to perceive their sober indifference as hostility. And as a recipient of so much disdain, he begins to feel worthless. He may sometimes feel that he does not really exist. This is the ultimate rejection. Having been disregarded by everyone he sees, he becomes dubious about "being" there at all. After all, if someone exists, other people acknowledge his existence. If they don't....

Such a situation is of course extreme. But it illustrates very forcefully what rejection can mean. Rejection is a powerful form of disparagement because, beside deflating the PR image, it annihilates the person's sense of self. When the rejection is universal, therefore (that is, when one is ostracized), it can have detrimental effects. But ostracism can be experienced even when it is not intended.

One girl, for example, was not invited to a social gathering by one of her friends. When she learned of the affair, she became terribly depressed and anxious. Two weeks later, she learned that the gathering had been called in secret in order to arrange a surprise party for her. She had tortured herself needlessly because she had misperceived the event.

Disparagement is one of the most destructive wounds that the ego can suffer. But it is largely a self-inflicted one. A person is only vulnerable to insults because he is sensitive in a certain area. His sensitivity is like a sore spot which feels pain at the slightest touch. It is therefore the person's own fears that lead to his devaluing himself.

DISPARAGEMENT AND THE ROLE OF WOMEN

Women are more easily disparaged than men in our society because they have been given an almost impossible role to fill. In the first place, the American woman is put into two completely contradictory positions regarding sex.[1] On the one hand, she must deny her own sexuality. ("Nice girls don't do such things. They don't even *think* about such things.") On the other hand, she is expected to be sexually attractive. That is, she is supposed to be seductive but not to be seduced; to be desirable but to have no desire. Since the primitive heroine is always a virgin with absolutely no trace of libido until it is miraculously awakened by the hero, the American woman has often had to pretend that she has no sexual feelings. Sometimes she does this all to well, and the resulting denial of her normal, natural appetites has led her to seek refuge in a world of fantasy filled with a sterile kind of romance where men bow and dance and bring gifts but never "do bad things."

But this is not all. She also has to play the subservient role without protest. She is expected to be passive, quiet, fastidious, prim, and neat. In short, she is expected to be a mannequin rather than a human being. Such demands are so flagrantly opposed to her real nature that she is forced to employ a great deal of repression in order to conform to this pattern. And this, of course, results in all kinds of defensiveness. Thus any suggestion that she is failing in any of these areas is seen as a defect and leads to anxiety, depression, or other neurotic reactions.

Another concession that she must make is that she must never be more intelligent than the man of her choice. This is the most pernicious demand of all. For in this regard she suffers either way. If she is more intelligent than the man, she is shunned and rejected. And if she is less intelligent, she comes to perceive herself as inferior to men and generally less capable and valuable to society. It is this latter image that feminist groups are so concerned with changing.

But such a change in the image of women is frightening to many men for it is seen as a threat to the male ego. The PR image of the male involves being dominant and one cannot be dominant over someone more intelligent than himself. Moreover, the male has defined the woman's role in such a way that *he* does all the interesting things in life and she gets all the routine duties that he would rather avoid. There appears to be a great deal of truth, therefore, in the complaint that women, like black people, brown people, and other "different" groups, are systematically denied opportunities that would lead them to actualize potentialities that are now suppressed.

Women also at times have the fear that they are valued by men only as objects of sexual gratification and for nothing else. And in fact, this is sometime true. But from the woman's standpoint, it presents several problems. In the first place, she perceives this as a disparagement since she is not accepted as a *person* but as a *thing*. In the second place, since she has probably been brought up to believe that sex is evil, or dirty, she sees this kind of attractiveness as "bad." To be wanted "only for one's body" is not very flattering.

A woman's perception of herself as a mere instrument of a man's desire adds to the already considerable feeling of inferiority imposed upon her by society. She is not really important to the man as a human being. Any other woman would probably do. She sees herself left out of all the things that are exciting and interesting, and she comes to feel that her presence is only tolerated because she can satisfy the man sexually.

A classic presentation of this image is the gangster's girl. She is always very flashy, sensual, somewhat gaudily made-up, wearing skintight clothing over a curvacious figure, but she is a moron. When anything serious is to be discussed, she is summarily thrown out of the room or she is sometimes given money (bribed) to spend more time elsewhere and sent on her way while the men get down to business. The girl is clearly (1) a decoration, (2) an object for ridicule or contempt, and (3) a body for sexual gratification on demand.

This image is, of course, the exaggerated version of the sex object, but it does represent the way in which women are sometimes perceived.

To be forced into such a situation is crippling to the ego of the young girl. She must always be on guard against "being used" as an object by men. She is in constant doubt about the "intentions" of the men in her life. Even when they claim that they consider her more than just a source of gratification, she must continue to be suspicious. After all, they may merely by *saying* such things for their own ulterior motives.

Even after marriage the woman may come to feel that her husband has no use for her beyond the sexual sphere because he seldom includes her in his other pursuits. He spends time with his male friends. He prefers to watch televison rather than take her places. He goes off on weekend hunting trips but would never consider taking *her* away for a weekend.

Women in our society are sometimes treated as pampered pets, sometimes as mother figures to whom we can go for comfort, sometimes as a necessary evil, but they are seldom valued as persons. They come therefore to expect such treatment and to take precautions against it. But like a person in an empty house during a storm, everything that happens tends to increase their suspicion that what they fear is actually happening. The woman perceives every incident of neglect, every inattention, every omission or oversight on the part of her man as proof of the thing she dreads. She is not a human being to him. She is a convenience. This is a humiliating experience.

Another thing that contributes still further to the conflicts in this area is the fact that a woman may also be insulted when she is *not* desired sexually. If her husband is indifferent, or attracted by other women, or is impotent with her, she may feel that she is not feminine enough. She is not a complete woman. Biologically she needs to be desired. Culturally she is afraid that she might be desired *only* biologically. The dilemma places her in constant conflict. Should she use sex to get the attention she needs, or should she use other means? If she concentrates on one, will it be to the neglect of the other?

Thus the female in American society often comes to perceive herself negatively no matter what happens. In a sense she cannot win. If she is too attractive, she may be used as an object. If she is not attractive enough, she may not be desirable at all. If she is intelligent, men may be afraid of her; if she is stupid, she will be treated like an article of furniture. If her sex drive is high, she is a tramp. If it is low, she is not a woman. It is no wonder, therefore, that women in our culture find it extremely difficult to develop their real potentialities without experiencing a great deal of emotional turmoil and stress.

PREJUDICE AND DISPARAGEMENT

The treatment of minority groups in the United States has for a long time been tinged with a particularly damaging form of disparagement. The idea, implicitly held and transmitted in many kinds of media throughout the society, that one or another group of people is evil, inferior, dirty, stupid has often been widespread. Such ideas are sometimes perceived as being valid by the disparaged group itself. This results from the fact that there is almost no information to the contrary available anywhere. Under these circumstances it is unusually difficult for anyone to disbelieve so great a mass of one-sided informationl

These kinds of beliefs tend to help fulfill their predictions since people who perceive themselves as inferior come to behave and perform that way. Ideas of this kind, therefore, produce the very thing that they begin by asserting. To counteract the devastating effects of such beliefs, minority people in the United States have begun searching for new means to express their own identities. By looking at themselves in new ways, they are attempting to undo the effects of the disparagement which they have been subjected to and to develop self-images with which they can satisfactorily identify.

COMPETITIVENESS AND THE PUT-DOWN

Ten men line up at the starting blocks and take their positions for a race. The gun sounds and they burst forward, sprinting down the track at top speed. Gradually some pull ahead and some fall behind and as they approach the finish line, one of the ten takes the lead and breaks the tape a few tenths of a second before any of the others can reach it. He is the *winner*. He receives a trophy. His name gets into print. And he is generally treated as a hero.

This event is a kind of model for many endeavors which are competitive in nature. Where there are many contenders and only one winner, there must always be a large number of losers. And since only the winner is afforded any recognition or esteem, the losers may all experience disparagement. It is interesting to note that in the above situation, all the runners were almost equally as good; the difference between them was very small. Yet only the one who broke the tape received any kind of recognition for his performance.

Although this is a hypothetical situation, such occurrences are common in everyday life. The man whose business succeeds, gets all the glory (and money) while his competitor who fails gets nothing but derision. He who wins receives a distinct kind of designation; everyone else is an "also-ran." It is for this reason that the Hopi Indians, when staging a race, arrange for everyone to cross the finish line together. This establishes their spirit of cooperativeness, in stark contrast to the competitive nature of many other cultures.

It is important, therefore, to consider the consequences of competition on the people who in a competitive society are the "also-rans." It turns out that, from a psychological point of view, almost everyone in such a culture perceives himself as a loser a good part of the time. This occurs because all the methods for evaluation in competitive enterprises are stacked against everyone but a minority of winners. Let us suppose that in the race described above, the winner had been unable to compete. Then the man who finished second in the race would have been the winner and would have been the recipient of all the approval, benefits, rewards, and so on. The winner in this case is somewhat slower than in the original race. But that makes no difference at all. It does not matter how *good* one is, only *whether one is better than the others*. A number of losers are therefore necessary for the creation of a winner.

Those who are "back in the pack" may perceive themselves as inferior. This is particularly likely if they have such an experience often; and in a competitive way of life, most people do. Many people entering therapy reveal a profound sense of disappointment in themselves, which on further investigation turns out to be a feeling that was expressed by a patient as "being a champion of nothing."

It is not to be inferred that competitiveness must always lead to this kind of result. It need not do so. But the tendency will be greatest where the winners are overvalued and those who perform less well are either spurned or ignored. Competition can lead to a sense of self-esteem if the entire enterprise is viewed as an opportunity for each contestant to give his best performance. In such a case the real credo of sport becomes the watchword of the undertaking. "It matters not whether we win or lose, but how we play the game." Each person accepting the challenge and giving the best he has to give fulfills the conditions for being fully accepted. The differentiation between winners and losers becomes somewhat obscured under such conditions, and in a sense they are all perceived as champions.

SELF-DEVALUATION IN GENERAL

Human beings have always been concerned with their status in the hierarchy of nature. From the time that men became aware of their being, they have looked for indications of their worth as a species wherever they could. For the most part they were able to show that they were the most important and most powerful of all God's creatures and they came to enjoy this position and to protect it.

However, certain events occurred in the history of mankind which were to shatter man's collective ego. One of the earliest and most important came out of the disclosures made by Copernicus. For many thousands of years, the view of learned man about man's place in the universe had been based on Ptolemy's astronomical theory. The earth was the fixed center of the universe and every other body revolved around it. Some bodies had rather erratic orbits; nevertheless, even these completed a revolution around the earth, thus demonstrating that no other world occupied so central a position. The implications of such uniqueness of necessity carried with it the impression of importance. For to be at the focus of things is, of course, a heroic position. The earth, and therefore the people of the earth, were the most important (that is, valuable) of all the creatures in the cosmos. This was not only a secular, but also a religious view.

Now Copernicus was a troublemaker. For one thing, he made extremely careful and accurate observations. For another, he evidently did not feel threatened by the idea that man might be moved from the center of things out somewhere to a less imposing locale. By putting the *sun* in the center of the universe, he reduced the earth's importance by an exponential factor (that is, from a winner to an also-ran). Here we were just one of several other bodies circling the "real" center, the sun. Things of course were to get worse before they got better, for we were to soon learn that even the sun held a rather unimportant position somewhere near the edge of an unimpressive galaxy.

But Copernicus's discovery caused a great deal of consternation among the learned men of the period, many of whom simply refused to accept the theory. In psychological terms, they denied the existence of facts that would give rise to a devaluation of their self-image. They simply would not believe that they were not God's reason for creating the universe in the first place. For such a belief would force them to accept a much more humble position in the scheme of things.

Man hardly recovered from one trauma before he was confronted by another. Copernicus, Kepler, Galileo, and Newton each helped to move man further away from his favored position. However, what they did to diminish man in his own eyes was nothing compared to what was done by a certain biologist named Charles Darwin.

If the astronomers had moved us away from the heart of things, we were at least divine creatures, made in God's image, and meant to have dominion over all the beasts of the earth. Or were we? Not according to the interpreters of Darwin. We were just highly developed apes. We could talk and write, but these were minor differences. We were merely a continuation of the lower life forms. Nothing unique. Perhaps not even divine. We were merely a slightly higher form of gorilla.

This was too much. We would never accept the humiliation of being a mere animal. Darwin, like Copernicus, was met with scorn and derision. When truth clashes with the ego, truth does not always fare too well.

But science was not yet through. Victorian Europe was shortly to be confronted by a bombshell delivered by one Sigmund Freud. Not only are we all well-educated apes, Freud told a startled world, but we are not very nice apes at that. We are wild beasts, driven by powerful instincts for destruction and aggression which must always be held in check by the restraints of society. We are little more than dressed-up gorillas, controlling our sexual, destructive urges by a complex series of conventions that we have introjected from our parents and the rest of society. The only difference between us and the other crawling creatures is that our animal lusts are repressed.

Whether or not Freud's theories were sound is not important at the moment. Like those of Copernicus and Darwin, his ideas required a good deal of refinement as time went on. And new findings continue to shed more light on all these areas of inquiry. But the reception that all these men received was similar. Their theories were rejected not merely because they clashed with the then current orthodoxy but because they demeaned man's picture of himself in his own eyes. In a word, they were perceived as disparagement.

DISPARAGEMENT AS A WEAPON

Insults, embarrassments, humiliations, and deprecations are all used by people against one another. The aim of such treatment is usually to injure the other person by piercing the armor of his PR personality. Such conduct on the part of one person against another is an agressive act that employs psychological weaponry. The most serious use of such a tactic occurs when it is directed against children.

The child is the crucible in which the concept of self-esteem is forged. And true self-esteem is, as we have noted earlier, a confidence in one's own worth. A child's self-esteem develops out of contacts with significant others who communicate his worth to him in many ways. But a lack of this feeling can easily be engendered in a child by parents or others who continually make derisive remarks about him.

Imagine, on the one hand, a child who is continually praised and encouraged by his parents for his many and varied efforts; and on the other hand, a child who is always berated, made fun of, and told of his stupidity. The former is likely to develop a feeling of confidence in his own capacities, while the latter may come to perceive himself as incompetent, inept, and worthless.

The victim of these devaluing perceptions will often be subjected to what is sometimes called pathological anxiety. Brandon refers to it as "a crisis of self-esteem—any threat to a man's ego—anything which he experiences as a danger to his mind's efficacy and control—is a potential source of pathological anxiety" (Brandon, 1969).

Although disparagement is a devastating weapon when used against a child, it is also quite potent when directed against adults as well. Many of the arguments that people engage in are really exchanges of verbal barbs directed from one person to another in an attempt to undermine the other's self-image. Some cocktail parties are virtual battlegrounds for insult flinging where women can criticize one another's clothing and men can ridicule each other's romantic prowess.

Once again, it is the person with doubts about himself who is more vulnerable to these kinds of attacks. Some people are literally terrified when entering a room full of people for fear that they will say or do something that will bring shame down on them and make them the butt of ridicule. To humiliate, shame, or embarrass someone is therefore a powerful kind of disparagement, especially in front of a large number of other people.

There are many ways in which these weapons are made potent. Almost any indication that a person is not up to par in some conventionally accepted virtue is enough to evoke strong feelings of inferiority. The man who is cowardly, the girl who is promiscuous, the woman whose house is messy, the man who is impotent or the woman who is frigid, the boy who strikes out, the girl who is unpopular, the businessman who is revealed as a swindler, the sick person; all may feel that they are something less than they would like to be. And others, by calling attention to their particular shortcoming, can cause them a great deal of anguish.

Sometimes a person with the best of intentions may do something that is seen by another person as an insult. There is, for example, a very fine line drawn by many people between sympathy and pity. Although most of us will accept and appreciate sympathy from others, pity is something else. The reason for the different reactions lies in the subtle differences in the implications of the two terms.

Sympathy is an understanding or, as one dictionary puts it, "a fellow feeling or correspondence of sensation of affections." It is therefore an expression of feeling between equals. The recipient of sympathy perceives himself on the same level as the one who expresses the feeling.

Pity, on the other hand, has come to carry an intimation of derision. "I pity him" has come sometimes to be a kind of insult. This results from the fact that pity establishes the person pitied as lower in status than the pitier. It is for this reason that people often object to being helped by others, especially if that help appears to come out of a feeling of pity.

Help itself can also be perceived as a disparagement if it is offered in a condescending way. If the attitude that accompanies it seems to say, "You poor thing, I've got to help you because you are so unfortunate" (that is, helpless, unheroic, and so on), the help will more often be resented than appreciated.

Of course anything that lowers the status of another person is seen as disparagement. Therefore, any kind of treatment, from discrediting a person's reputation to taking away his key to the executive washroom, qualifies.

Some kinds of disparagement occur in industry, where certain status symbols can be dispensed or withheld. Packard (1959) describes cases where the furnishings of an office can subtly tell an executive that his status is lower or higher than another. The size of the office is one indication. So is the wood out of which the desk is made. Plush carpeting and furniture also attest to the standing of the person, as does the view from his windows. Use of the executive dining room and company paid membership in a country club are other kinds of evidence.

Sometimes there is a kind of backbiting conflict between people in industry who are all struggling to improve their status in the hierarchy of the organization. When new college-trained men and women are placed in higher positions than oldtime "managerial" people, they are viewed as "college punks" by the "regulars," who have a grand time "batting down or slyly sabotaging bright ideas staff men have for improving their own methods of operating."

Anything that can be made to puncture the facade that a person tries to present to the world is fair game. A member of the family can easily embarrass the other members by doing something in public which would cast aspersions on their "respectability," "integrity," "right-mindedness," and so on. Father coming home drunk, daughter living with a man, little Jimmy being expelled from school, Aunt Sarah being put away in a mental institution. All of these, if made public, may cause great concern among the members of the family while they may be almost ignored if they don't come to light. The concern in such cases is usually "What will the neighbors think?" Translated into therapeutic language, "What are you doing to our image in the neighborhood?"

The interesting thing to notice in this syndrome is that the other people involved who are supposed to be concerned with the welfare of the "deviant" are actually far more disturbed by the fact that whatever has transpired will reflect badly on *themselves*. The fact that Jimmy or Aunt Sarah have a problem which may be very difficult and distressing to them is a secondary consideration, if it is considered at all. It is the concern with the image that is paramount here, and such concern is susceptible to disparagement.

A mother much concerned with her image traveled a great deal about the country with her children. They would stop en route to have their meals in restaurants wherever they happened to be at mealtime. The mother always admonished the children to "leave some food on their plate" so that the waiters would not think "we are pigs." Even if the children were still hungry, they were not allowed to finish their food. The woman felt greatly threatened by the fact that perfect strangers might have a low opinion of her if she and her children did not conform to certain "respectable" forms of behavior. Her great fear was to be perceived as a person without breeding. This fear was greatly exaggerated because of the fact that she had come from very humble beginnings. Anything, therefore, that appeared vulgar or indecorous was extremely demeaning if it was associated with her in any way.

SEX AS A WEAPON

Sex can be used as a weapon in a number of ways. Since sexual behavior is often considered bad, dirty, or sinful in our society, people frequently come to be ashamed of their own sexual feelings or behavior. Some men use sex as a weapon of destruction against women.

J. had a pathological hatred for women because of a strong repressed hatred for a domineering, castrating mother. Sex, he believed, was degrading both to men and women, but most especially to women. (This has been a very generally held belief in America, and a clear statement of the double standard, with which we will deal later.) The way for J. to destroy women was therefore to seduce them. He was rather handsome and smooth, and so he was reasonably successful in his pursuits. He did not enjoy sex most of the time and found that he could feel respect only for those girls who refused him. He finally married a frigid woman and held her in very high esteem until, through therapy, she acquired the ability to have orgasm. This precipitated so much friction that the couple separated a number of times and were finally divorced.

Another way that sex can be used as a weapon is through the use of rejection. A woman rejecting a man's advances or a man turning down an obvious offer by a woman are both making an implicit statement to the victim about his or her sexual attractiveness. Since sex is highly valued by most people, such treatment is not always accepted graciously, although the outward behavior may attempt to conceal this fact. The rebuffed person often feels terribly depressed, because sexual attractiveness is the heroic trait that leads to the greatest rewards. The hero is, of course, never rejected completely. He may occasionally be forced to overcome some token resistence, but this is a kind of parrying in the jousting between lovers. In the end he always gets his woman. Moreover, he is desired by all women, so rejection is impossible for him. An even worse rejection is to be informed *after* intercourse that the partner did not enjoy it. This is particularly devastating, as sexual prowess is an extremely important heroic virtue.

Sex is often used by parents as a weapon against children. Adults often do not realize what damage they can do to a child in this way. The disparagement comes from the parents' vindictive attitude toward the child's normal sexuality. Their disapproval and punishment for any kind of sexually related behavior, from mere curiosity to masturbation, may stigmatize the child in his own mind. Moreover, threats of punishment (such as castration, insanity, or blindness) may produce a conditioned fear or distaste that will accompany any erotic thought or action for many years thereafter, giving rise to a feeling of self-reproach whenever sexual stimulation occurs.

Sexuality itself, high sex drive, or promiscuity in sexual behavior has been perceived as disparaging, especially for women, for a long time. A woman pointed out and whispered about was often persecuted mercilessly for her "misbehavior" and was generally considered unacceptable in the presence of "decent" people. Derogatory names (hussy, slut, tramp, harlot) were hurled at her and she was generally ostracized by all but those in the same circumstances. Nathaniel Hawthorne's novel *The Scarlet Letter* clearly depicts the attitudes of early America with regard to childbearing out of wedlock. The heroine, Hester, was forced to wear a brightly colored letter sewed to her dress so that all could see her "disgrace." She was thus stigmatized in the eyes of the community and treated as an undesirable. Although this took place in sixteenth-century Salem, the attitude toward female sexuality, although not the treatment, has endured until relatively recent times.

OTHER KINDS OF DEROGATION

People sometimes feel humiliated by certain societal conditions which are not always intended to have such an effect. People on relief during the Depression were often ashamed to let their neighbors know their plight, and those on welfare today often feel stigmatized when they have to present their food stamps in the neighborhood market. While these poeple are affected by their inability to earn a living, some workers feel that *they* are being taken advantage of by these very same people. The workers generally have hard, unpleasant jobs which they have held for a lifetime with little or no advancement, and they see welfare recipients doing almost as well financially without working at all. These workers therefore come to "feel like suckers," especially because their taxes are paying to "support those free-loaders."

A person who finds himself in an environment that is generally peopled by those of a "higher" station in life can also begin to feel extremely uncomfortable.

A man with little education was invited to a party where most of the guests were professional people. Their conversation was polite and often directed to him. But his discomfort continued to grow. How could he respond to such statements as: "The criteria for any kind of judgment in such an area have to be empirical." He wasn't sure about two words in the sentence and besides that, he was not clear about what "area" they were discussing. As the evening wore on, he found himself left out of the activities more and more. First they stopped directing their words to him and finally they stopped looking at him entirely. This was not done out of malice, but merely because he continually failed to reinforce their earlier remarks by any kind of response. In the end, they came to act as if he were not there.

The same kind of feeling is reported when someone finds himself in a place where, because of his clothes, dialect, or appearance, he is shown to be "beyond his social depth." In such a situation, even though those present may try to ignore the obvious breach of decorum, their very politeness may be perceived as insulting, since there is an unspoken condescension built into the situation itself.

Mr. and Mrs. B. were invited to a country club dance by a relative somewhat more successful in the business world. Mrs. B. wore a rather fashionable party dress and her husband looked terribly uncomfortable in his rented tuxedo. Although the guests at their table were gracious and considerate, the couple could not shake the feeling of embarrassment which plagued them all evening. The more considerate the others were, the more they were made to feel like clods. The message that was communicated to them was: "You are not as polished and genteel as we, but we are generous and kind and can overlook that. We like you in spite of your poor breeding and humble origins."

The waiters and waitresses were not as kind as the other guests and continually expressed their feelings in derogatory looks and gestures, which were seen only by the unfortunate couple. Afterward the help at the country club expressed their discontent at "having the Club degraded by allowing people of low station on the premises."

THE CONSEQUENCES OF DISPARAGEMENT

The victim of any kind of disparagement undergoes a variety of unpleasant experiences. Physiologically there are a number of autonomic changes, such as sudden changes in skin color (blushing or blanching); increase or decrease in pulse and blood pressure; alterations in the respiratory rhythm; perhaps the secretion of adrenalin or noradrenalin; increased muscular tension, especially in the gastrointestinal area; and other kinds of measurable responses, such as an increased GSR.[2]

Behaviorally there are other kinds of responses. There may be a kind of withdrawal physically, so that the person simply removes himself. Or there may be less complete withdrawal in which case the victim may merely lower his eyes, bow his head, or turn his attention to something else (Carlson, 1970). Some of his actions may be a kind of acknowledgement of his own error. He may cover his head with his hands or his his head with the heel of his hand. He may become visibly unnerved by the incident, manifesting various kinds of discomfort by fidgeting, shaking, twisting things in his hands, wringing his (empty) hands, furtively glancing about, or he may pace back and forth. His speech may be awkward, he may stammer, begin phrases and stop abruptly, the pitch of his voice may suddenly change, he may have to swallow hard and often, or he may be completely unable to speak.

Although these behavioral changes may inform others of his plight, the subjective experiences that accompany feelings of deprecation are by far the most important as well as the most disturbing.

One of the most common responses to almost all disparaging situations is, as noted earlier, a diminution of self-esteem. Any evidence that a person is not as "good" as he thought himself to be is met with a good deal of disappointment. In such a situation, the person becomes dissatisfied with himself, feels unhappy because of his limitations, and tends to berate himself.

Such a response is particularly true of one whose PR image is extremely important to him. Since the PR image is unrealistic, such a person is continually meeting with disappointments in his expectations about himself. That is, he hopes (expects) to be "good" or "successful" at many things, but he keeps falling short of his mark. Each of these "failures" causes him to reassess his value in this new light, and every instance is met with a further lowering of his self-esteem.

The lowering of self-esteem in turn gives rise to frustration, hostility, depression, or anxiety. It also often gives rise to compensatory measures intended to bolster the tottering self-image. Such measures raise the entire conflict to a higher level by attempting to further inflate the PR image. But these tactics are doomed to failure, for just as the earlier expectancies were disappointed, so will these later ones fail to materialize.

The feeling of shame is another subjective experience which accompanies disparagement. Shame has been defined as the discrepancy between the idealized self (that is, the PR image) and the self as it is actually perceived in those moments when it is unmasked. Actually, the feeling of shame is usually associated with the fact that others can, at least potentially, see the discrepancy which the person is trying to hide. This gives one the feeling that he is literally "naked" or "undressed" and that others are witnesses to his predicament.

The experience induces a strong desire to hide, to withdraw, in order to be out of the sight of others. It is as if the actual glances of other people induce a kind of psychic pain which can only be alleviated by getting out of their presence. It is an extremely uncomfortable feeling, but it does diminish slightly as soon as the victim gets out of sight of other people.

The feeling does not disappear completely, however, for there is always one observer who cannot be avoided. That one is, of course, the self. Therefore, shame is felt when a person does not live up to the criteria which he himself has set. It is true, of course, that many of these criteria have been accepted by him because of the influence of others—parents, peers, authority figures—but it is only *his* acceptance of such standards, his belief that these criteria are valid in some sense, that affects his feelings so strongly. If a person, for example, did not believe that being poor was a disgrace, he would not feel ashamed to have this fact brought to light; in fact, there have been times when being "poor but honest" was a badge of honor for many.

A person may also experience shame when he deviates too far from the norm in an attribute that he cannot control. Goffman (1963) refers to "abominations of the body," by which he means various kinds of physical deformity. People with these kinds of problems often feel extremely uncomfortable in the presence of "ordinary" people. This occurs, he believes, because the "normals believe the person with the stigma is not quite human." One can readily see how devastating such an attitude must be on the victim. If, in fact, the disabled person believes that all normal people view him as something less than human, he may come to perceive himself in that light. His feelings of depreciation will therefore be very intense indeed.

> A young girl who had been born with a clubfoot was continually made fun of by other children. She gradually began to shy away from them because she thought that she was a kind of freak who should not associate with other children. Although their taunts hurt her deeply, she became convinced that they were justified and began to perceive herself as a cursed individual who had probably done something terrible in an earlier life.

The permanently disabled person may suffer from an overwhelming feeling of depression. There is a powerful sense of futility in his life because he can do nothing about his plight and he has been led to see it as a mark of inferiority, inadequacy, abnormality, or worthlessness. Although he may try to hide his infirmity, the usual defensive techniques will not work well here. Denial, for example, is useless when one is afflicted with a defect that is clearly visible to all.

The consequences of disparagement are not always merely personal. They may be global. The feeling of disgrace suffered by the German people as a result of their defeat in World War I was never quite forgotten. For years they carried with them a sense of humiliation that they were anxious to overcome. They were in great need of a new philosophy which would change the image that they hated so.

Hitler was acutely aware of this feeling in the people and probably in himself also. He seized upon this great need to introduce into the thinking of the German people the new national PR image. "You are not failures," he explained. "You could have won the war, for you are more than mere men. You are Supermen. You didn't really lose to the enemy. You were betrayed from within. The Jews betrayed you and *they* are responsible for your shame."

Thus in one stroke Hitler absolved the German people of blame for their humiliating defeat, created a scapegoat, and at the same time presented the people with a new public image which they were eager to embrace. His technique was extremely successful, and he was able to win great numbers of people to his side, change the direction of an entire nation, and finally, involve most of the civilized nations of the world in a global war of massive proportions.

DISPARAGEMENT AS ANNIHILATION

The person who has made a great investment in his PR image has, of course, more to lose from attacks upon it. As was pointed out in Chapter 2, the more anxiety one feels regarding his real worth, the more he will try to inflate the value of his public self. In some cases a situation may be reached in which the person has totally lost touch with his real nature and believes himself to be, in fact, the false image that he has created. Under such circumstances, if one should suffer a severe disparagement, he may feel completely destroyed. Having no self but the one that he has invented, the disappearance of this image is the disappearance of the entire person. Extremely disturbed individuals sometimes believe that they are living in a shadow world in which nothing exists and that they themselves are unreal (Coleman, 1964). Rejection of the self, therefore, which comes as a result of rejection by others, can lead to severely painful feelings of nonbeing.

Another related kind of annihilation occurs as a result of what might be termed "existential emptiness." Experiments in sensory deprivation have shown that man needs sensory input if he is to retain his sanity (Bexton, et al., 1954). Clinical experience tends to show that emotional input is similarly essential.

If a person has lost touch with his own feelings as a result of denial, he has erected a psychological barrier against emotional input which is as real to him as any physical one. He may therefore suffer from emotional deprivation, with the result that most of his experiences reach him without having any impact. By screening out the emotional content of his awareness, his experience is impoverished. A feeling of nonbeing (existential emptiness) can easily become overwhelming under such circumstances. If, added to this, a person suffers continual rejection by people who are important to him (that is, he is ignored in situations where he feels he should be noticed), the result may be a sense of "not being there," of being a nonentity, of being invisible, lost, dead. The feeling is illustrated by the nihilistic delusions, which occur in severe form in paranoia. In these psychotic states, the person may believe that he has no brain, no insides, no feelings, or no experiencing (that is, no awareness).

Sometimes the prospect of death itself may be perceived as the ultimate form of humiliation. The idea of nonbeing, beside provoking a certain amount of fear, can also be seen as another form of valuelessness. For this and other reasons, many people refuse to face the fact that one day they will die. As May (1967) points out, by facing this (existential) fact of life one is able to experience "normal anxiety" about death. However, by repressing the normal anxiety (that is, by not dealing with the fact that one day he will no longer exist), a person is forced to project (blame) his anxiety on other things. Since this anxiety is misdirected, it is neurotic anxiety.

The need to continue to exist after "death" is, of course, reflected in many of man's myths. And as pointed out earlier, the hero, especially in American mythology, is often immortal. A belief in immortality, however, need not always be a reflection of a *need* for continued existence. It is true that in many cases it obviously is nothing more than that. But there are other reasons why men come to believe the things they believe. Psychologists must be careful in assigning the causes of all behavior to need (that is, deficiency states). As Maslow (1970) has shown, there are other kinds of motivation which may be more revealing of the nature of man.

If our heroes are immortal, then death is not heroic (that is, a deprecation). To some extent, our rituals with regard to death and burial are attempts to deny the finality and reality of death. We prepare the bodies of our deceased relatives in such a way as to simulate life. We are sometimes expected to be comforted in some way by the fact that so-and-so "looked so natural." The implication is, of course, that the departed person is not *completely gone*. Other ceremonial procedures intended to assure us of the continuation of the individual personality beyond the grave have similar effects. Although many of these rituals are intended to comfort the survivors, they also serve to communicate to the living that *they* will never die.

PSYCHOTHERAPY AS DISPARAGEMENT

One of the most important reasons that people seek psychotherapy is their concern with their perceptions of themselves. Almost the first complaint that one hears in the early interviews are such statements as, "I don't like myself," "I can't do anything," "I am worthless, useless—a nothing." In short, the person sees himself as an incompetent human being who is unable to manage his affairs with any kind of efficiency. He finally gives up and goes to an "expert," who he hopes will solve his problem for him. But this very action places him in the midst of a dilemma.

On the one hand, he ostensibly wants to become more competent, more useful, more autonomous, more self-sufficient. But by seeking the help of an expert, he is actually admitting that he is incapable of just such action. The feeling that one *cannot* do certain things is often a critical factor in this very inability. Moreover, in some psychotherapeutic relationships there may be a subtle communication from the therapist to the client which runs something like the following: "You are disturbed, ill, unbalanced, unlucky, and unfit (that is, you are unheroic). I, who am healthy, well, competent, and heroic, will put you on the right track."

Such a communication, although not intended, can be very clearly implied in the relationship, especially to one who is insecure about his capabilities anyway. The result can be one more bit of evidence confirming the suspicions which the client has had about himself all along. Perhaps one reason for the great success of group therapy is that it all but eliminates this problem. In a group setting, the client is more likely to perceive the others as people like himself, who help him with his problems, and *whom he helps with theirs*. The importance of helping others toward the development of a positive self-image cannot be overestimated. To be the "psychiatrist" instead of the "patient" is proof of one's worth and capability. No amount of advice or encouragement by another person is as helpful in aiding a person to gain a sense of mastery.

DEALING WITH DISPARAGEMENT

The feelings that have been described in connection with the syndrome are powerful, painful, and difficult to annul. The nature of the self-image is such that it is peculiarly vulnerable to disparaging attacks. In a sense, the self-image is perhaps the most valuable "possession" a person has. It is for *its* benefit that other "valuable" commodities are sought. A person seeks riches, fame, status, respect, and so on, to gain a view of himself that *he* can value. Some of these things may be worthwhile in themselves, but they are particularly useless if they do not also help a person develop a real feeling of self-esteem. Disparaging attacks, intended or not, have the effect of undermining this very important feeling.

What, then, can a person do to minimize or entirely eliminate the damage that disparagement can do? There are a number of things. Some kinds of responses are more effective than others.

defensive responses

A usual attempt to deal with threats against the ego (self-image) is to become very defensive about the particular trait. If someone attacks our intelligence, we may try to make a great show of erudition in order to disprove their allegation. Responses of this kind are unsatisfactory since they merely increase the falsity of the PR image and lead to greater problems later.

Another attempt to handle this kind of attack is to withdraw. In this situation we may feel that if we take ourselves out of the situation, we are no longer vulnerable. Although this may be the case, it is really avoiding the question rather than facing it. To leave the scene either physically or psychologically is a temporary palliative measure at best. It does not help a person's perception of himself to know that he had to run away from the threat of being insulted or humiliated. It merely confirms his own suspicion that he in fact deserves such treatment.

Another way to deal with the effects of disparagement is to try to build a kind of shell which says in effect, "I am invulnerable, I cannot be hurt by others." The difficulty with such a stance, however, is that there is a tendency under such conditions for the person to deny his real feelings. And in so doing, as noted earlier, he becomes alienated from himself. Health, whether physical or psychological, demands that one be in tune with all the vital functions of his body. Denial of feeling is hardly a step in that direction.

There are a number of therapies that attempt to deal with disparagement. Most of these will be considered in Chapter 13. For our purposes in this chapter we shall consider one therapeutic approach to altering one's evaluation of himself.

the rational method

Albert Ellis (1958) has tackled head-on the problem of disparagement. His approach is really quite simple. Ellis feels that most people base their beliefs and behaviors upon assumptions that in many cases are "irrational." These irrational beliefs lead to contradictions between thought and feelings. And such contradictions lead to various maladaptive kinds of behavior. To break this pattern, Ellis suggests that we reexamine our assumptions and consider more rational alternatives in their place.

For Ellis the very first irrational assumption is "the idea that it is a dire necessity for an adult to be loved or approved by almost everyone for virtually everything he does." Another assumption is related to the first. It is "the idea that one should be thoroughly competent, adequate, intelligent and achieving in all possible respects. . . ." These two assumptions, taken together, are the essential elements underlying most negative feelings about the self. Such attitudes practically guarantee disaster, for they ask the impossible. They demand infallibility and they are satisfied with nothing less. A person accepting these assumptions (and they are extremely widespread in our society) can permit nothing short of perfection in himself. And such impossible (unrealistic) ambitions must lead to serious disappointments.

an altered approach to obligation

Mrs. A., a young mother, sought help at a nearby clinic because she had been having extremely severe anxiety attacks. She was an intelligent woman of twenty-three who had been taught to believe that a woman's place is "taking care of her home and family without complaint." "A woman," her mother had always said, "should not want other things in life." But Mrs. A. *did* want other things. Moreover, she could not accept the things she thought she *should* want. She hated housework and wanted to go back to school to study law. As a result, she developed an image of herself as a worthless human being. In her mind, a woman who could not be happy in the role of wife and mother was "no good." Her anxiety attacks reflected her feelings of inadequacy.

The idea that one *ought* to want certain things is a prevailing one in our culture. Moreover, we are indoctrinated with these "oughts" at an extremely early age before we are able to develop critical judgment. But a person cannot *will* the feelings that he has. He cannot love someone simply because he *ought* to. Nor can he love the style of life that someone else has set for him. As a result, the person who cannot be what he has been told he *should* be feels that he has failed.

A solution to some of these kinds of problems lies in an altered view of what a person is *obligated* to do. As Ellis points out, most of our ideas about the things we should be and do are based upon irrational assumptions about the nature of man, the nature of woman, the nature of the universe, and so on. A reconsideration of some of these ideas may lead to a better way of being who we are instead of who we are supposed to be.

Psychologists of whatever persuasion generally agree that a person must be true to his own nature before he can become "well." What this means in terms of obligation is that one is obliged to acknowledge his own feelings without fearing their consequences. We must know how we feel. And we must accept our feelings without prejudging them by someone else's standards. If psychologists have discovered anything of which they can be reasonably certain, it is the fact that individual differences exist on any measure we wish to use. Each human being (and probably each animal as well) is separate and unique and can be compared to others only by ignoring these differences. *It is therefore irrational to make any general statement about all women, all children, all boys, and so on.*

To return to the problem of Mrs. A.: had she not believed that women *must* accept their role as prescribed by her mother and others, she would have had no problem. It was her acceptance of an irrational idea about the obligation of women that made her feel so worthless. Her obligation was *not* to acquire in her role but to *acknowledge her own nature and then strive to fulfill it.* When in the course of therapy she began to do this, her self-image began to change and her anxieties largely disappeared.

an altered approach to self-evaluation

The notion that one must be competent and achieving in all things and that he must also be loved and approved by everyone with whom he comes in contact is the underlying assumption of the PR personality. Along with this idea goes the belief that happiness is only possible when these requirements are met. In order to fulfill these demands, a person will have to play the role of the hero or suffer the humiliation of being the ordinary guy. But beside the fact that demands of this type lead to certain failure, the idea that happiness is only achievable when one is universally admired and/or completely expert in everything is an illusion. It is therefore an irrational belief. Happiness has very little to do with how *others* experience you, but *how you experience you.*

We are taught from childhood that we must excel, we must compete, we must be liked, admired, sought after, and respected. And we come to believe that our happiness, even our very psychological existence, depends upon such things. These beliefs can be shown to be false by empirical procedures: the incidence of unhappiness, suicide, and the like, is just as high among those who have great abilities and popularity as it is among those who apparently do not. But, more importantly, such beliefs are self-defeating. They can lead to only one result—destruction of one's evaluation of himself.

These kinds of beliefs therefore do not bring about the results for which they are originally adopted. Their purpose is to increase the happiness of the organism, but the adoption of these beliefs actually has the opposite effect. It increases the misery of the organism by presenting it with impossible goals.

It is not necessary to accept an idea simply because it happens to be commonplace. Most people once accepted the idea that the earth was flat. If the beliefs that we have been exploring subvert their purpose, what other beliefs might we consider that would not?

In order to understand what is about to be said, we must be prepared to jar our thinking into an unfamiliar path. We must be willing to drop all our usual assumptions and consider some very different ones. Let us see what they might be:

1. All human beings are intrinsically valuable because of the very fact that they exist.
2. Each individual is special and important because he is *unique.*
3. Each human being can and must accept his imperfections as parts of his uniqueness.
4. A person need not feel degraded, useless, worthless, because he "fails" in certain endeavors.
5. The concept of "worthiness" can exist without its opposite, "worthlessness." Every concept does not necessarily have to be countered by a contradictory one. This is simply a convention of Western civilization. But there is no law that states that all values must have negative counterparts.
6. There need be no rank ordering of value among human beings. All individuals are appraised as universally valuable.

The last assumption is a particularly difficult one for Americans. We have been conditioned to make most of our evaluations by comparisons. Our only criteria for judging ourselves and others is whether or not we are bigger, stronger, taller, prettier than someone else. And because there are superficial differences of these types which can be observed, we make the mistake that the taller, stronger, or prettier one is somehow more worthwhile. If, however, we can come to realize that each of us, no matter what his attributes, has an intrinsic, unchangeable worth, then our self-esteem need never be shaken by any external event.

We can approach this problem from another point of view. If a human being is to be valued for what he *is*, then it is necessary for us to redefine his *is-ness.* As we have seen, we can view an individual objectively, as a collection of *attributes*, or existentially as a center of awareness. But viewing a person in terms of his attributes forces us to *compare* him with others. This leads to differing evaluations of individuals. The person who has more heroic attributes becomes more valuable than those who are less well endowed. But is it rational to make such appraisals in terms of human beings?

Do we really want to say that someone who is younger, or taller, or prettier, or stronger, or healthier, or even kinder than someone else is therefore really more worthwhile in a real sense?

It is irrational to evaluate human beings in this way for two reasons. In the first place, it is unlikely that anyone really believes that handsome people, for example, are really more valuable than homely ones. In the second place, if we use such criteria, every one of us will find ourselves inadequate, and therefore experience disparagement, in any number of areas. This makes the use of such a criterion self-defeating.

There is another problem related to the person-as-collection-of-attributes model. Since no two people perceive an individual in exactly the same way, *there is no real person-as-object*. There are as many different perceptions of an individual as there are observers, so the attributes we like or dislike in ourselves may not even exist for someone else. But if the self-as-object is unreal, what self *is* real?

The one reality that we can all accept, is the reality of our own existence. Descartes said, "I think, therefore I am." Our own experience is the proof of our being. We are the ongoing process which informs us of the fact that *anything* exists at all. We may not be the center of the universe in the way that Ptolemy believed, but we are certainly the center of the only universe that we will ever know.

Each of us is *a vortex of awareness, a focus of experience, a center of consciousness*. This is what we are most certainly, and if we think of ourselves in this way, how can we ever say that one individual consciousness is in any way more or less valuable than any other? Although my attributal self may be compared with others, my existential self is beyond all comparison. Its value is in its very existence. It cannot be disparaged because it is void of any qualities that can be compared with any other consciousness.

One young man was asked by a solicitous questioner what he could do better than anyone else. It was the assumption of the person who asked the question that everyone has some attribute at which he excels. Thus the question was intended to help the young man discover this attribute in order to increase his self-esteem. But the answer that the questioner received was one that he was probably not prepared for. For the young man, who seemed very comfortable and self-assured, replied, "I can be *me* better than anyone else in the world."

This is the real answer to the question. Each one of us can be the unique individual self that we are, better than anyone else. And it is impossible to compare such individuals because it is like comparing apples and oranges. *We are all best at being different and unique.* If we can come to perceive ourselves this way, we cannot be disparaged. And the feelings that accompany that experience will largely disappear from our lives.

This is, of course, an ideal statement of what our aims might be. Although we may never reach the state in which we are completely invulnerable to derisive attacks, from a practical standpoint all we need do is to make progress in approaching this goal. A clear vision of a person's intrinsic worth makes him almost impervious to disparagement of any kind. Moreover, this vision dispenses with the necessity for an exaggerated PR image. Once a person perceives himself as worthwhile, he has no need to continue to present falsified versions of himself and the world.

disparagement and the healthy individual

A person with a firm idea of who he is is free to experience his own feelings. Insults and disparaging situations do not touch him very deeply. He knows who he is and he likes who he is. Or if there is something about himself that he does not like, he can face that fact and perhaps try to change it. But he can only change something about himself when he admits it exists. If he denies it because it is "bad," then he can do nothing about it.

The authentic person is in touch with his own being in a very intimate sense. And he comes to admire himself partly because of this intimacy. But the essential fact about the healthy person is that he can explore his own experience without fear that it may betray him as a worthless individual. He can also feel comfortable with other people because he knows that revealing his true nature to others will bring them closer to him.

[1] Although changes are beginning to occur in this area, many American women are still influenced by traditional standards.

[2] Galvanic skin response—a measure of the electrical conductivity of the skin, which tends to increase with increased tension or emotion.

VI / Educational Implications of Self Theory

So long as he keeps his self-respect, an individual can endure anything no matter how grievous. But let him lose that and he will be incapable of joy, creativity, perhaps even of life itself.

Rabbi Milton Steinberg

Educational Implications

Wallace D. LaBenne and Bert I. Greene

What does self-concept theory mean for schools, education and teaching? What current practices does it question, negate, or support? What new directions does it suggest for curriculum, methodology, and classroom experience?

Self-Concept and the Education Process

When the child enters kindergarten, he does not arrive as a simplified personality with singular attitudes, ideals, feelings, and traits. Instead, he arrives in a malleable state which is the result of the interaction of many past experiences. It is highly unlikely that these experiences were all similar, that is, that they were all either negative or positive. Rather, it is to be expected that the impact of some of these experiences arose from their competing with some of his other experiences. His present concept of self, and his relationship to the other children and to the teacher, is profoundly affected by such factors as his social-class membership, family structure, parental behaviors, ethnic background, religion, and the language spoken in the home. If his self-concept could be seen at this particular time, it would probably be labeled "developmental" (in-process). Although the child has already developed a concept of himself, he has also experienced the variability of human nature. That is, he knows he may succeed at many of his endeavors, but he should also expect that he might fail to attain some of his goals. At this point, however, his image of himself is not fixed and rigid.

The feelings one develops about oneself are formed quite early in life and are modified by subsequent experiences. The fact that the significant people who come and go in a child's life, leaving an indelible mark on how he views himself, are many and varied leads us to believe that the basic factor in the development of self-image is flexibility. This is perhaps the most important point for the educational practitioner to keep in mind—that the child's self-concept is not unalterably fixed, but is modified by every life experience, both in and out of the classroom, at least through the maturing years. If this were not the case, then we would have to face the alternative of suggesting that there is really little or nothing educators can do to enhance a

From Wallace D. LaBenne and Bert I. Greene, EDUCATIONAL IMPLICATIONS OF SELF-CONCEPT THEORY. Copyright © 1969 by Goodyear Publishers, Inc., pp. 22-34. Reprinted with permission.

student's feelings about himself. This premise is self-defeating, because it appears that future success or failure is preordained, that the action one takes will have little impact on what one can become, and that there is a special mysticism surrounding all educational practice. To accept such a premise is to suggest that some people must live with hopelessness and futility, and this denies the basic premises upon which our educational system is built.

On the other hand, the suggestion that teachers are among a number of significant others in a student's life, and that there might be some competition in their influence, is not meant to imply that teachers can take their task too lightly. Exactly how important a teacher can be in the life of any child can be seen in the countless testimonials given each year by people who recall that the most significant person in their lives was their teacher. The opposite is equally true. There are untold thousands who were psychologically maimed by teachers while they were in school. Many of these people have since married and now have children of their own in school. These parents subtly transmit their own fears, anxieties, and hostilities toward school and school personnel to their children. It is little wonder that teachers may have difficulty explaining their function to some parents. A parent who has been hurt by a teacher will jealously guard his child from the onslaught of another teacher.

Evidence of Self-Concept Influences

Empirical and experimental data clearly indicate a direct relationship between the child's self-concept and his manifest behavior, perceptions, and academic performance. Lecky[1] was one of the first investigators to demonstrate that low academic achievement was often due to a child's definition of himself as a nonlearner. Walsh[2] found that "high ability, low achievers" had a negative self-regard when matched with "high ability, high achievers." Benjamins,[3] Reeder,[4] and Buckley and Scanlan[5] presented additional data to demonstrate that a person's self-concept has a direct bearing on his intellectual efficiency.

Brookover, Thomas, and Paterson[6] found a statistically significant positive correlation between self-concept and perceived evaluations of significant others, general performance in academic subjects, and achievement in specific subject-matter fields. Perkins[7] found that teachers who had taken certain course in mental hygiene and child development were able to promote healthier personality growth in children. Healthy personality growth was defined in terms of the degree of congruence between the real self and the ideal self. Cutler and McNeil[8] demonstrated that when mental health consultants worked directly with teachers, the teachers developed greater skill in child management which had beneficial effects for the student indirectly. Davidson and Lang[9] showed that the more positive the children's perception of their teacher's feelings toward them, the better was their achievement and the more desirable was their classroom behavior. In a study of emotionally handicapped children, LaBenne[10] found a highly significant relationship between the teacher's self-concept and the pupil's perception of himself in the classroom

Self-concept as a factor which influences behavior patterns and adjustment was studied by Martire[11] and Steiner[12] Both of these investigators found corraborative evidence for a positive relationship between self-concept and social adjustment. Sheerer[13] demonstrated that there was a positive correlation between acceptance of self and acceptance of and respect for others. Stock[14] also found that when a person's feelings about himself changed, his attitude toward others changed in the same direction.

Other researchers have reported finding similar effects of the self-concept on learning and behavior. More important perhaps is the fact that most experienced teachers can recite a great many examples in which a student's conception of his abilities severely restrict his achievement, even though his real abilities may be superior to those which he demonstrates. It is not infrequently that some students will insist they cannot do a task, almost before they have an opportunity to examine the nature of the work. Nor is it unheard of for some students to offer an apology before they answer a question. Which teacher has not heard some modification of the comment, "I'm probably wrong..." or "This may be a silly question, but...'"? This type of behavior should be carefully noted, because it might provide, along with additional behavioral evidence, some information about the student's self-concept.

In addition, teachers who gain a measure of intimacy with students can report the many cases in which objectively attractive young people avoid social situations because of subjective feelings of unattractiveness. The point to be made here is that the "facts" as they may seem to an outsider do not necessarily appear to the behaver in the same way. It is not the objective event itself which elicits the specific response, but rather the individual's subjective experience of the event. People react to the same circumstances in different manners, and the way a person behaves is a result of how he perceives the situation at the time of his action. How a person acts and learns is a product of unique and personal meanings, which may, and often does, vary from one person to another.

EDUCATIONAL INFLUENCES

In any consideration of the educational implications of self-concept, a relevant aspect is the student's concept of his ability to learn certain types of academic behaviors. Combs points out that the circular effect of a given concept of self is inability to read:

> Such a child is likely to avoid reading, and thus the very experience which might change his concept of self is bypassed. Worse still, the child who believes himself unable to read, confronted with the necessity for reading, is more likely than not to do badly. The external evaluation of his teachers and fellow pupils, as well as his own observations of his performance, all provide proof to the child of how right he was in the first place! The possession of a particular concept of self tends to produce behavior that corroborates the self-concept with which the behavior originated.[15]

Some people have firm images of themselves as people who cannot learn foreign languages, mathematics, statistics, or some other subject. It is an interesting question to ponder whether a person cannot learn mathematics because he does not like it, or whether he does not like it because he cannot learn it. The answer is academic and not readily apparent, but the two factors appear to vary together; that is, they are correlated. It is probably true that a person's attitude toward a subject is an overriding factor. On the other hand, there is no denying that his attitude is often reinforced by his poor performance. Any attempt to separate these two factors is like arguing over whether length or width contributes more to the area of a rectangle.

The conceptions of an inability to learn appear to be self-fulfilling prophecies. That is, the types of experiences that might alter the notions a student holds about himself are purposely avoided. Instead of obtaining more practice in an area of weakness, the student avoids any further experiences with the subject. The resultant effect is that low-ability level is perpetuated. If, however, for some reason he must take a test or otherwise demonstrate some competency in the area, his attitude will be influenced by his ability, and in this instance both may be rather weak.

Social psychologists clearly state that a person's self-concept is learned through interpersonal encounters with significant others. This becomes a very important dimension of the teaching-learning act, and provides the teacher an opportunity to become a significant other in the life of a student. Any person who is intimately involved in the administration of rewards and punishments is in a position to become a significant other. Rather, it is the manner in which he uses his authority that causes him to have a potent impact.

The influence of schooling, in the narrow sense of the term, or education in the broader sense, may have a positive, negative, or neutral effect on a child's concept of self. Whether planned or unplanned, the influence of the school or, more specifically, the teachers, has a great deal to do with the developing self-concept. We should like to examine some teaching activities, therefore, which have specific reference and meaning for the development of the self-image.

TEACHERS MUST BE HONEST

We have indicated that people behave in terms of how they see themselves, and this perception in turn influences how things appear to them. The principle implied here is that behavioral change will not occur until the concept of self has been modified. What does this mean for teachers? Some teachers conscientiously avoid making any reference to a student's ability even though they use ability groupings in their classroom. They divide their class into three or four reading groups, call them after a color or species of bird, but never make any reference to the ability level of each of these groups. This game teachers play with themselves amuses the students. Each student is not only aware of which group he is a member, but he is also able to rank-order the groups according to ability. Where ability grouping is used throughout an entire school, the students have little difficulty in distinguishing the various ability levels. A low-ability class once shocked the teacher, because some of the students noted that they were in the "dumb room." This was not said in malice or hurt, but was an honest appraisal. Teachers, however, fear to be as blunt with their students as the students are with the teacher. Instead, they continue to act and treat the class as if each student were identical with the next. They forcefully refrain from making any reference to the varying abilities and other differences among students.

In contrast, another condition which frequently exists in our schools is that teachers take the opportunity to talk with the student about his abilities. During these discussions, it is not unusual for teachers to purposely distort the evidence and go out of their way to provide false praise for poor performance. The student is not fooled by this sham; he knows who he is and what he can do based on actual experience. No passing grade can make him deny his experiences when he must work alongside his classmates each day. This does not mean that the student does not want to get a good grade, or does not want to believe that he is doing his work satisfactorily. Whatever he wants to believe must ultimately be tested against the reality of his experiences. Teachers who behave in this fashion probably do so out of a false notion of kindness. Perhaps they feel that by withholding the truth and providing praise they will not hurt the student's feelings. The kindest approach, however, would be to be completely honest with the students.

When children have the security that the teacher accepts them for what they are as worthy beings, there is no need to give false praise or to disguise the facts with sugarcoating. If children know the teacher is "on their side," they can profit from the truth about their achievements and constructively build upon the knowledge of their needs and current weaknesses. Indeed, there is no other way to assist them in appraising their present progress and establishing next-step plans in terms of what is yet to be accomplished. Confrontation with reality in an atmosphere of warmth and acceptance is imperitive for an accurate view of self.

We have in education today something that is known to teachers as "social promotion." It is not our purpose to examine all the pros and cons here, but we would like to examine one instance in which this system might be damaging to children in the developmental stage of self-concept. Many teachers take advantage of this situation to avoid confronting students with their abilities as manifested in their classroom performance. The most they can hope to accomplish by this action is to postpone the reckoning that must come sooner or later. We have seen children in the later elementary grades who have finally had to come to grips with their abilities. Many of these children seemed to believe that they could perform at a level much higher than they actually did. The reason they gave for this belief was that, after all, they had been promoted every year since they entered school. We do not mean to imply here that social promotion is a dangerous process or that it is harmful to students. What we are saying is that it *could* be harmful, and the antidote is for teachers to be honest with students and help them recognize their weaknesses as well as their strenghts. Furthermore, teachers must become convinced of the value of rewarding each student for gains that are made in respect to individual desires. There is no reason why students must always be compared to a total class or group. Somewhere in the curriculum and during each day, students must be given opportunities to work to their own expectations, and they should be rewarded when they make significant gains in these endeavors.

It has been said many times before that "Nothing succeeds like success." This, however, does not mean that we can tell a student he is doing well when he is not. This axiom can be made operational only when teachers provide meaningful activities in which students can explore and discover the personal meaning of events for themselves. To do this demands that teachers know the students and select for them experiences that provide, at a minimum, the opportunity for success. Studies in achievement motivation have documented that when the task is seen as being virtually impossible of attainment, there is no shame in failure. Where the task is viewed as being ridiculously easy, there is no desire to perform. The most adequate tasks, in terms of incentive and satisfaction, are those which contain a probable chance of success. The mandate is clear: To help a child develop a positive self-concept, one must help him select experiences which provide a challenge, and at the same time help him maximize his opportunities for success.

This mandate is more easily said than done, because it demands a clear recognition that there can be no predetermined standards for an entire class. Each student must be viewed as a separate entity and learning tasks must be tailored, insofar as possible, for each student even though the entire class is being taught at the same time. To insist that class standards exist is not only to ignore the fundamental principles of child growth and development which state that each child grows, develops, and learns at differing rates, but is also a clear distortion of the concept of a class average. A class average is obtained by a statistical consideration of the performance of all the students. This means that some students are above average and some are below. If all students were performing at a high level, then the class average would be higher, but there would still be some students above and below the average.

PREDETERMINED DECISIONS

One of the most damaging and vicious practices in our public schools today is the tendency on the part of some teachers to make judgments about a student on the basis of his cumulative record, without ever having seen the student. This practice denies the student any credit for growth that might have been made during the summer months. Furthermore, it often reinforces the bias of the preceding teacher without an opportunity to collect the evidence firsthand. Teachers might be further ahead if they did not avail of the opportunity to view the cumulative recurd until after the first marking period. This approach would force them to base their evaluations on behavioral evidence rather than hearsay. Perhaps this procedure would be unnecessary if all teachers really believed that it was their function "to take the child where he is," but unfortunately this is not the case. The many years that this slogan has been preached by professors of education has had relatively little impact on teachers. For some strange and undefined reason, there is a great deal of security in following a lock-step curriculum.

Many teachers cry out to be creative and innovative, but surprisingly few are willing to provide similar opportunities for the students. What teachers fail to recognize is that quite often students know more about the teacher than he knows about the students. The well-developed grapevine works most effectively among students. We recall quite vividly a second-grade teacher who conducted a unit on chickens each year. It wa amazing to observe the responses of children upon learning that they would be in her room for the following year. Although they knew almost exactly what she would do, they all wanted to go through the experience themselves. There are two points to be made here: (1) the students enjoyed the security of knowing what would be forthcoming, and (2) although they knew in advance what the teacher would do, they never behaved in a manner to force her to modify her teaching.

Students certainly deserve every bit as much consideration as teachers themselves. Even if a teacher knows firsthand about a student, he has an obligation to give the student a fair trial when he arrives in the new class. To classify him on the basis of another teacher's experience with him is to do a grave injustice to the student and to make a mockery of the word "education."

STUDENTS BECOME WHAT THEY ARE THOUGHT TO BE

The teacher who believes in the fixed or static character of pupil abilities, interests, traits, and values is quite likely to convey this attitude and provide experiences that maintain and perpetuate these same self-concepts. If a teacher believes that a student is a failure, he may provide him with experiences so shallow that he could not possibly fail. The challenge will not be there, and the student will view it as "mickey mouse." Or, the teacher may not adjust the program to the pupil's abilities so that he will consistently do less well than other students. In either case, the student will soon learn that he does not belong. If he is provided with failure after failure, we can expect that sooner or later he will come to believe he is a failure and will act like one.

None of us would long continue to drive a car if each time we got into a car we also got into an accident. Sooner or later we would run out of excuses and begin to believe that we are "accidents about to happen." The same is true of children: they cannot long tolerate consistent failure without having something happen to them. Indeed, what happens is that they begin to see themselves as being persistent failures in school and are just waiting for the time they can leave school. These students are psychological dropouts long before they become physical dropouts. The evidence is mounting to support the theory that dropouts are made in the elementary school, not in the secondary school. When they do finally leave school (which, because of compulsory attendance, is quite likely to be the high school), their departure will be based on a decision that was a long time aborning; it will not be a hastily made decision.

As we said earlier in this chapter, the student entering school is malleable; his self-concept is in the process of developing. How teachers treat him and react toward him becomes a factor in how he views himself. Experiences may cause him to become locked in a certain stage of developmental progression. The consequence is tragic for the child who happens to be slower at the onset of his academic career. The student who is seen by his teachers to be handsome but slow, brilliant but careless, average but mischievous, talented but lazy will behave accordingly. Until a student is presented with other evidence and experiences, he will remain incarcerated in these pockets of self-concept.

SUMMARY

In this chapter the central place of the teacher as an agent influencing the developing self-concept of the student is emphasized. Numerous studies indicate a direct relationship between the child's self-concept and his manifest behavior, perceptions, and academic performance. The manner of the teacher in presenting the subject matter is of critical importance,

166

because teaching activities have specific reference and meaning for the development of the student's self-concept. Some of these activities are internalized by the student as being self-defeating, and the circular effects of these conceptions reinforce an inability to learn certain kinds of academic material.

The need for honest student appraisal and evaluation, while at the same time avoiding comparisons with other students, is a necessity. Confrontation with reality in an atmosphere of warmth and acceptance is imperative if one is to get an accurate view of self. False praise for poor performance is seen by the students as a sham. Here it is emphasized that students must be provided real experiences in which they can have success and from which they can draw the inference that they are successful.

The common practice of establishing pre-set standards for groups of children is viewed as frankly damaging to the self-concepts of many individual children within the group. Teacher expectancies and goals for the student must be set individually; each student must be provided experiences that are in concert with his own particular inventory of abilities, needs, and interests. That these traits are transient should have meaning for the teacher in terms of his classroom techniques. The teacher who believes in the fixed or static character of pupil abilities, interests, traits, and values is likely to convey this attitude to the students and provide experiences that maintain and perpetuate these same self-concepts.

Although the practice of using cumulative records and heresay as a basis for student evaluations is not unusual, one would hope that current behavioral evidence would be more influential in determining the evaluation. It is difficult to argue with the idea of using all available evidence, but the teacher cannot overlook the fact that last year's information may be out of date. Nor can the teacher forget that this information may be biased. Students have a right to expect that they will be judged on their current performance, not on what other teachers think of them.

1. P. Lecky, *Self-Consistency: A Theory of Personality* (New York: Island Press, 1945).

2. A.M. Walsh, *Self-Concepts of Bright Boys with Learning Difficulties* (New York: Bureau of Publications, Teachers College, Columbia University, 1956).

3. J. Benjamins, "Changes in Performance in Relation to Influences Upon Self-Conceptualization," *Journal of Abnormal and Social Psychology*, 45 (1950). 473-80.

4. T.A. Reeder, "A Study of Some Relationships Between Level of Self-Concept, Academic Achievement, and Classroom Adjustment," *Dissertation Abstracts*, 15 (1955), 2472.

5. H. Buckley and K. Scanlan, "Faith Enough for Both," Childhood Education, 32 (1956), 230-32.

6. W.B. Brookover, S. Thomas, and A. Paterson, "Self-Concept of Ability and School Achievement," *Sociology of Education*, 37 (1964), 271-78.

7. H.V. Perkins, "Factors Influencing Change in Children's Self-Concepts," *Child Development*, 29 (1958), 221-30.

8. R.L. Cutler and E.B. McNeil, *Mental Health Consultation in Schools (Unpublished, Ann Arbor, Michigan, 1963)*.

9. *H.H. Davidson and G. Lang, "Children's Perceptions of Their Teachers' Feelings Toward Them," Journal of Experimental Education*, 29 (1960), 109-18.

10. W.D. LaBenne, "Pupil-Teacher Interaction in a Senior Ungraded School for Emotionally Handicapped Boys" (Unpublished Ph.D. dissertation, University of Michigan, 1965).

11. J.C. Martire, "Relationship Between the Self-Concept and Differences in the Strength and Generality of Achievement Motivation," *Journal of Personality*, 24 (1956), 364-75.

12. I.D. Steiner, "Self-Perception and Goal-Setting Behavior," *Journal of Personality*, 30 (1957), 344-55.

13. E.J. Sheerer, "An Analysis of the Relationship Between Acceptance of and Respect for Self and Acceptance of and Respect for Others in Ten Counselling Cases," *Journal of Consulting Psychology*, 13 (1949), 169-75.

14. D. Stock, "An Investigation Into the Interrelationships Between the Self-Concept and Feelings Directed Toward Other Persons and Groups," *Journal of Consulting Psychology*, 13 (1949), 176-80.

15. A.W. Combs, "Intelligence from a Perceptual Point of View," *Journal of Abnormal and Social Psychology*, 47 (1952), 669-70.

SELECTED READINGS

Andrews, R.J., "The Self-Concept and Pupils with Learning Difficulties," *Slow Learning Child*, 13 (1966), 47-54.

Bruck, M., and R.F. Bodwin, "The Relationship Between Self-Concept and the Presence and Absense of Scholastic Underachievement," *Journal of Clinical Psychology*, 18 (1962), 181-82.

Combs, A.W., *The Professional Education of Teachers*. Boston: Allyn and Bacon, Inc., 1965.

————, "Intelligence from a Perceptual Point of View," *Journal of Abnormal and Social Psychology*, 47 (1952), 662-73.

Fink, M.B., "Self-Concept as it Relates to Academic Under-Achievement," *California Journal of Educational Research*, 13 (1962), 57-62.

Hamachek, D.E., *The Self in Growth, Teaching, and Learning*. Englewood Cliffs, N.J.: Prentice-Hall, Inc., 1965.

Holt, John, *How Children Fail*. New York: Pitman Publishing Corporation, 1964.

Hott, L., and M. Sonstegard, "Relating Self-Conception to Curriculum Development," *Journal of Educational Research*, 58 (1965), 348-51.

Morse, W.C., "Self Concept in the School Setting," *Childhood Education*, 35 (1964), 195-201.

Roth, R.M., "Role of Self-Concept in Achievement," *Journal of Experimental Education*, 27 (1959), 265-81.

Samler, J., "The School and Self-Understanding," *Harvard Educational Review*, 35 (1965), 55-70.

Sears, P., and V.S. Sherman, *In Pursuit of Self-Esteem*. Belmont, California: Wadsworth Publishing Company, Inc., 1964.

Shaw, M.C., and G.J. Alves, "The Self-Concept of Bright Academic Underachievers: II," *Personnel and Guidance Journal*, 42 (1963), 401-3.

Shaw, M.C., K. Edison, and N.R. Bell, "The Self-Concept of Bright Underachieving High School Students as Revealed by an Objective Check List," *Personnel and Guidance Journal*, 39 (1960), 193-96.

Stevens, P.H., "An Investigation of the Relationship Between Certain Aspects of Self-Concept, Behavior, and Students' Academic Achievement," *Dissertation Abstracts*, 16 (1956), 2531-32.

Wattenberg, W.W., and C. Clifford, "Relation of Self-Concept to Beginning Achievement in Reading," *Child Development*, 41 (1964), 461-67.

Self-Concept in Teaching and Learning
by Jack Canfield and Harold Wells

I am happy. I am sick. I am good. I am beautiful.
I'm a loser. I'm a winner. I am dumb. I am fine.
I'm okay. I am bad. I am clumsy. I am a gossip.
I'm neurotic. I am a bore. I'm a mess. I'm cool.
I am successful. I'm a failure. I'm lovable. I'm sexy.
I am sad. I'm smart. I am a good teacher.
I am a good person. I'm a slow learner. I'm not okay.

Which of these sentences describe you? Go back and draw a circle around each sentence that expresses how you feel most of the time. Go ahead do it now.

How many of your circled sentences please you? There are twenty-six sentences: thirteen are essentially "positive" and thirteen "negative." When you look at your responses in this light, what kind of picture do you get of yourself? That picture is a little glimpse of a tiny part of your *self-concept!*

Your self-concept is composed of all the beliefs and attitudes you have about yourself. They actually determine *who you are!* They also determine *what* you think you are, what you *do*, and what you can *become!*

It's amazing to think that these internal beliefs and attitudes you hold about yourself are that powerful; but they are. In fact, in a very functional sense, they are your *Self.*

Imagine the "glob" on page 1 as a representation of your Self. You are an entity that hangs together in an organized, consistent, reasonably firm and permanent state, yet you also have the quality of fluidity—something like a strong jellyfish! The dots in the glob represent the thousands of beliefs you hold about yourself. They fit together in a meaningful pattern or "system" each complimenting the others so that they form an integrated whole.

Notice that some of the dots are more "internal" than others. The more central a belief is to your Self, the more value—either negative or positive—you attach to it. For example, most teachers feel that to be smart is more important than to be a good swimmer. (Not everyone feels that way.) Most teachers' beliefs and attitudes about their own intelligence, then, are more central in their Self systems than their beliefs and attitudes about their swimming ability.

HOW IS THE SELF FORMED?

It is evident that the Self is learned. It is not inherited. From our earliest moments of life we begin to accumulate data about ourselves and our world. New impressions flood in upon us. We soon learn what eases pain and what makes us comfortable, what satisfies our hunger, what it takes to get attention, and so on. As our experiences multiply, our developing Self becomes a perceptual screen through which subsequent impressions must pass. For example, if an infant has been fed at the breast for weeks, he will not be satisfied with a spoon. His perceptual screen will reject the spoon as the wrong shape, and too hard and cold, and he will scream for the object he *knows* is right!

In the same manner we gradually formulate impressions and attitudes about ourselves. A crawling baby reaches out to grasp a figurine on a low coffee table. The mother says, "No, no, no! Mustn't touch. Bad boy!" Repeated exposure to such responses teaches the child—"I do things wrong. Things are more important than I am. I'm bad!" This, of course, is not at all what the parent wanted to teach, but nevertheless is precisely the message that many infants receive in such situations.

This example illustrates how vitally important early childhood experiences are in forming the kind of persons we become. We are especially vulnerable to the responses we get from our parents (particularly mother) because of the amount of time spent with them and our total dependence on them.

THE SELF IS CONSISTENT

Let's return to our illustration of the "glob." Any new experience you have is interpreted in light of all the beliefs and attitudes you've accumulated within your Self. If a new experience is consistent with what you believe, it is enveloped and your Self becomes a little larger. On the other hand, if the new experience is not consistent with your Self, it is ignored or rejected. Your "glob" simply withdraws a little where the new experience hits and moves right on past it, filling itself in as though nothing has occurred. This is a wonderful protective quality, actually. It keeps us together! There are some problems with it, however. It makes change in self-concept extremely difficult because to *significantly change anything* requires modification of the whole system in order to retain a consistency of Self. Here is an illustration of this concept:

> Jack is a good kid. He's a typical boy, so he sometimes gets into little scrapes, but never anything too bad. However, on this occasion Jack is playing with some other boys and they decide to steal some cigarettes and hide somewhere and smoke them. Jack is scared, but excited, too. Jack's little brother hears about what has happened and tells their father, who raises the roof with poor Jack. What does Jack say? What does he *really* believe about this incident? "I didn't want to steal but—well, the gang kind of—you know. Besides *I* didn't steal the cigarettes. Charley did! I only smoked one and I hated it. It was a good lesson. I'll never smoke those awful things again."

Sounds like a lot of kids you know, doesn't it? Now why did Jack respond like this? It's simple, really. Jack, *just as every other human being alive, must protect his self-esteem—his feelings about himself.* He did that in this instance by rationalizing about being kind of "forced" into the situation and by figuring what a great lesson it was. He may, in time, actually come to believe he did it as an experiment; a lesson to himself on how bad cigarettes taste so he'll never again be tempted by the habit. See how smart that makes him, and how good he can feel about himself? So, two things have happened. First, Jack's image of himself as a "good kid" is retained. He has taken an objectively "bad" incident and filtered it through his Self system in such a way as to maintain this consistency of his concept of himself. Second—and this is closely related—he has maintained or increased his self-esteem. *This is the prime motivation for all "normal" behavior.* It is perhaps our most important ability as human beings. We must, in spite of everything, be able to accept our own behavior. The strangest, most bizarre, and often most hideous behavior can be accounted for by this motivation to maintain and enhance one's Self *in one's own eyes.*

It is difficult for others to see how some behavior can possibly be Self-maintaining—but it is. We would have to be inside the skin of the other person to fully comprehend his actions, which of course is not possible, but we can keep this idea in mind and try to probe for data that will help us understand his rationale, no matter how distorted it may seem in *our* eyes.

LEARNING AND SELF-CONCEPT

By the time a child reaches school age his self-concept is quite well formed and his reactions to learning, to school failure and success, and to the physical, social, and emotional climate of the classroom will be determined by the beliefs and attitudes he has about himself. There is considerable evidence to support this view. Perhaps the most dramatic is that of Wattenberg and Clifford,[1] who studied kindergarten youngsters in an attempt to see if self-concept was predictive of reading success two and a half years later. It was. In fact, it was a better predictor than IQ! Children with low (poor) self-concepts did not learn to read or did not read as well as children with high (good) self-concepts.

Other studies affirm the position that self-concept is related to achievement in school; they also indicate that the relationship is particulary strong in boys, that it begins to make itself evident as early as the first grade, and that learning difficulties experienced in early school years persist.

WHAT YOU CAN DO
ABOUT STUDENTS' SELF-CONCEPTS

Theory is helpful, but the heart of the matter is what we can do about students'self-concepts. We can extract several principles from what has been said above:

1. **It is possible to change self-concepts, and it is possible for teachers to effect the changes—either way, both positive and negative.**
   Many of us teach because we had a teacher or two who really had a significant impact on us. The impact was related to our self-concept. The teacher somehow communicated a sense of caring and a sense of our own personal worth. On the other hand, many of us have also experienced a teacher who humiliated us or our classmates through sar-

casm and ridicule. These teachers make learning a negative experience. Teachers can and do effect pupils' self-concepts every day. You have a choice over what kind of effect you will have.

2. **It isn't easy. Change takes place slowly, over a long period of time.** This is not written to discourage you, obviously, but simply to caution you not to expect sudden and dramatic changes in the way a child feels about himself. Self-concept builds the same way muscles do, slowly and often, at first, imperceptibly.

3. **Efforts that aim at more central beliefs have greater impact on the student even though they are harder to change.** Our society puts very heavy emphasis on academic ability. If you can help the child see himself as capable of learning you are dealing with a central belief. If you help a mischievous boy see himself as kind and helpful, or a doubting girl see herself as intelligent and attractive, you've make a significant difference in the life of the child.

4. **Peripheral experiences are helpful.** Many successes are required to help a person feel better about himself in a basic sense. The development of talents is important, for example. Almost anything you do, from calling a student by his name to complimenting him on his new shoes helps to create a sense of self-worth.

5. **Relating successes or strengths to one another is important.** You can strengthen the impact of any enhancing experience by relating it to others the student has had. For example, when a child produces a good piece of art work, you can say, "I really like your picture, Harold. You learned to use charcoal very quickly, I noticed!" This relates his artistic talent to what may be a more central belief about himself—his ability to learn.

There are some additional things you can do about pupils' self-concepts. Perhaps most important is creating an environment of mutual support and caring. Soar[2] has shown that growth is optimized in a supportive environment that contains a little dissonance. For the most part we don't have to create dissonance deliberately—there is usually more than enough to go around! The crucial thing, however, is the safety and encouragement students sense in the classroom. They must trust other group members and the teacher to the extent that they can truly express their feelings openly without ridicule or derision. Further, they must recognize thay they are valued and will receive affection and support. This can't be stated strongly enough. Without the critical environmental dimensions of trust, caring, and openness the teacher's efforts to enhance pupils' sense of self-esteem will be seriously limited.

CREATING AN OPEN, CARING ENVIRONMENT

The subject of the creation of an open and caring environment could well be a book in itself! We can only outline some of the more important concepts here.

Let's start with the basic teacher-pupil relationship. Abraham Maslow describes the self-actualizing teacher with these words:

Our teacher-subjects behaved in a very unneurotic way simply by interpreting the whole situation differently, i.e., as a pleasant collaboration rather than as a clash of wills, of authority, of dignity, etc. The replacement of artificial dignity—which is easily and inevitably threatened—with the natural simplicity which is *not* easily threatened; the giving up of the attempt to be omniscient and omnipotent; the absence of student-threatening authoritarianism, the refusal to regard the students as competing with each other and with the teacher; the refusal to assume the "professor" stereotype and the insistence on remaining as realistically human as, say a plumber or a carpenter; all of these created a classroom atmosphere in which suspicion, wariness, defensiveness, hostility, and anxiety disappeared.[3]

This sets the direction for us. We must strive for a natural, human, democratic relationship. This means involving students from the beginning in creating the environment. They must help in decision-making about the physical setting (the arranging of the room, care for equipment, bulletin boards, etc.). Students also must be involved in planning the academic environment. This includes decisions about content, sequence of activities, and even methods of study. All this must take place within the limits defined by school district policies, of course, but these too must be openly acknowledged and confronted.

Students have a vested interest in the emotional environment of the classroom as well. Teachers and students should sit down together and freely discuss cooperation and competition, trust and fear, openness and deceit, and so on. These and many other topics discussed in classroom meetings help create the kind of climate that fosters total pupil growth.

Additional factors that appear to contribute to a "positive" classroom milieu are enumerated by us in our self-concept-self-identity curriculum,[4] in which elements of a supportive classroom climate are cited as including such important teacher behaviors as:

climate are cited as including such important teacher behaviors as:

1. Accepting pupil contributions without judgment
2. Maintaining a "you can do it" attitude
3. Listening, listening, listening
4. Being, in all ways, a friend

It is interesting to compare this brief treatment of this subject with Hamachek's[5] summary of the research on qualities of effective teachers:

We can sketch at least five interrelated generalizations from what research is telling us about how effective teachers differ from less effective teachers when it comes to perceptions of others. In relation to this, effective teachers can be characterized in the following ways:

1. They seem to have a generally more positive view of others—students, colleagues, and administrators.
2. They are not prone to view others as critical, attacking people with ulterior motives, but rather see them as potentially friendly and worthy in their own right.
3. They have a more favorable view of democratic classroom procedures.
4. They have the ability and capacity to see things as they seem to others, i.e., the ability to see things from the other person's point of view.
5. They do not see students as persons "you do things to" but rather as individuals capable of doing for themselves once they feel trusted, respected, and valued.

If you as a teacher behave in a way consistent with the principles and characteristics enumerated in this introduction, your teaching will build children rather than destroy them! Is there anything more important?

THE RELATIONSHIP OF SELF-CONCEPT TO LEARNING

One of the questions often asked by teachers regards the relationship of self-concept to the learning of subject matter. The research literature is filled with reports indicating that cognitive learning increases when self-concept increases. The data suggesting this conclusion is quite extensive and overwhelming.[6]

We have developed a theory to explain this phenomenon which we call the "poker chip theory of learning." We see all learning as the result of a risk-taking situation somewhat akin to a poker game (or any other gambling situation, for that matter). In any potential learning situation, the student is asked to take a risk: to write a paper that will be evaluated, to make a recitation which may be laughed at, to do board work that may be wrong, to create an object of art that might be judged, etc. In each situation he is risking error, judgment, disapproval, censure, rejection, and, in extreme, cases, even punishment. At a deeper level the student is risking his or her self-concept.

Imagine that each student's self-concept is a stack of poker chips. Some students start the learning game, as it were, with a lot of poker chips; others with very few. The students with the higher number of chips have a great advantage. To continue the poker analogy, the student with one hundred chips can sustain twenty losses of five chips each. The student with only fifteen chips can only sustain three losses of five chips each. The latter student will be much more cautious and reticent about stepping into the arena. This kind of student manifests a variety of behaviors indicating his reluctance to risk learning. They range from "This is stupid, I don't want to do it" (translation: "I am stupid; I'm afraid I can't do it") and withdrawn silence on one extreme to mischievous acting out on the other.

The student who has had a good deal of success in the past will be likely to risk success again; if he should fail, his self-concept can "afford" it. A student with a history predominated by failures will be reluctant to risk failure again. His depleted self-concept cannot afford it. Similar to someone living on a limited income, he will shop cautiously and look for bargains. One obvious recommendation in this situation is to make each learning step small enough so that the student is asked to only risk one chip at a time, instead of five. But even more obvious, in our eyes, is the need to build up the student's supply of poker chips so that he can begin to have a surplus of chips to risk.

If a student starts out, metaphorically speaking, with twenty chips and he gains fifteen more through the exercises contained in this book, then, even if he loses ten in a reading class, he is still ahead of the game. But if he loses ten from a starting position of twenty he is now down to ten and in a very precarious psychological position. Viewed in this way, self-concept building can be seen as making sure that every student has enough chips to stay in the game.[7]

[1] W.W. Wattenberg and C. Clifford, *Relationship of Self Concept to Beginning Achievement in Reading*, U.S. Office of Education, Cooperative Project No. 377 (Detroit: Wayne State University, 1962).

[2] S. Robert Soar, "Humanizing Secondary Schools," unpublished paper (mimeograph) distributed by the Institute for Development of Human Resources, University of Florida, College of Education, Gainesville, Florida, 1968.

174

[3] Abraham H. Maslow, "Self-Actualizing People: A Study of Psychological Health," in Clark E. Moustakas, *The Self: Explorations in Personal Growth* (New York: Harper and Row, 1956) pp. 190-91.

[4] Harold C. Wells and Jack Canfield, *About Me*, Teacher's Guide (425 North Michigan Avenue, Chicago, Ill.: Encyclopedia Britannica Educational Corp., 1971), p. 76.

[5] Donald E. Hamachek, *Encounter with the Self* (New York: Holt, Rinehart and Winston, 1971), p. 202.

[6] See William W. Purkey, *Self-Concept and School Achievement* (Englewood Cliffs, N.J.: Prentice-Hall, Inc., 1970), for a comprehensive review of the research.

[7] For a list of other materials currently available and workshops offered in the areas of humanistic education and self-concept development, write to the Institute for Wholistic Education, Box 575, Amherst, Massachusetts 01002.

Relationship Between the Self Concept and Success in School

William W. Purkey

Teachers want to be significant forces in the lives of their students. As Moustakas (1966) declared, every teacher wants to meet the student on a significant level, every teacher wants to feel that what he does makes a difference. Yet in order to influence students it is necessary to become a *significant other* in their lives. We are seldom changed by people whom we see as insignificant or unimportant. The way the teacher becomes significant seems to rest on two forces: (1) what he believes, and (2) what he does.

WHAT THE TEACHER BELIEVES

No printed word nor spoken plea
Can teach young minds what men should be,
Not all the books on all the shelves
But what the teachers are themselves.

Anonymous

A basic assumption of the theory of the self concept is that we behave according to our beliefs. If this assumption is true, then it follows that the teacher's beliefs about himself and his students are crucial factors in determining his effectiveness in the classroom. Available evidence (Combs, 1969) indicated that the teacher's attitudes toward himself and others are as important, if not more so, than his techniques, practices, or materials. In fact, there do not seem to be any techniques which are always associated with people who are effective in the helping relationships. Rogers (1965) reported that personality changes in therapy come about not because of such factors as professional qualifications and training, or knowledge or skill, or ideological orientation, but primarily because of the attitudinal characteristics of the relationship. Attitudes play an important role, and so we need to examine the teacher's beliefs about himself and his students in some detail.

WHAT THE TEACHER BELIEVES ABOUT HIMSELF

There seems to be general agreement that the teacher needs to have positive and realistic attitudes about himself and his abilities before he is

From William Watson Purkey, SELF CONCEPT AND SCHOOL ACHIEVEMENT, © 1970, pp. 45-58. Reprinted by permission of Prentice-Hall, Inc., Englewood Cliffs, NJ.

able to reach out to like and respect others. Numerous studies (Berger, 1953; Fey, 1954; Luft, 1966) have reported that there is a marked relation between the way an individual sees himself and the way he sees others. Those who accept themselves tend to be more accepting of others. (Trent, 1957) and perceive others as more accepting (Omwake, 1954). Further, according to Omwake, those who reject themselves hold a corresponding low opinion of others and perceive others as being self-rejecting. From these studies it seems clear that the teacher needs to see himself in essentially positive ways. The manner in which this can be accomplished needs further investigation, but Jersild and Combs have given us some clues.

Jersild (1952, 1960, 1965) has been a pioneer in emphasizing the importance of the attitudes that teachers hold about themselves. He argues that the self-understanding of teachers is a necessary factor in coping with their feelings and in becoming more effective in the classroom. The personal problems of teachers often interfere with their effectiveness in teaching, and an understanding of the influence of those and other attitudes and emotions is vital in working with students. Jersild has suggested that we need to encourage in-service group counseling situations for teachers, in which their attitudes and feelings can be safely explored with others. This, it is hoped, would result in increased understanding of and sensitivity to oneself, and to more effective teaching in the classroom.

A similar view is reported by Combs and his associates (1963, 1964, 1965, 1969) in their research on the perceptual organization of effective helpers. They found that effective teachers, counselors, and priests could be distinguished from ineffective helpers on the basis of their attitudes about themselves and others. Such findings as these have long-range implications for the professional education of teachers. In fact, the suggestion that teacher preparation should be based on a perceptual, self concept approach has already appeared in Combs' *The Professional Education of Teachers* (1965), and an experimental program of teacher training using the perceptual approach was introduced at the University of Florida in 1969.

The way the evidence points is that each teacher needs to view himself with respect, liking, and acceptance. When teachers have essentially favorable attitudes toward themselves, they are in a much better position to build positive and realistic self concepts in their students.

WHAT THE TEACHER BELIEVES ABOUT STUDENTS

The ways significant others evaluate the student directly affects the student's conception of his academic ability. This in turn establishes limits on his success in school. Teachers, in their capacity of significant others, need to view students in essentially positive ways and hold favorable expectations. This is particularly important at the elementary level, but is vital in all grades. Several studies bear directly on the importance of what the teacher believes about students.

Davidson and Lang (1960) found that the student's perceptions of the teacher's feelings toward him correlated positively with his self-perception. Further, the more positive the children's perceptions of their teacher's feelings, the better their academic achievement and the more desirable their classroom behavior as rated by the teacher. Clarke (1960) reported a positive relationship between a student's academic performance and his perception of the academic expections of him by significant others.

One of the most comprehensive studies of the self concept of ability and school success was that of Brookover and his associates (1965, 1967) which we considered, in part, earlier. Brookover and his associates conducted a six-year study of the relation between the self concept of academic ability and school achievement among students in one school class while in the seventh through twelfth grades. A major porpose of the study was to determine whether improved self concept results from the expectations and evaluations held by significant others as perceived by the students. As Brookover, Erickson, and Joiner conclude: "The hypothesis that students' perceptions of the evaluations of their academic ability by others (teachers, parents, and friends) are associated with self concepts of academic ability was confirmed" (1967, p. 110). The almost unavoidable conclusion is that the teacher's attitudes and opinions regarding his students have a significant influence on their success in school. In other words, when the teacher believes that his students can achieve, the students appear to be more successful; when the teacher believes that the students cannot achieve, then it influences their performance negatively. This self-fulfilling prophecy has been illuminated by the research of Rosenthal and Jacobson (1968a, b).

The basic hypothesis of Rosenthal and Jacobson's research was that students, more often than not, do what is expected of them. To test this hypothesis, the two researchers conducted an experiment in a public elementary school of 650 students. The elementary-school teachers were told that, on the basis of ability tests administered the previous spring, approximately one-fifth of the students could be expected to evidence significant increases in mental ability during the year. The teachers were then given the names of the high-potential students. Although in fact the names had been *chosen at random* by the experimenters, when intelligence tests and other measures were administered some months later, those identified as potential spurters tended to score significantly higher than the children who had not been so identified. Also, Rosenthal and Jacobson found that these children were later described by their teachers as happier, more curious, more interesting, and as having a better chance of future success than other children. The conclusion drawn by Rosenthal and Jacobson is that the teacher, through his facial expressions, postures, and touch, through what, how, and when he spoke, subtly helped the child to learn. This may have been accomplished, according to the researchers, by modifying the child's self concept, his expectations of his own behavior, and his motivations, as well as his cognitive style. They summarized their study by stating that the evidence suggests strongly that "children who are expected by their teachers to gain intellectually in fact do show greater intellectual gains after one year than do children of whom such gains are not expected" (1968b, p. 121). The full educational implications of the self-fulfilling prophecy remain to be explored, but it seems certain that the ways the teacher views the student have a significant influence on the student and his performance.

WHAT THE TEACHER DOES

As we have seen, the key to building positive and realistic self-images in students lies largely in what the teacher *believes* about himself and his students. These beliefs not only determine the teacher's behavior, but are transmitted to the students and influence their performance as well. Yet we cannot ignore what the teacher *does* in the classroom, for the behavior he displays and the experiences he provides, *as perceived by students*, have a strong impact in themselves. In this section we will consider two important aspects of the teacher's role: (1) *the attitudes he conveys;* and (2) *the atmosphere he develops.*

THE ATTITUDE THE TEACHER CONVEYS

It is difficult to overestimate the need for the teacher to be sensitive to the attitudes he expresses toward students. Even though teachers may have the best intentions, they sometimes project distorted images of themselves. What a person believes can be hidden by negative habits picked up long ago. Therefore, teachers need to ask themselves:

Am I projecting an image that tells the student that I am here to build, rather than to destroy, him as a person? (Spaulding, 1963, reported that there is a significant relationship between a student's positive self concept as reported, and the degree to which teachers are calm, accepting, supportive, and facilitative, and a negative relationship between a student's self concept and teachers who are threatening, grim, and sarcastic.)

Do I let the student know that I am aware of and interested in him as a unique person? (Moustakas, 1966, maintains that every child wants to be known as a unique person, and that by holding the student in esteem, the teacher is establishing an environmental climate that facilitates growth.)

Do I convey my expectations and confidence that the student can accomplish work, can learn, and is competent? (Rosenthal and Jacobson, 1968*b*, have shown that the teacher's expectations have a significant influence on the student's performance.)

Do I provide well-defined standards of values, demands for competence, and guidance toward solutions to problems? (Coopersmith, 1967, has provided evidence that self-reliance is fostered by an enviroment which is well-structured and reasonably demanding, rather than unlimitedly permissive.)

When working with parents, do I enhance the academic expectations and evaluations which they hold of their children's ability? (Brookover, et. al., 1965, has illustrated that this method yields significant results in enhancing self concept and improving academic achievement.)

By my behavior, do I serve as a model of authenticity for the student? (Both Jourard, 1964, and Rogers, 1965, suggest that a most important factor in the helping relationship is the helper serving as a model of genuineness, without "front.")

Do I take every opportunity to establish a high degree of private or semi-private communication with my students? (Spaulding, 1963, found a high relationship between the pupil's self concept and the teacher's behavior when it involved personal and private talks with students.)

The above questions are samples of how the teacher may check himself to see if he is conveying his beliefs in an authentic and meaningful fashion. As Gill reported, teachers' attitudes toward students are vitally important in shaping the self concepts of their students. Gill summarized his study by saying that "teachers should consider self concept as a vital and important aspect of learning and development which the school, through its educational process, should seek to promote and foster in every child" (1969, p.

10).
THE ATMOSPHERE THE TEACHER CREATES

Six factors seem particularly important in creating a classroom atmosphere conducive to developing favorable self-images in students. These are (1) challenge; (2) freedom; (3) respect; (4) warmth; (5) control; and (6) success. A brief discussion of each of these may be helpful.

Challenge Because of the focus of this book, little has been said about high standards of academic accomplishment. This omission should not be taken to mean that achievement should be minimized. As we have seen, high academic expectations and a high degree of challenge on the part of teachers have a positive and beneficial effect on students. A good way to create challenge is to wait until the chances of success are good, and then say "This is hard work, but I think that you can do it." The teacher chooses the right moment to put his trust on the line with students. Of course, an important part of challenge is relevance. If the required learning is relevant to the student's world of experience and has some personal meaning to him, then he is likely to work hard—*if* he feels free to try. This brings us to the question of freedom.

Freedom It is difficult for self-esteem to grow in an environment where there is little or no freedom of choice. If the student is to grow and develop as an adequate human being, he needs the opportunity to make meaningful decisions for himself. This also means that he must have the freedom to make mistakes, and even to laugh at his inadequacies. Carlton and Moore (1966, 1968) have shown that the freedom of self-directed dramatization improved the reading ability and enhanced the self concept of elementary-school youngsters. This general emphasis on freedom has been highlighted by Moustakas, who wrote: "Self values are in jeopardy in any climate where freedom and choice are denied, in a situation where the individual rejects his own senses and substitutes for his own perceptions the standards and expectations of others" (1966, pp. 4*f*). When the student has a say in his own development and is given personal decisions to make, he develops faith in his own judgments and thoughts.

Closely related to the notion of freedom of choice is the idea of freedom from threat. Children seem to learn and develop best in an atmosphere characterized by much challenge and little threat. Kowitz has noted, for example, that if the child feels evaluation takes place with "vicious assault upon his self concept" (1967, p.163), there can be little real freedom. In fact, some students fear failure so much that they avoid achievement whenever they can and, when they cannot, do not try to succeed. In this way, they can avoid the task of trying to achieve. A comprehensive study of the person who fears failure is provided by Birney, Burdick, and Teevan (1969).

What this means to the teacher is that students will learn, provided the material appears to be relevant to their lives and provided they have the freedom to explore and to discover its meaning for themselves. We know that exploration is curtailed in an atmosphere in which one must spend most of his time avoiding or reducing the experience of anxiety brought about by threat to the self. Sarason (1961) has reported that a poor performance by anxious subjects occurred only when the task was presented as a threat.

When anxious subjects were told that failure was normal and expected, they actually outperformed subjects who were less anxious. The freedom to try without a tiger springing at you if you fail is essential to a healthy atmosphere in the classroom.

In considering the factors of freedom and challenge, the classroom teacher can ask himself:

Do I encourage students to try something new and to join in new activities?

Do I allow students to have a voice in planning, and do I permit them to help make the rules they follow?

Do I permit students to challenge my opinions?

Do I teach in as exciting and interesting a manner as possible?

Do I distinguish between students' classroom mistakes and their personal failure?

Do I avoid unfair and ruthless competition in the classroom?

Questions like these can help the teacher evaluate himself and the classroom climate he creates.

Respect A basic feeling by the teacher for the worth and dignity of students is vital in building self concepts in them. No aspect of education is more important than the feeling on the part of the teacher that the individual student is important, valuable, and *can* learn in school. Sometimes teachers forget the importance of respect and run roughshod over the personal feelings of students. Using both the official and unofficial school practices which we cataloged in Chapter 3, teachers sometimes lower the feelings of worth of many young people. One of my students told me why he could never get along with his previous English teacher. It was because, although his name is Cribbiddge, "She always called me cabbage whenever she called roll, and then laughed." The rule seems to be that whenever we treat a student with respect, we add to his self-respect, and whenever we embarrass or humiliate him, we are likely to build disrespect in him both for himself and for others.

If the teacher genuinely values and respects students, it will be reflected in everything he does. Davidson and Lang (1960) found that when students feel that teachers value and respect them, they are likely to value and respect themselves. Moustakas summed it up this way: "By cherishing and holding the child in absolute esteem, the teacher is establishing an environmental climate that facilitates growth and becoming" (1966, p. 13).

The need for respect is particularly important in working with culturally disadvantaged students. These are the children whose behavior makes them most difficult to respect, but who probably need respect the most. Teachers must make an extra effort to communicate to these young people a feeling of trust, positive regard, and respect. Closely related to respect is the concept of warmth.

Warmth There is considerable evidence to support the assumption that a psychologically safe and supporting learning situation encourages students to grow academically as well as in feelings of personal worth. Cogan (1958) reported that students with warm, considerate teachers produced unusual amounts of original poetry and art. Christensen (1960) found the warmth of teachers significantly related to their students' vocabulary and achievement in arithmetic. Reed (1962) concluded that teachers characterized as considerate, understanding, and friendly, and with a tolerance for some release of emotional feeling by students, had a favorable influence on their students' interest in science.

Relating more directly to the task of building favorable self concepts, Spaulding's research (1964) supported the findings of previous investigators regarding positive attitudes toward the self. He found significant correlations between the height of the self concept and the degree to which the teachers in his study were calm, accepting, supportive, and facilitative. It is interesting to note that significant negative correlations with the height of pupils' self concepts were found when teachers were dominating, threatening, and sarcastic.

An important part of warmth is commitment. Teaching has been described as a delicate relationship, almost like a marriage, where, in a sense, the teacher and student belong to each other. The student says "There is *my* teacher" and the teacher says "These are *my* students." The process of commitment is illustrated by the story of the chicken and pig who were walking down a country lane: The chicken excitedly told the portly pig of his latest business idea. "We'll prepare and franchise the best tasting ham 'n eggs money can buy, and we'll make a fortune." The pig thought it over for a moment and replied: "It's easy for you to get enthused. For you it's an occupation, but for *me* it means *total* commitment!" Perhaps total commitment is asking too much of teachers, but certainly they need to feel that their work with students is more than an occupation. A warm and supportive educational atmosphere is one in which each student is made to feel that he belongs in school and that teachers care about what happens to him. It is one in which praise is used in preference to punishment, courtesy in preference to sarcasm, and consultation in preference to dictation.

Some practical questions about respect and warmth which the teacher might ask himself are:

Do I learn the name of each student as soon as possible, and do I use that name often?

Do I share my feelings with my students?

Do I practice courtesy with my students?

Do I arrange some time when I can talk quietly alone with each student?

Do I spread my attention around and include each student, keeping special watch for the student who may need extra attention?

Do I notice and comment favorably on the things that are important to students?

Do I show students who return after being absent that I am happy to have them back in class, and that they were missed?

It is in ways such as these that we tell the student that he is important to us.

Control Coopersmith (1967) has suggested that children who are brought up in a permissive environment tend to develop less self-esteem than those reared in a firmer and more demanding atmosphere. The assumption that clearly established and relatively firm guidance produces more self-esteem in children can also be applied to the classroom. It is important for the teacher to maintain discipline, for the type of control under which a child lives has considerable effect on his self-image. It is yet another way of telling the student that the teacher cares about him and what he does. Classroom control does not require ridicule and embarassment. The secret seems to be in the leadership qualities of the teacher. When he is prepared for class, keeps on top of the work and avoids the appearance of confusion, explains why some things must be done, and strives for consistency, politeness, and firmness, then classroom control is likely to be maintained. When punishment is unavoidable (and often it *can* be avoided), then it is best to withdraw the student's privileges. Of course, this means that teachers must be sure that there *are* some privileges in school which can be withdrawn. Poor control procedures would include punishing the entire class for transgressions of a few, using corporal punishment, or using school work as punishment.

In considering classroom control, teachers might ask themselves:

Do I remember to see small disciplinary problems as understandable, and not as personal insults?

Do I avoid having "favorites" and "victims"?

Do I have, and do my students have, a clear idea of what is and what is not acceptable in my class?

Within my limits, is there room for students to be active and natural?

Do I make sure that I am adequately prepared for class each day?

Do I usually make it through the day without punishing students?

Questions such as these help the teacher to estimate his ability to handle students in a way which maintains discipline, and, at the same time, builds positive and realistic self concepts in students.

Some teachers believe that warmth and firmness are in opposition to each other, but this is not so. Warmth is more than the obvious display of affection, it is also expressed by firmness which says to the student, "You are important to me and I care about the ways in which you behave."

Success Perhaps the single most important step that teachers can take in the classroom is to provide an educational atmosphere of success rather than failure. Reviewing over a dozen experiments, Wylie (1961) made the tentative statement that students are likely to change their self-evaluations after experimentally induced success or failure. This statement has been echoed in more recent studies. Costello (1964) found that over-all, regardless of the task or the ability of the students, praise produces more improvement in performance than blame. Ludwig and Maehr (1967) showed that the approval of significant others caused an increas in self-ratings and an increased preference for activities connected with the criterion task, and that disapproval resulted in lowered self-rating and a decreased preference for related activities. Moreover, the reaction to the evaluation was followed by a spread of effect, from the areas of self-regard.

A number of writers have pointed out some of the steps involved in giving honest experiences of success. Page's (1958) research showed that pupils' performance improved significantly when teachers wrote encouraging comments on their written work. A control group, given conventional grades without comment, lost ground. Walsh (1956) explains that it is helpful to show students that they have mastered even the smallest step, rather than vaguely saying "That's nice" about everything.

The sensitive teacher points out areas of accomplishment, rather than focusing on mistakes. Continuing awareness of failure results in lowered expectations, not learning. According to Combs and Snygg (1959) a positive view is learned from the ways people treat the learner. People learn that they are able, not from failure but from success. Questions about success which the teacher might ask himself when he thinks about success experiences for students include:

Do I permit my students some opportunity to make mistakes without penalty?

Do I make generally positive comments on written work?

Do I give extra support and encouragement to slower students?

Do I recognize the successes of students in terms of what they did earlier?

Do I take special opportunities to praise students for their successes?

Do I manufacture honest experiences of success for my students?

Do I set tasks which are, and which appear to the student to be, within his abilities?

What all of this discussion hopes to say to teachers is that a backlog of challenge, freedom, respect, warmth, control, and success develops positive self-images in students and encourages academic achievement. The absence of these factors makes for the person who is crippled psychologically.

THE SENSITIVITY THE TEACHER DEVELOPS

You can know me truly only if I let you, only if I want you to know me. . . . If you want me to reveal myself, just demonstrate your good will—your will to employ your powers for my good, and not for my destruction.
Sidney Jourard, *The Transparent Self*

"Sensitivity" is a term which is used to serve many purposes and to describe various processes. In this book it is defined as the ability to sense what an individual feels about himself and the world. Sensitivity first requires the honest *desire* to become aware of how others are experiencing things. This sounds simple, but the fact is that many people don't take the necessary time and trouble to be sensitive to others. After the desire must come the habit of really listening, and listening for meanings rather than words. For instance, a student might say that he does not wish to try, when he means that it is better not to try than to try and be proved wrong.

Entering a person's private world in order to understand how he is seeing things is difficult, for the individual self can only be approached through the perceptions of some other person, perceptions filled with all sorts of prejudices, aspirations, and anxieties. Fortunately, however, most teachers have a great supply of sensitivity, as do most humans. It's just a matter of applying this sensitivity more deliberately to teaching. To the degree to which a teacher is able to predict how his students are viewing themselves, their subject, and the world, to that degree he is in a position to become a successful teacher.

Throughout this book the idea has been stressed over and over that the teacher must give the self concepts of students far greater empahsis than is presently given. The purpose of this section is to assist teachers to become more competent in assessing the self concepts of the students with whom they work. For a long time, many of us in education and psychology have been saying that theory about the self has a vital role to play in the educative process and that teachers should be made more aware of the importance of how students view themselves. Yet little has been done to equip teachers and counselors with simple clinical techniques and instruments which would enable them to be more sensitive to their students. It would seem that we in education have the responsibility, within the limits of our training, to investigate, to understand, and to utilize the self concept as a means of facilitating scholastic success. What a person says about himself, and the inferences we draw from his behavior, are valuable data for teachers.

How Child Sees Himself May Relate To How Teacher Sees Himself

Robert Allen Blume

If we want mentally alert, healthy youngsters to emerge from our schools, we must do whatever we can to help children build strong selves.

The important question is: How can we help our students to acquire positive attitudes toward self?

No doubt teachers are nearly as important as parents to the growing self all through school, and they are particularly significant persons in regard to the child's self-concept as a student.

A few years ago research was conducted at the University of Michigan which examined the relationship between the self-concepts of children and those of their teachers.

By comparing self-esteem scores of 26 teachers with the children in their classes, it was possible to determine the extent of their similarity. As was suspected, it was quite high.

The data included scores on the children in each teacher's class for two consecutive years. Each teacher's self-esteem was compared to that of both of his or her classes.

The results were the same for both years; teachers who scored high in self-esteem tended to have groups of pupils who scored high as well.

It would seem that if we want to develop children with high self-esteem, we should first of all provide them with teachers who have high self-esteem.

This is the job of colleges of education, school administrators, boards of education, hiring officials, teachers themselves, and parents and lay citizens.

Each of these groups of people has an important role to play in providing children with teachers who think well of themselves.

The colleges of education must recruit students who have positive feelings and beliefs about themselves and nurture this attitude with good counseling and good teaching. It should be the purpose of teacher educators to produce people who have positive self-concepts.

Once the college has done its work, it is up to hiring officials to select for their schools the applicants who have the most self-confidence and who

Reprinted by permission from the MICHIGAN EDUCATION JOURNAL, © November 1, 1968, pp. 9-11, by the Michigan Education Association.

seem to think well of themselves.

Frequently administrators look for academic excellence in prospective teachers, but grades do not tell much about self-esteem. A shrewd observer and skillful interviewer can make a good guess, however, if that is his purpose.

After the teacher has been hired it is primarily up to the school administration—especially the principal—to maintain the kind of school in which teachers will be able to enhance their self-concepts rather than to feel them diminish.

It is a time-worn cliche among educational consultants who regularly visit many schools that the principal's personality can be predicted after a five-minute hallway tour.

Just as the teacher is the key to the child's school self-concept, the principal is the key to the teacher's school self-concept.

Does the principal treat teachers with respect or with disdain? Does he consult them concerning future plans, or does he consult only "experts" from the central office and universities?

Does he make decisions for them, or does he present problems for their decisions? Does he associate with his staff, or does he see himself on a higher level?

Doe the school district provide teachers with the amenities other professionals take for granted (offices, secretaries, non-professional help for routine chores, petty cash budget, released time to attend conferences) or are teachers expected to put up with adverse conditions through a sense of dedication?

The attitude of administrators toward teachers are clear for all to see in their behavior toward teachers. It is small wonder that many teachers feel less worthy the longer they teach, just as many pupils feel less worthy the longer they attend school.

Although their role is very important, administrators alone cannot do the job of maintaining a school in which teachers will develop positive self-concepts. Teachers themselves must be aware of their own self-attitudes and those of their colleagues.

Statements like "I don't know what she did with these kids last year, but they sure aren't ready for fourth grade!" are detrimental to the teacher in question.

Teachers must be more protective of each other, not to the extent of condoning incompetence, but in order to help each other maintain a sense of security.

At the very least teachers must not "run each other down" in public, because the negative feedback from lay citizens tends to lower each teacher's self-esteem.

The parents and other citizens have a role, too, in helping teachers maintain a positive view of self. When parents are supportive of teachers, when they work to pass millage elections, they communicate a message to teachers which is self-enhancing.

On the other hand, when parents become hypercritical and put teachers on the defensive, low teacher self-esteem emerges.

How can a teacher improve his own self-concept? Although it may appear that I am saying here that teachers' self-concepts are in the hands of other people to mold in whatever way fate will have it, nothing could be further from the truth.

The self-concept is a result of the *perception* one has of the reactions of other people toward him. This means that it emerges from the interaction of one's perceptive mechanism, one's behavior, and one's populated environment.

The individual can affect his own self-esteem in two ways: in what he does (which will be perceived by others and reflected back to him) and in how he perceives others.

Our perceptions of others are influenced by our attitudes, and our attitudes are partially within our own control.

What we tell ourselves is important in how we perceive others, and specifically how we perceive their perception of us. Therefore the teacher *can* decide to improve his own self-concept, and set about to do just that.

Next, he must throw off the guilt which he has collected because he has not succeeded in helping every pupil learn everything he expected him to learn. The fact is that teachers cannot do everything they "should" do to help children learn.

Furthermore, all children are not going to learn everything we "teach" them. It is unrealistic and self-defeating to expect a whole class to achieve at any given grade level.

Instead, we must do our best to help each child achieve as much as he can, recognizing that there will be a wide range in the class at the beginning of the term, and a wider range at the end.

This is inevitable and even desirable. No teacher should feel guilty about it. No administrator, colleague, or parent should contribute to such a feeling.

The next thing a teacher can do is to direct his efforts more toward *communication* with children and less toward *manipulation* of them. He can spend less time grading papers and more time holding brief conferences with each child. He can spend less time telling the entire class and more time listening to individuals and small groups.

Frequently teachers have been more successful than they realize. By talking with students they learn about their successes, as well as the areas in which they need to do more in order to be successful.

Teachers can also do a great deal to improve their own self-concepts by joining with others to assert their position on professional matters. The present movement toward a more militant teaching staff is beneficial for this reason.

One's self-concept is altered by his membership in groups. By choosing positive, voluntary groups to belong to, an individual can enhance his self-concept.

In asserting one's ideas as a militant member of a group, it is important, however, not to assume a posture of negativism toward all administrators or all administrative decisions.

Such negativism transfers from one aspect of an individual's perceiving to others, and sometimes children become the recipients of some of the negativism originally aimed at the administration.

And of course, negativism is usually reciprocated, which doesn't help the self-concept, and in fact, engenders more negativism toward self and others.

The school *can* help children build healthy self-concepts, but first it must look to the self-concepts of teachers. When teachers have positive feelings about themselves, they are able to converse with children in a way that enhances their self-concepts.

Teachers then feel less guilty and more open to new ideas, and they have fewer negative feelings toward boys and girls. Students who have positive self-concepts provide teachers with positive feedback, and consequently teachers become more capable of liking their students and enjoying their work.

Much responsibility for helping teachers maintain healthy selves rests with administrators. However, the colleges and public at large must each do their share to make teaching a self-enhancing profession.

VII / New Activities for Building Self-Esteem

*The more each person strives and is able
to seek his profit, that is to say, to perserve
his being, the more virtue does he possess;
on the other hand, in so far as each person
neglects his own profit he is impotent.*
Baruch Spinoza

Teaching Human Beings to Love Themselves

Jack Canfield and Paula Klimek

> If I were to search for the central core of difficulty in people as I have come to know them, it is that in the great majority of cases they despise themselves, regrading themselves as worthless and unlovable.
>
> —Carl Rogers

> I had a great feeling of relief when I began to understand that a youngster needs more than just subject matter. Oh, I know mathematics well, and I teach it well. I used to think that that was all I needed to do. Now I teach children, not math. I accept the fact that I can only succeed partially with some of them. I have found further that my own personhood has educatable value. When I don't have to know all the answers, I seem to have more answers than before when I tried to be the expert. The youngster who really made me understand this was Eddie. I asked him one day why he thought he was doing so much better than last year. He gave meaning to my whole new orientation. "It's because I like myself now when I'm with you," he said.
>
> —A teacher quoted by Everett Shostrom in
> *Man, the Manipulator*

Overcoming negative self-concept is one of the most prevalent problems facing educators today at all levels—kindergarten through college. Students of all ages seem to be suffering from the same basic problem of not liking themselves. They come into our classes with their self-concept development having been retarded by well-meaning but psychologically ignorant parents, similarly well-meaning but ignorant teachers and equally wounded peers.

Herbert Otto conducted a study with college freshmen at two universities in which he asked them to list their strengths and their weaknesses. He found that they listed six weaknesses to every one strength. Their positive self-regard was almost non-existent![1]

I recently conducted a demonstration class in a junior high school in Connecticut. I asked the class to sit in a circle and to take turns sharing with the rest of us something they had done in the past year that they were proud of. I was stunned to find out how difficult this was for almost all of them. They simply did not believe that they had done anything worthy of remembering let alone mentioning. I have seen the same lack of positive

Reprinted by permission from the authors, copyright © 1978.

self-awareness in elementary classrooms.

It is astounding to me how negatively focused our culture has become. We always seem to focus on what's wrong with something or somebody rather than what is right. The result is incredible psychic pain and waste. But perhaps even more relevant to us as educators, the result is also less personal growth, less academic achievement and less learning.

There is an increasing amount of research that indicates that one's self-concept is directly related to his or her achievement in school. The literature is filled with reports indicating that cognitive learning increases when self-concept increases. The data suggesting this conclusion is quite extensive and overwhelming.[2]

I have developed a theory to explain this phenomenon which I call "the poker chip theory of learning."[3] I see all learning as the result of a risk taking situation somewhat akin to a poker game (or any other gambling situation, for that matter). In any potential learning situation, the student is asked to take a risk: to write a paper that will be evaluated, to make a recitation which may be laughed at, to do board work that may be wrong, to create an object of art that might be judged, etc. In each situation he is risking error, judgement, disapproval, censure, rejection, and, in extreme cases, even punishment. At a deeper level the student is risking his or her self-concept.

Imagine that each student's self-concept is a stack of poker chips. Some students start the learning game, as it were with a lot of poker chips; others with very few. The students with the higher number of chips have a great advantage. To continue the poker analogy, the student with one hundred chips can sustain twenty losses of five chips each. The student with only fifteen chips can only sustain three losses of five chips each. The latter student will be much more cautious and reticent about stepping into the arena. This kind of student manifests a variety of behaviors indicating his reluctance to risk learning. They range from "This is stupid, I don't want to do it." (translation: "I am stupid; I'm afraid I can't do it.") and withdrawn silence on one extreme to mischievious acting out on the other.

The student who has had a good deal of success in the past will be likely to risk success again. If perchance he should fail, his self-concept can "afford" it. A student with a history predominated by failures will be reluctant to risk failure again.

His depleted self-concept cannot afford it. Similar to someone living on welfare, he will shop cautiously and look for bargains. One obvious recommendation in this situation is to make each learning step small enough so that the student is asked to risk only one chip at a time, instead of five. But even more obvious, to our eyes, is the need to build up the student's supply of poker chips so that he can begin to have a surplus of chips to risk.

If a student starts out, metaphorically speaking, with twenty chips and she gains fifteen more through the exercises contained in this book, then, even if she loses ten in a reading class, she still is five ahead of the game. But if she loses ten from a starting position of twenty she is now down to ten and in a very precarious psychological position. Viewed in this way one can see self-concept building as a sort of pump priming to the academic learning process.

Before I share with you a number of specific exercises to help students build positive self-concepts, let us first briefly explore the three general areas which I see as essential to self-concept development in the classroom. I like to refer to them as a sense of belonging, a sense of competence and a sense of worthwhileness. These happen to be the same categories that Donald Felker refers to in his book, *Helping Children to Like Themselves*.[4] Interestingly enough several other educators have independently arrived at these same three areas. Gerald Weinstein refers to them as connectedness, power and identity.[5] Uvaldo Palomares and Harold Bessell refer to them as social interaction, mastery and awareness.[6] Sid Simon in his now famous IALAC story[7] refers to a sense of lovableness (belonging and worthwhileness) and capability (competence) as the key needs of students and William Glasser in *Schools Without Failure* states that the need for love and the need for self-worth are the two most basic needs of any person.[8]

The importance to me of all this cross-referencing of terms is to illustrate that almost all of the major writers in the field of affective education have independently discovered the importance of these basic ingredients to healthy personality growth. It provides a validity check for their assertion that we must attend to these three needs of belonging, sense of competence, and sense of worth if we are to truly enhance the self-concepts of our students. Let us look briefly at each of these needs.

Belonging. All of us want to belong, to be liked, to be valued and to be cared for. We seek affirmation of our existence from others. We have a need to share who we are and touch the lives of others. We need to discover our basic unity as well as our uniqueness. This can only be done in a group. Therefore, one of our first goals in developing self-concept is the promotion of what I call group rapport. There are many methods that have been developed to help students learn to overcome their initial reservations about self disclosure and to discover the basic humanity that is common to themselves and their classmates.

Feeling Competent. All of us need to feel that we are competent, that we can do things well, and that we can successfully neet our needs in the world. Most of us are very competent in many areas that we take for granted and that we have failed to learn to properly appreciate. Again, because of our negative focus, we have been taught to focus on what we have not yet mastered. We have all heard the story about the student who brings home a report card with four A's and one B. The father responds with "What is this B doing here?"

The first step in learning to feel competent is to focus on what we already can do well, have done well and are doing well right now. Once a positive psychological base is developed the student can then branch out and take risks in new areas that he or she would like to become competent in. We will explore several classroom activities to achieve these ends in a moment.

Feeling Worthwhile. Feeling worthwhile consists of the basic belief that "I am ok. I am good, not bad." In my experience this feeling is derived from four areas: mental, emotional, physical, and imaginal intuitive. To feel worthwhile I need to believe my mind works, the thoughts I have are valid, creative and helpful, and that my ideas are valued by others. Too often I hear parents and teachers saying things like "That's the stupidest thing I ever heard." "How can you be so dumb?" "Do you really believe that?" "I'm not interested in your opinion. I want to know the facts." Those are all statements that I am sure we've all heard. Even more destructive are the unstated put downs. If all that is ever allowed to be discussed is the curriculum, then the students begin to say to themselves "What I think and feel are not important; the only thing that is important is science or math or whatever."

To feel worthwhile a student must learn to believe that her feelings are ok. We are currently raising a generation of kids who are being taught to believe that anger, sadness, pain, grief, fear, aggression, pride and exuberantly expressed joy are all taboo. Boys are told that they are little men now and should not cry. Young girls are told that it's not lady-like to get angry and stand up for themselves. Peer pressure dictates that it is not "cool" to be afraid or to be proud. Feelings are! They just happen. They flow through us in no predictable pattern. They are complex and often confusing and seemingly contradictory. Yet they must be accepted and expressed. A student must come to believe that it's natural and acceptable to get angry, to feel sad, to cry, to get excited, to laugh and shout.

Feelings must not be talked away. I remember an incident where a third grade boy came in alone from recess. He was obviously very upset. The teacher asked him what the matter was. He said that no one liked him because he couldn't play on the swing. He was on the verge of tears as he spoke. He was obviously very sad and feeling quite rejected. Instead of accepting these feelings and encouraging their expression, the teacher immediately tried to talk the boy out of his feelings. "Oh, come on now, Johnny! There's nothing to get upset about. Lots of people like you. Billy likes you...etc." In her well-intentioned attempt to cheer Johnny up and avoid "a scene," she not only helped Johnny repress his feelings, she invalidated his perception of reality at that moment. She helped Johnny take another step in the long march toward self-alienation and negative self-concept. It is probably quite true, as the teacher suggests, that lots of people like Johnny. However, when one needs to discharge feelings, he needs to discharge feelings. It is only then that he can re-evaluate his concomitant thoughts about the situation.

To feel worthwhile a student must feel good about his or her body — not just how it looks, but how it functions, how it feels and how he feels in it. In the classroom this has boiled down to helping students appreciate what they look like (some first grade children in the inner city have never even seen themselves in a mirror!), helping them become more aware of their senses of touch, taste, smell, and hearing, helping them to learn to comfortably touch others and be touched without fear, and helping students to *enjoy* their bodies through the use of movement exercises, dance, and non-competitive sports.

Finally, a student must also learn to value and trust his unconscious world which manifests itself to him through intuition, imagination, dreams, daydreams and fantasy. Not only have we failed to develop the imaginal capacity in children through the proper use of guided imagery and fantasy, we have actually retarded its development with statements such as "Sally, are you daydreaming again?" "Look, there's nothing to be afraid of; it was only a dream." "Tommy, you always live in a fantasy world. Why don't you come down to earth." Television has largely replaced reading and the radio. People are no longer required to create images in their head to "get a picture of" what they are reading. Instead, they are passive receivers of pre-packaged images — often very manipulating and self-destructive images, such as those presented in today's advertisements, *Playboy* magazine and the other media.

The business of image creation is an extremely important one when dealing with self-concept because self-concept is synonomous with self-*image,* how I *imagine* myself to be. Once a person can learn to create and control their internal images they can begin to decide what images to allow and what images to disallow. To give yourself a sense of how important the images you hold are, try the following experiment with your wife, husband, roommate, students, etc.

Ask them to close their eyes and to imagine (i.e., see inside their head as if it were actually happening) that they are standing in the middle of a very small terrace on top of the tallest skyscraper in the world...and that this terrace has no railing. Then ask them to imagine walking to the edge and looking down at the street very, very far below. Next ask them to imagine walking along the edge to another side of the terrace, and finally back to the middle of the terrace. After they open their eyes, ask them not to tell you what they saw but what they actually experienced in their physical body as they took this brief guided imagery trip. They will invariably report some sort of physical reaction such as fast heart beat, sweaty palms, tightness across the chest, nausea, shallow breathing, etc.

The point of this experiment is that they had a physical reaction to the fantasy experience as if it were actually happening to them—*as if it were real!* To relate this to education you only need think of the student who images himself to be a poor student, unathletic, inarticulate, not mechanically inclined, etc. For the most part, these are images of who we are that we live up to and respond to rather than who we really are. For example, a student who images himself as unable to make friends, will react physiologically with fear reactions such as shallow breathing, shaking, aversion of his eyes, tightened voice, etc. to a new social situation in response to his fantasized or imagined fear of rejection rather than to the situation that really is present. He may in fact act so shy and nervous that people do in fact reject him, thus completing the circle of self-fulfilling prophecy. What would happen if this same student spent ten minutes a day imagining people reacting favorably to him in social situations? Maxwell Maltz claims that the unconscious mind cannot distinguish between an imagined event and a real one.[9] He cites research on students making basketball foul shots. Those who only "warmed up" in their minds, by imagining successfully sinking ten consecutive shots, did equally well or better than those who actually took ten warmup shots.

A number of educators and psychologists have recently turned their attention to the development of the student's ability to image. For specific techniques consult the following resources:

•*Put Your Mother on the Ceiling: Children's Imagination Games* by Richard deMille. New York: The Viking Press, 1967; revised edition, 1973.

•*The Power of Pretend* by Maurice Rapkin. Available from Claude Nolte, Box 38, Forest Falls, California 92399. Cost: $5.50. Copyright 1973.

•*Scamper: Games for Imagination Development* by Robert F. Eberle. Available from D.O.K. Publishers, 771 East Delevan Avenue, Buffalo, New York 14215. Copyright 1971.

•*Fantasy in the Classroom* edited by Jack Canfield and Paula

Klimeck. In press.
•*Learning Through Fantasy* by Thomas B. Roberts, Frances V. Clark
and Benjamin S. Westheimer. In press.
•"Fantasy and Imagination" by Frances V. Clark in *Four Psychologies Applied to Education* edited by Thomas B. Roberts. Cambridge, Mass.: Schenkman Publishing Co. (distributed by John Wiley and Sons), 1975, pp. 498-513.

So now...let us begin to look at specific classroom activities that you can use to enhance the self-concepts of your students. Most of the exercises that appear below are taken from the book *100 Ways to Enhance Self-Concept in the Classroom* written by Harold C. Wells and myself (Englewood Cliffs, N.J.: Prentice-Hall, 1976). They have all been used successfully in hundreds of classrooms from Massachusetts to California with all age groups. I have divided the activities into the three categories I discussed earlier: belonging, feeling competent, feeling worthwhile. You will also notice that the exercises encompass all four domains of mental, emotional, physical and imaginal. I have found it best to usually start with some sort of physical warmup so that people become totally involved. Two examples of physical warmups are Thumb Wrestling and Mirroring. Here's how to play them.

THUMB WRESTLING

Ask the students to pick partners. Then ask them to interlock their right hands with their thumbs free at the top. The goal is to pin their partner's thumb down for the count of three. Ask them to see who can win the best three out of five competitions. When they have completed the exercise, ask them to close their eyes and answer the following questions silently to themselves:

1) How did you feel winning or losing?
2) Did you make any statements or judgments about yourself to yourself?
3) If you won, did you say anything out loud to make your partner feel better?
4) If you lost, did you say anything internally or out loud to excuse yourself?
5) How seriously did you get involved? Do you think of yourself as a competitive person?
6) Did you develop a strategy during the competition?

Ask the students to open their eyes and talk about their responses to the question with their partners.

MIRRORING

Again ask the students to choose a partner and designate who is A and who is B. Tell them that in the first round A's will be leaders and B's followers. A and B stand directly facing each other. A is to move in any way he or she wants to—the more bizarre and ridiculous the better. The movement should include facial expressions as well as body movement. B is to act like a mirror and imitate every movement that A makes. A should feel like he is looking into a mirror. After about three to five minutes, reverse roles so that B is the leader and A the mirror.

After the exercise is over, ask them if they enjoyed it. Then ask the class to talk about which role was easier for them—leading or following? What is difficult about leading (fear of being judged, feeling the pressure to be creative or funny, feeling awkward, etc.) and about following (giving my authority to another, feeling inferior to my partner's leading, not getting to do what I want to do, making mistakes in following my partner's movements)?

BELONGING

The following activities are designed to help establish a feeling of positive rapport in the classroom. They will increase each student's sense of belonging.

THE NAME GAME

This two-part exercise has several learning goals. It can be used to help one learn others' names, and to establish positive feelings toward oneself and his classmates. In the event that the students are already well-acquainted start with part B.

A. Have the class sit in a circle. Start by saying, "I am Miss (Mr., Mrs.) Jones." The first student to her right says, "I am Billy and that's Miss Jones." Continue this process around the circle until the last person has repeated everybody's name.

B. The second time around in addition to their name, each person must add something he is good at. For example, "I am singing Miss Jones." "I am basketball-playing Billy, and that's singing Miss Jones." "I am cookie-baking Sally, and that's basketball-playing Billy, and that's singing Miss Jones," and so on around the circle.

AUTOBIOGRAPHICAL SHARING

In order for the child's self-concept to grow she needs to be in an environment of trust and rapport so that she can feel secure enough to take risks. One of the best methods for developing an environment of trust is mutual self-disclosure.

Ask the students to sit in a circle. Tell them that each student will have one (two or three) minutes to share with the group an autobiographical sketch of his life. Appoint one student with a second hand on his watch to be the timer. If you're working with elementary students, you may have to supply the watch. When working with a small group of eight to ten students, you may wish to use a three-minute egg timer.

Ask the students to share those important experiences throughout their lives, beginning with early childhood, which they consider of importance in the sense of leaving a strong impression on their personalities.

In this type of exercise it is a good idea for you to be the first one to share in order to model the behavior you are after with the students. Your going first also creates an environment of less risk.

SUCCESS SHARING

Another way to help students focus upon the positive aspects of themselves is to have them publicly share their accomplishments with the group.

In small groups of five or six, or with the entire class, ask the students to share with their group a success, accomplishment or achievement they had before they were ten years old. Next ask them to share a success they had between the ages of ten and fifteen; then between the ages of fifteen to the present time. Obviously, these age ranges will need to be revised depending on the ages of the students in your class.

At first some students may have difficulty remembering some of their earlier successes, but as others share theirs, it will trigger their minds. Children with extremely low self-concepts often report that they haven't had any successes. If this happens, you will need to help prod the students with questions such as:

"Well, you've been taking care of your younger brothers and sisters for two years; I consider that an accomplishment, don't you?" "Can you remember when you learned to ride your bicycle? Did you feel good about that achievement?"

STRENGTH BOMBARDMENT

Have the students break into groups of five or six students each. Focusing on one person at a time the group is to bombard him with all the strengths they see in him. The person being bombarded should remain silent until the group has finished. One member of the group should act as recorder, listing the strengths and giving them to the person when the group has finished.

The students should be instructed to list at least fifteen strengths for each student. They should also be cautious that no "put-down" statements are allowed. Only positive assets are to be mentioned. At the end of the exercise ask the students to discuss how they felt giving and receiving positive feedback. Was one easier than the other? Which one?

In some groups it is wise to spend ten minutes discussing with the class the different types of strengths that exist, as well as developing a vocabulary of strength words they can use. It may be a good thing to list all the words that are "brainstormed" on the chalkboard for the students to look at during the "bombardment" sessions.

To reinforce this activity, have your students also ask their parents to list the strengths they see in them. The new list could be added to that which is collected in class. This additional exercise will also provide the student with some very important positive feedback from his parents.[10]

Note to teachers: Haim Ginnot in his book *Teacher and Child* (New York: Macmillan, 1972) makes the following useful distinction between evaluative feedback and appreciative feedback: evaluative feedback is characterized by judgment—i.e., the teacher is the judge and the student is to be judged. Examples of this kind of feedback are: "This is a B- poem." "You are a good artist." "You are funny."

Appreciative feedback is characterized by letting the student know how you, as a person, have been affected by what they have done. Examples of appreciative feedback are: "*I* was deeply moved by your poem, *The Me I Never Dared to Be*. As *I* read it I identified with the many fears you wrote about. *I* guess we are similar in more ways than *I* had imagined." "I enjoyed your pictures. *I* like the way you use colors to express motion and power." "*I* appreciate the way you are always able to relax the tension in the classroom with a joke or a story. *I* enjoy your humor."

Try as much as possible to use appreciative feedback with the students in both formal (papers, artwork, etc.) and informal (personal feedback, group discussions, etc.) situations. Try discussing this distinction with your students and encourage them to also use appreciative rather than evaluative feedback with each other. The key to the difference is that most evaluative feedback starts with the word "you"; most appreciative feedback starts with the word "I."

THE IALAC STORY

The IALAC Story is told to illustrate how one's self-concept can be destroyed by others. If done with feeling and imagination, it can be a very powerful and moving experience. I have found that it is appropriate for students of all ages.

Take a sheet of paper and write the letters IALAC (pronounced I-ah-lack) on it in large bold print. Holding this to your chest so that the students can see it, tell them, "Everyone carries an invisible IALAC sign around with them at all times and wherever they go. IALAC stands for 'I am lovable and capable.' This is our self-concept, or how we feel about ourselves. The size of our sign—or how good we feel about ourselves—is often affected by how others interact with us. If somebody is nasty to us, teases us, puts us down, rejects us, hits us, etc., then a piece of our IALAC sign is destroyed. [Illustrate this by tearing a corner piece off the sign.] I am going to tell you a story to illustrate how this happens in everyday life." Then proceed to tell the students about a boy or girl who is the same age they are. Pick a name that no one in the class has. As you tell the story, try to be as emotional and dramatic as you can without burlesquing it too much. An outline is provided below. You will have to fill it in with your own imagination. Some teachers we know have the children help create the story as they go along. As you describe each event that negatively effects the student's IALAC sign, tear another piece off the sign until at the end you are left with almost nothing.

A possible outline for the IALAC story is as follows. Feel free to adapt, add to, change, and embellish it in any way you want: A seventh-grade boy named Michael is still lying in bed three minutes after his alarm goes off. All of a sudden his mother calls to him, "Michael, you lazy-head, get your body out of bed and get down here before I send your father up there!" (rip!) Michael gets out of bed, goes to get dressed and can't find a clean pair of socks. His mother tells him he'll have to wear yesterday's pair. (rip!) He goes to brush his teeth and his older sister, who's already locked herself in the bathroom, tells him to drop dead! (rip!) He goes to breakfast to find soggy cereal waiting for him. (rip!) As he leaves for school, he forgets his lunch and his mother calls to him, "Michael, you've forgotten your lunch; you'd forget your head if it weren't attached!" (rip!) As he gets to the corner he sees the school bus pull away and so he has to walk to school. (rip!) He's late to school and has to get a pass from the principal who gives him a lecture. (rip!)

Continue the story through the school day with appropriate examples. Some of the possibilities are:

Forgetting his homework

Getting a 68 on a spelling test

Being called on for the only homework question he can't answer

Making a mistake in reading so that all the kids laugh

Being picked last to play ball at recess

Dropping his tray in the lunchroom, with everybody applauding

Being picked on by bullies on the way home from school

Being referred to as "Hey you!" in gym class

You can think of other examples or get the students to help you.

When Michael gets home from school some typical negative events might include not being able to watch the baseball game because his mother is watching her favorite soap opera or because he's not yet finished his homework, or being told to wash the dishes for the third night in a row because his older brother has band practice, etc.

End the story by showing Michael going to bed with an IALAC sign about as big as a quarter! When you're finished, ask the kids to discuss the following questions:

How does *your* IALAC sign get torn up? What things affect you the most?

What do you do that destroys the IALAC signs of others—in school, family, etc.?

How do you feel when your IALAC sign is ripped? When you rip someone else's?

What can we do to help people enlarge their signs rather than make them smaller?

FEELING COMPETENT

The following activities are designed to help students focus on the sense of competence—to help them acknowledge their past achievements and to set realizable new goals and accomplish them.

PRIDE LINE[11]

Pride is related to self-concept. People enjoy expressing pride in something they've done that might have otherwise gone unrecognized. Our culture does not encourage such expressions and it is sometimes difficult for people to actually say, "I'm proud that I...."

Ask the students to make a statement about a specific item, beginning with "I'm proud that I...." For example you might say, "I'd like you to mention something about your *letter writing* that you'd be proud of. Please begin your response with "I am proud that I...." Students may say "I pass" if they wish.

Below are some suggested items for use in the Pride Line.

1. Things you've done for your parents.
2. Things you've done for a friend
3. Work in school.

4. How you spend your free time.
5. About your religious belief.
6. How you've gotten some money.
7. Something you've bought recently.
8. How you usually spend your money.
9. Habits you have.
10. Something you do often.

SUCCESS-A-DAY

At the end of each day, have the students briefly share with the rest of the class the successes they have experienced during the day.

Some students will find this difficult at first, but as others begin to share, they too will realize they have had some of the same successes. It has also been our experience that if a student says he has had no success, that some of his classmates will chime in with successes they have seen him accomplish. The sensitive teacher will also look for successes to be pointed out to the child with extremely low self-esteem.

I LEARNED STATEMENTS

A typical dialogue which occurs between parents and students goes like this:

"What did you learn in school today?"

"Oh, nothing."

Of course, this is usually not the case; however, many kids are not explicitly aware of what they have learned. This lack of awareness impedes self-concept development, for a person needs to know he is expanding his skills and his knowledge in order to feel competent. Our task as teachers then is to help students to be able to articulate what in fact they have learned. One way that I have found particularly helpful is having the students make "I learned..." statements. There are two kinds of "I learned..." statements. The first covers traditional subject matter, skills and facts, for example: "I learned how to multiply fractions today." "I learned how to use the card catalogue today." "I learned where Afghanastan is located." "I learned how bees communicate."

The second kind of "I learned..." statement is of a more personal nature—focusing on self-awareness. This kind of "I learned..." statement requires a second "I."

It would read "I learned that I...." Examples of this form might include: "I learned that I don't like to dissect animals." "I learned that I find it hard to study when I'm angry." "I learned that I get embarrassed when I receive positive feedback." "I learned that I am very competitive."

I generally use "I learned" statements in two ways—immediately after a lesson and again at the end of the day. I take a few minutes and write people's "I learned..." statements, usually paraphrased to save time, on the chalkboard. I just have the kids shout them out to me as I write. After about a week or two most classes can fill up a whole board with "I learned..." statements. There is a tremendous amount of self-validation that occurs as students recall their day and realize what they have learned.

SUCCESS SYMBOLS[12]

All of us have symbols of success, things which remind us of our past successes. We have photographs, medals, certificates, dried-up corsages, dance books, ticket stubs, autographed baseballs, newspaper clippings, bronzed shoes, mounted golf balls, fish and antlers, trophies, plaques, and ribbons. Most of us save these objects because they remind us of our abilities and competences and our likability and popularity.

Have the students bring to class five tangible objects that recall or symbolize some past successes or accomplishments they have had.

During the next class period have each student share one or more of his "success symbols" with the rest of the class. Instruct the students to share the feelings and meaning connected with the specific object as well as the success it symbolizes.

A variation of the success symbol concept is to have the students list five success symbols they do not have, but would like to acquire in the next year, five years, etc. This activity could be used in conjunction with goal-setting. Be sure to discuss the choices or goals without judgment; be open to whatever the students come up with.

As a teacher, what are your success symbols? Take a walk through your house or apartment and see how many are visible. If they are all stored away in drawers and closets, consider how you might make them a more *integral* part of your environment.

WISHING

Dreams and wishes range from the simple to the fantastic. One may simply desire a new toy or he may imagine himself walking on the moon. A child can easily imagine himself to be anything or anyone he chooses. While wishes may often seem impossible and far-fetched, they are very often expressions of real needs—such as the common need to be accepted by one's peers. Once wishes are expressed and recognized as normal, they can be used as a motivating force behind action. With the use of goal setting a child can begin to realize that, with action, a wish may be attained.

Genies and magic fairies often grant people three wishes. Ask the children to imagine they had three wishes. What would they be? Ask them to imagine they had three wishes for someone else whom they liked very much. What would they wish for them?

If they could relive the previous day, what would they wish to have been different? To have been the same?

Did you ever wish to be someone else? Who? Why? Do you think someone might wish to be you? Why would she want to be you?

Did you ever have a wish come true? Tell about it. Is there anything you can do, besides just wishing, to help you get your wish?

THE GOAL POST

Decorate a bulletin board in the form of a football goal post. Each day, as the kids come into class, ask them to set a goal for that day or for that night at home. Record the goal on a 3 × 5 index card and post it on the bulletin board below the cross bars of the goal post.

At the end of the day, or the following day, ask all those who completed their goals to move their index card above the cross bar. If you are working in a group situation, ask the kids to share their goal and how they completed it with the group. This provides the goal achievers with the attention of their peers as a reinforcement of their successful action.

I CAN'T...I WON'T...

Ask the students to find partners. Ask them to take turns saying sentences that start with the words "I can't...." Ask them to consider their school life, their social life, their home life, etc., as possible areas from which to draw these statements.

After about four or five minutes, ask them to go back and repeat all the sentences they have just said with one change: replacing the word "can't" with the word "won't" or "I don't." Explain to them that the words "I won't" may not feel right to them the first time they say them, but that it is like going into a clothing store and trying on a coat. It may not fit you, but you won't know that until you try it on. Just because you say it, doesn't mean you are stuck with it forever. It is simply an experiment to discover how we experience ourselves differently after saying "I won't" instead of "I can't."

Ask them to repeat exactly what they said before except for the substitution of "won't" for "can't," and to take the time to be aware of how they experience saying each sentence. Again, give them about five minutes to do this.

Bring the class back together and ask them what they experienced as they did the exercise. Did they experience any difference between saying "I can't" and "I won't"? Usually responses will include such statements as:

I felt more powerful when I said, "I won't!"

I felt like "I can't" was a copout.

I felt like I was more in charge with "I won't."

When I said "I can't," it was as if there was some outside force controlling me. With "I won't" I realized that the decision to do it or not to do it was all in me.

I sounded whiney when I said, "I can't."

"I won't" sounded more true to me.

Ask them to consider whether their "I can't" statements are really statements of something that is impossible, or whether it is something possible that they simply refuse to do. Ask them to become aware of and to affirm their power of refusal. "I can't" implies being unable, crippled, and controlled from the outside. "I won't" affirms the responsibility for their actions. Often this reaffirmation of responsibility even leads to the transformation of an "I can't" to an "I will."

After you have used this exercise with your class, make a habit of correcting people in class who say "I can't." Ask them to repeat whatever they have said with the words "I won't."

FEELING WORTHWHILE

The following activities are designed to validate and affirm the students' thoughts and feelings as ok. They also help the students to form a clearer picture of their true identity—who they really are, not who they pretend to be.

COLLAGE OF SELF

Instruct your students to make a collage entitled "Me!" Provide each student with a 12 × 18-inch sheet of thick construction paper or thin cardboard. They should collect and cut out pictures, words, and symbols that are representative of themselves—things they like to do, things they own, things they would like to own, places they've been, people they admire, etc. Then they are to paste these pictures, words, and symbols onto their sheets of construction paper to make a collage. Instruct the students not to sign them.

After the individual collages are completed, display them in the classroom. First, have the students try to guess who made each collage. Next have each student explain to the class all the items in his collage. Note for the class that the collages are all somewhat different—unique—just as each person, while having much in common with all others, is a different and unique individual.

You will probably need several class periods to complete this project. Try to have a lot of magazines with pictures available for the students. Magazines such as *Ms.*, *Ebony*, *Black Sports*, *Women in Sports*, *Auto World*, etc. should be included. The greater the variety of magazines, the better.

ON MY MIND

Ask the students to pair up and draw a large profile or silhouette of one another's heads. Then they are to cut out words, pictures, etc. that represent their personal thoughts, thus making a collage of their current concerns. Later these pictures can be shared with the class.

This activity legitimizes the private thoughts of each student as proper subject matter and as reasonable data to share, as well as allowing the teacher to see what are the primary concerns of his or her students. Another outcome is that students usually begin to realize that they are not alone in many of their concerns. The realization that others share their concerns and feelings often helps students feel "less wierd," "less strange," and more "normal," thus enlarging their self-concepts.

THE OWL GAME[13]

The old owl just sits there and repeats, "Who? Who? Who?" Maybe his "who" is not a question—but then, it might be. In the Owl Game the "owl" does ask a question, and asks it over and over. He asks his question with sincerity, empathy, and integrity. The respondent must trust his "Owl" so he can say whatever pops into his mind. A long philosophical treatise is not an appropriate response; simply a word, phrase, or brief sentence will convey what the respondent is thinking at the moment.

This exercise seems to go better with students of high school age and over.

Ask the students to each find a partner—someone with whom they feel comfortable. Tell them to find a place to sit across from each other and to decide between them who is to be "A" and who is to be "B." After this has been determined, tell the A's that they can only ask the question "Who are you?" The B's are to answer each time with a word or a short phrase. Ask them to continue this until you tell them to stop. Let them go at this in rapid-fire fashion for two to five minutes. Then have them switch roles with B asking "Who are you?" and A answering. Tell the students to say whatever comes into their heads, no matter how crazy, absurd or repetitive it may sound. If they don't, they'll get stuck. Next instruct the A's to ask the question, "Who do you pretend to be?" The B's are to answer as before. Again allow two to five minutes. Then have them switch roles again.

This exercise can be extended or repeated in a variation of this form by using the questions: "What do you want?" and "What are you feeling right now?"

I strongly advise you to allow time for discussion of this activity with the whole class reconvened. Discussion of personal results makes it possible for the students to become aware of both their unique and their common patterns of response. Tuning in to these patterns heightens one's self-awareness.

MOTORCYCLE FANTASY

In several places in this article I have used different mental images or fantasies to help a student get some insight into his personality. This is another such exercise. It has special appeal to older children and youth because motorcycling is currently so popular with them.

Prepare your class for a brief fantasy experience. The children should be relaxed, happy, sitting with their eyes closed. Speak softly but clearly and pause briefly between sentences so they have time to visualize your directions.

Imagine that you are a motorcycle. Notice what kind you are and what make. You are being ridden now. Notice who your rider is. How do you get along with each other? Have a dialogue with your rider; finish the dialogue and become aware of how fast you are going. Notice where you are. What kind of condition are you, the motorcycle, in? Notice all of your various parts. Is everything working smoothly? Any badly worn parts about to cause trouble? Where are you now? Notice how you feel being a motorcycle. Your left handlebar has a brake grip for the front wheel and your right handlebar has the acceleration grip. Carry on a dialogue or conversation between the front wheel brake grip on the left and the accelerator on the right. Notice carefully what each is saying and feeling. You are being stopped now. Where did you stop and how? How do you feel after the ride?

The fantasy usually leads to an animated discussion. Don't interpret or suggest "good" and "bad" concerning any fantasy content. Let your students take what they can from the activity without pressing for insight.

STUDENT OF THE WEEK[14]

Place the names of all your students in a box. Each week, in front of the class, draw one of the names from the box. The student whose name is drawn becomes the student of the week.

Ask the rest of the class to state the things they like about the chosen student. Be patient and encouraging; stress that everyone has many good qualities. You might also wish to tell the students that it is important to take this seriously because they too will one day have a turn. Try to get six to ten concrete statements listed. It is also a good idea to try to keep the lists equal in length.

Have the student of the week bring in a picture of herself, or take one of her with a Polaroid camera. Post his or her picture, name, and list of good qualities on the bulletin board. You may change this bulletin board each week, or you may wish to make a cumulative bulletin board of students of the week.

To assure that all class members receive recognition within a shorter period of time, you may wish to have three students a week (Monday, Wednesday, Friday) or three on one day of the week.

POSITIVE MANTRAM[15]

No matter what you say or do to me, I am a worthwhile person!

Ask the students to close their eyes and repeat in unison with you the chant: "No matter what you say or do to me, I am a worthwhile person!" This seemingly simple exercise has a very powerful impact if done repeatedly. It implants a new seed thought in each of the students; it acts as an antidote to all the negative thoughts and statements already implanted in their thinking.

A way to heighten the effect of this exercise is to ask students to imagine the face of someone who has put them down in some way in the past—parent, teacher, coach, friend, fellow student, Girl Scout leader, policeman, etc.—each time they begin to say "No matter...." Have them stick out their chins and repeat the sentence strongly and convincingly.

After they get the hang of it you might interject statements like "You're stupid, ugly, etc." and let them respond to these with "No matter what you say or to to me, I am a worthwhile person."

POSITIVE FEELINGS

Working with a small group or the whole class, ask the children to arrange their chairs in a circle so that everyone can see everyone else's faces. Ask them to tell about something that makes them feel very good. You might first ask them to draw a picture or write a story about it and then share it in the circle.

A variation is to ask the children to share something they did that made someone else feel happy. You might start out by saying:

"Yesterday I told Jane that I like the dress she was wearing. I thought the dress was very colorful. She smiled, and I think my comment made her feel good. Would you share with us something you have said or done for someone else that made him or her feel good? How did it make that person feel good?"

Another variation is to ask the children to respond to the following instruction:

"Can you think of something that a grownup did or said to you this week that made you feel good? Could you share that thing with the group and tell us why it gave you a pleasant feeling?"

This exercise could be used substituting teachers, best friends, pets, etc. for grownup participants. Some examples of past use of this exercise are: It made me feel good when the playground supervisor told one of the other kids to stop picking on me. I felt good because she noticed I was being hurt. I felt good when my mother said we could make cupcakes together and that I could bring them to school.

INCOMPLETE SENTENCES

Incomplete sentences provide the student with an opportunity to get more insight into himself based on the unrehearsed quality of the answers that emerge from completing sentences listed below with whatever pops into their heads first. Incomplete sentences can be used one at a time as a basis for starting a discussion, as a cue for journal writing, or they can be used several at a time to give students a lot of data from a similar subject (such as "friends") from which they can extract a pattern about their responses.

In their book *Toward Humanistic Education: A Curriculum of Affect*, Gerald Weinstein and Mario Fantini suggest that there are three areas of concern that people seem to spend most of their time thinking about:

Identity basically deals with the question "Who am I?" Various forms of this question are: Why am I a girl? Why was I born black? What do I really feel about things? How come I act the way I do? How come I'm in the dumb class? What's really important in life? What can I do to be more happy?

Connectedness deals with the issue of my relationships with others in my world. Typical concerns from this area are: Who are my friends? What are my values? To whom do I owe my allegiance? How do I make new friends? What do I want from other people? What am I willing to give up of myself to get what I want from others?

Power refers to the sense of control over one's own life. Typical expressions about one's concern with power are: I can do anything I set my mind to! Why should I even try; nothing ever works out the way I want it to. I don't have a chance, man; I have to do what they say. How can I get a good job with a "C" average?

What I've done below is to list incomplete sentences divided into the three areas of identity, connectedness, and power. Most of these have been brainstormed by teachers that have been in my training workshops. A group of five teachers can usually generate over fifty sentence stubs in a period of five or six minutes. So, when you run out of these, get together with some teachers and invent some more. It's easy—and profitable!

IDENTITY

My favorite _____ is. . . .
If I could have one wish, it would be. . . .
I'm happiest when I. . . .
I feel the saddest when. . . .
I feel most important when I. . . .
One question I have about life is. . . .
I get angry when. . . .
A fantasy I enjoy is. . . .
A thought I keep having is. . . .
When I get angry I. . . .
When I feel sad I. . . .
When I get scared I. . . .
I get scared when. . . .
Something I want but I'm afraid to ask for is. . . .
I feel brave when. . . .
I felt brave when. . . .

I love to. . . .
I see myself as. . . .
Something I do well is. . . .
I worry about my. . . .
My greatest asset is. . . .
I worry about my. . . .
More than anything else, I would like to. . . .
If I were an adult I would. . . .
If I were a little kid I would. . . .
The best thing about being me is. . . .
I hate. . . .
I need. . . .
I wonder about. . . .

CONNECTEDNESS
People are. . . .
My friends are. . . .
The thing that makes me a good friend is. . . .
The things I look for in a friend are. . . .
My parents. . . .
My brother(s) sister(s). . . .
Other people make me feel. . . .
Older people are. . . .
Younger people are. . . .
I wish people would. . . .
I wish my family would. . . .
I like people who. . . .
I don't like people who. . . .
I believe. . . .
I value. . . .
I make friends by. . . .
My best friend. . . .
My teacher. . . .
I wish my teacher would. . . .
The other students in this class. . . .
Girls. . . .
Boys. . . .
People can get to me by. . . .
Teasing people is. . . .
When people tease me I. . . .
When someone tells me they like me I. . . .
People like me because. . . .
People think I am. . . .
I think I am. . . .
Someone I'd like to get to know better is. . . .
Something I do for my mother is. . . .
Something I do for my father is. . . .
I like it when somebody says to me. . . .
I wish I had told. . . .
I stop myself from talking in class by imagining that. . . .
I resent. . . for. . . .

I appreciate....
I demand....
I pretend to be...when I'm really....

POWER

Something I do well is....
Something I'm getting better at is....
I can....
I am proud that I....
I get people's attention by....
I get my way by....
My greatest strength is....
I can help other people to....
I taught someone how to....
I need help on....
I'm learning to....
I feel big when....
I have the power to....
I was able to decide to....
When people try to boss me around, I....
I don't like people to help me with....
Something I can do by myself is....
People can't make me....
I got into trouble when I....
I get praise from others when I....
The most powerful person I know is....
People seem to respect me when I....
I want to be able to....
I want to be strong enough to....
A time when I was a leader was....
I'm not afraid to....
Something that I can do now that I couldn't do last year is....
When I want my parents to do something, I....
I have difficulty dealing with....
People who expect a lot from me make me feel....
I have accomplished....
If I want to, I can....
People who agree with me make me feel....
Strong independent people....
If I were the teacher I would....
I bet....
I feel like my mother/father when....
I do my best work when....
My body is....
My face is....
I feel uncomfortable when....
The thing I'm afraid to talk about is....
I don't want to....
I am afraid to....
I wish I had the courage to....

These are just a few of the exercises that have been developed. All of them work. They have been used successfully in hundreds of classrooms with teachers reporting back tremendous differences in the tone of their classes as well as in the behavior of individual students. I hope you, too, will try them, adopt them, invent new ones, and experience the joy of seeing your students grow to believe in themselves and their ability to achieve their individual goals. It is a rewarding feeling.

1. Unpublished study conducted by Dr. Herbert Otto, National Center for the Exploration of Human Potential, 8080 El Paseo Grande, LaJolla, California 92037.

2. See *Self Concept and School Achievement* by William W. Purkey. Englewood Cliffs, N.J.: Prentice-Hall, Inc., 1970.

3. This theory originally appeared in "Self-Concept: A Critical Dimension in Teaching and Learning" by Jack Canfield and Harold C. Wells in *Humanistic Education Sourcebook* edited by Donald H. Read and Sidney B. Simon. Englewood Cliffs, N.J.: Prentice-Hall, Inc., 1975, pp. 460-468, and *100 Ways to Enhance Self-Concept in the Classroom* by Jack Canfield and Harold C. Wells, Englewood Cliffs, N.J.: Prentice-Hall, Inc., 1967, p. 7

4. *Helping Children to Like Themselves* by Donald W. Felker. Minneapolis, Minn.: Burgess Publishing Co., 1974, pp. 24-30.

5. *Toward Humanistic Education* by Gerald Weinstein and Mario Fantini. New York: Praeger, 1970.

6. *Methods in Human Development Theory Manual* by Harold Bessell. Human Development Training Institute, 7574 University Avenue, LaMesa, California 92041, © 1973.

7. *I Am Lovable and Capable* by Sidney B. Simon. Available from Argus Communications, Niles, Illinois.

8. *Schools Without Failure* by William Glasser. New York: Harper and Row, 1969, p. 12.

9. *Psychocybernetics* by Maxwell Maltz. Englewood Cliffs, N.J.: Prentice-Hall, 1960. Also available in paperback. For other books which explore the dynamics of mind power and mental imagery, see the following: (1) *Make Your Magic Mind Power Work For You* by Leslie M. LeCron. Greenwich, Conn.: Fawcett Publications, 1969, (2) *The Magic of Believing* by Claude M. Bristol. New York: Pocket Books, 1969. (3) *The Magic of Thinking Big* by David J. Schwartz. New York: Cornerstone Library (distributed by Simon and Schuster), 1965.

10. I learned this activity from Herbert Otto. We recommend his book, *Group Methods Designed to Actualize Human Potential*, which is available from The Holistic Press, 329 El Camino Drive, Beverly Hills, California 90212.

11. I learned this exercise from Sid Simon.

12. Suggested by Herbert Otto in *A Guide to Developing Your Potential* (New York: Charles Scribner's Sons, 1967).

13. I first learned this exercise from Bernard Gunther.

14. Suggested by Astrid Collins, Markham Junior High School, San Jose, California.

15. I learned this exercise from Leonard Smith.

Dr. Dov Peretz Elkins

Human Relations Trainer, Organizational Consultant, Group Facilitator, Educator, Counselor, Author. Available for training workshops and lectures.

TOPICS:

THE FAMILY
Raising Children in This Crazy World
Family Life Education
Marriage Enrichment
Building Self-Esteem
Human Sexuality

EDUCATION
Value Clarification
Self Concept Development
Fostering Creativity & Imagination
Experiential Learning
Teacher Effectiveness

ORGANIZATIONS
Creative Problem Solving
Management Development
Organizational Assessment
Team Building
Third Party Consultation
Communication Skills
Intergroup Relations
Holding Better Meetings
Handling the Dissenting Member

PERSONAL GROWTH
Building Self-Confidence
Assertiveness Training
Interpersonal Relationships
Being Single & Happy
Life & Career Planning
Leadership Skills
Gestalt Awareness Training
Spiritual Development
Death & Dying
Handling Stress & Burnout

Dr. Dov Peretz Elkins is a world-renowned platform speaker and workshop leader. Experiential sessions include active group involvement utilitizing the best resources of the modern behavioral sciences in a safe and accepting atmosphere.

Dr. Elkins is Founder and Director of Growth Associates, a human relations consulting and publishing firm in Rochester, NY. He does couple, family, individual and group therapy, as well as consulting in educational and organizational development. He has led in-service workshops for helping professionals throughout North America for a wide range of educational, community, industrial and religious organizations. Representative clients include Xerox Corporation, Automatic Data Processing (ADP), Indiana Office of Occupational Development, Boys Club of America, Clinton Valley Mental Health Center (Detroit), University of Rochester Department of Psychiatry, Cornell University, Dutchess Community College, Drug and Alcohol Council, YMCA, Vocational Guidance Teachers Association, American Personnel & Guidance Association, Association for Humanistic Psychology, National Humanistic Education Center, as well as scores of public and private school systems throughout the country.

His background is in training, consulting, personal growth, education and counseling. He was trained at leading growth centers throughout the country, including Esalen Institute at Big Sur, CA; NTL (National Training Labs) at Bethel, Maine; numerous Gestalt labs, and completed the University Associates Laboratory Education Internship Program. He is a certified instructor for Parent Effectiveness Training and Teacher Effectiveness Training.

Dov Elkins is author of over one hundred articles and fifteen books on psychology, education and religion, including TEACHING PEOPLE TO LOVE THEMSELVES, GLAD TO BE ME, and SELF CONCEPT SOURCEBOOK. He is now at work on a new volume called **One Hundred Ways to Foster Creativity & Imagination.**

FOR FURTHER DETAILS, WRITE OR CALL:
Growth Associates
Human Relations Consultants & Publishers
P.O. Box 8429
Rochester, N.Y. 14618
716/244-1225

Workshops and Resource Materials on Self-Concept Development

by Dr. Dov Peretz Elkins,
international authority on self-concept development,
counselor, educator, author, trainer, consultant

Send order form below to: Growth Associates, Box 8429, Rochester, NY 14618. 716/244-1225. **All orders must be prepaid.** Please send checks in US funds payable to Growth Associates. Prices include postage & handling.

●●

ORDER FORM

Name _____ Address _____

City _____ State _____ Zip _____

Quantity	Titles by Dr. Elkins	Total Cost
	Teaching People to Love Themselves: A Leader's Handbook of Theory and Technique for Self-Esteem & Affirmation Training. A book for trainers, educators, teachers, therapists & others who work with people. $17.50	
	Self Concept Sourcebook: Ideas and Activities for Building Self-Esteem. A collection of extended writings of the leading psychologists, philosophers and educators of recent times, including Rogers, Fromm, Canfield, Hamachek, Horney, Purkey & others, plus many new learning exercises. Can be used as high school & college text. $16. Quantity discount.	
	Twelve Pathways to Feeling Better About Yourself. An inspirational and idea-packed book for the general and professional reader. $7.50.	
	Glad To Be Me: Building Self-Esteem in Yourself & Others. A delightful, beautiful, inspiring collection of poems, sayings, insights and photographs about raising self-esteem in yourself, your family, students, employees, clients, and anyone you care about. $6.50.	
	Cassette Tapes: ($10 each) (a) The Magic of Self-Esteem (b) Relaxation and Self-Esteem Building Exercise	

Total Order (NY residents add 7% tax) $ _____

Workshops and Resource Materials on Self-Concept Development

by Dr. Dov Peretz Elkins,
international authority on self-concept development,
counselor, educator, author, trainer, consultant

Send order form below to: Growth Associates, Box 8429, Rochester, NY 14618. 716/244-1225. **All orders must be prepaid.** Please send checks in US funds payable to Growth Associates. Prices include postage & handling.

●●

ORDER FORM

Name _____ Address _____

City _____ State _____ Zip _____

Quantity	Titles by Dr. Elkins	Total Cost
	Teaching People to Love Themselves: A Leader's Handbook of Theory and Technique for Self-Esteem & Affirmation Training. A book for trainers, educators, teachers, therapists & others who work with people. $17.50	
	Self Concept Sourcebook: Ideas and Activities for Building Self-Esteem. A collection of extended writings of the leading psychologists, philosophers and educators of recent times, including Rogers, Fromm, Canfield, Hamachek, Horney, Purkey & others, plus many new learning exercises. Can be used as high school & college text. $16. Quantity discount.	
	Twelve Pathways to Feeling Better About Yourself. An inspirational and idea-packed book for the general and professional reader. $7.50.	
	Glad To Be Me: Building Self-Esteem in Yourself & Others. A delightful, beautiful, inspiring collection of poems, sayings, insights and photographs about raising self-esteem in yourself, your family, students, employees, clients, and anyone you care about. $6.50.	
	Cassette Tapes: ($10 each) (a) The Magic of Self-Esteem (b) Relaxation and Self-Esteem Building Exercise	

Total Order (NY residents add 7% tax) $ _____